X-O MANOWAR

EXODUS

ROBERT VENDITTI | RAFA SANDOVAL | ULISES ARREOLA | JORDI TARRAGONA

CONTENTS

Collection Cover Art: Rafa Sandoval and Jordi Tarragona with Ulises Arreola

Editors: Warren Simons (#38-39)
and Tom Brennan (#40-42)
Editor-in-Chief: Warren Simons

VALIANT.

Peter Cuneo
Chairman

Dinesh Shamdasani
CEO & Chief Creative Officer

Gavin Cuneo
Chief Operating Officer & CFO

Fred Pierce
Publisher

Warren Simons
VP Editor-in-Chief

Walter Black
VP Operations

Hunter Gorinson
Director of Marketing,
Communications & Digital Media

Atom! Freeman
Director of Sales

Matthew Klein
Andy Liegl
John Petrie
Sales Managers

Josh Johns
Digital Sales & Special Projects Manager

Travis Escarfullery
Jeff Walker
Production & Design Managers

Alejandro Arbona
Tom Brennan
Editors

Kyle Andrukiewicz
Associate Editor

Peter Stern
Publishing & Operations Manager

Andrew Steinbeiser
Marketing & Communications Manager

Danny Khazem
Editorial Operations Manager

Ivan Cohen
Collection Editor

Steve Blackwell
Collection Designer

Lauren Hitzhusen
Editorial Assistant

Rian Hughes/Device
Trade Dress & Book Design

Russell Brown
President, Consumer Products,
Promotions and Ad Sales

Geeta Singh
Licensing Manager

X-O Manowar®: Exodus. Published by Valiant Entertainment
LLC. Office of Publication: 350 Seventh Avenue, New York, NY
10001. Compilation copyright © 2015 Valiant Entertainment LLC.
All rights reserved. Contains materials originally published in
single magazine form as X-O Manowar #38-42. Copyright © 2015
Valiant Entertainment LLC. All rights reserved. All characters,
their distinctive likeness and related indicia featured in this
publication are trademarks of Valiant Entertainment LLC. The
stories, characters, and incidents featured in this publication are
entirely fictional. Valiant Entertainment does not read or accept
unsolicited submissions of ideas, stories, or artwork. Printed in the
U.S.A. First Printing.
ISBN: 9781939346933.

VALIANT ENTERTAINMENT PROUDLY PRESENTS

The Wedding of...

X-O MANOWAR®

Written By:
ROBERT VENDITTI

Pencils By:
RAFA SANDOVAL

Inks By:
JORDI TARRAGONA

Colors By:
BRIAN REBER

Letters By:
DAVE SHARPE

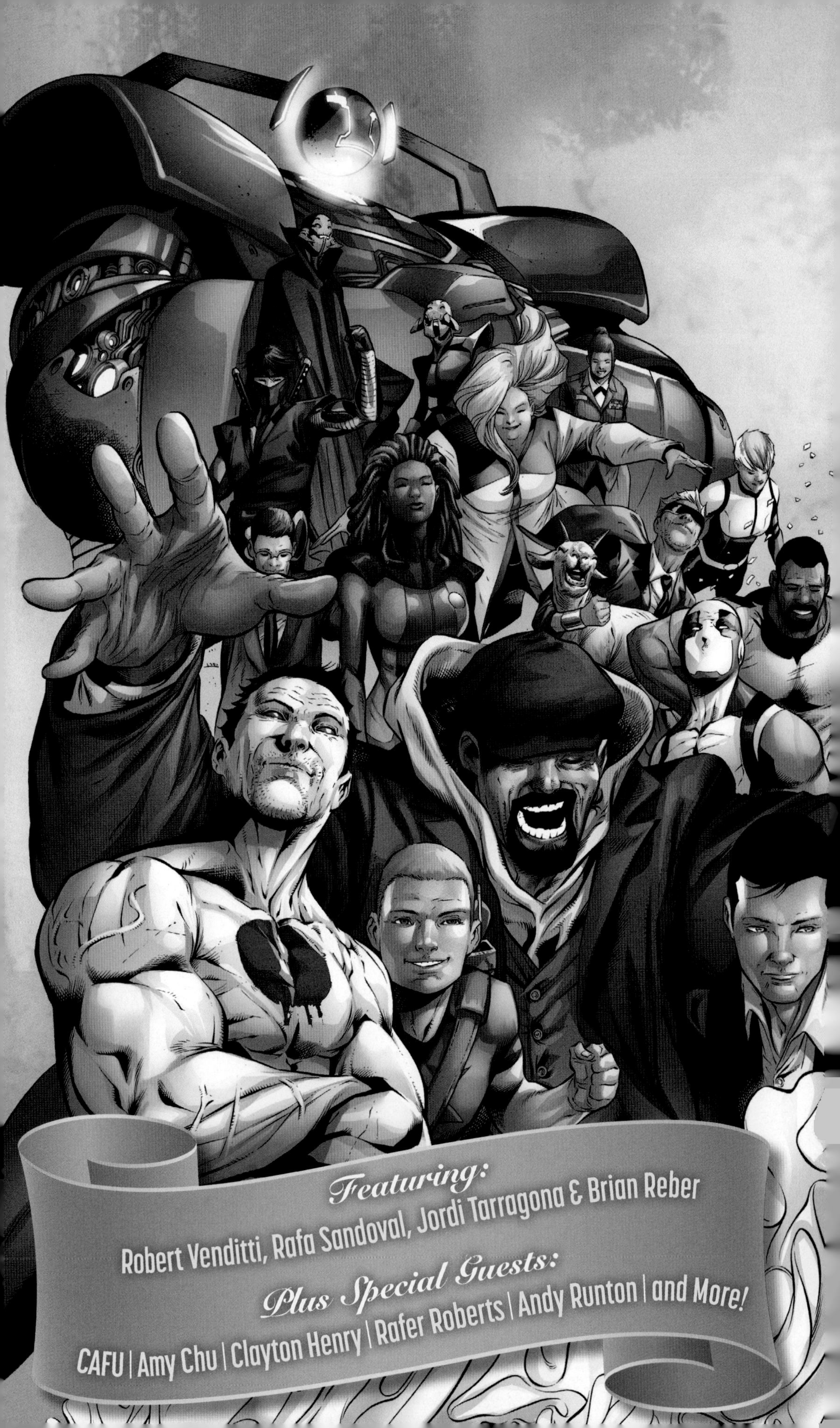
Featuring:
Robert Venditti, Rafa Sandoval, Jordi Tarragona & Brian Reber
Plus Special Guests:
CAFU | Amy Chu | Clayton Henry | Rafer Roberts | Andy Runton | and More!

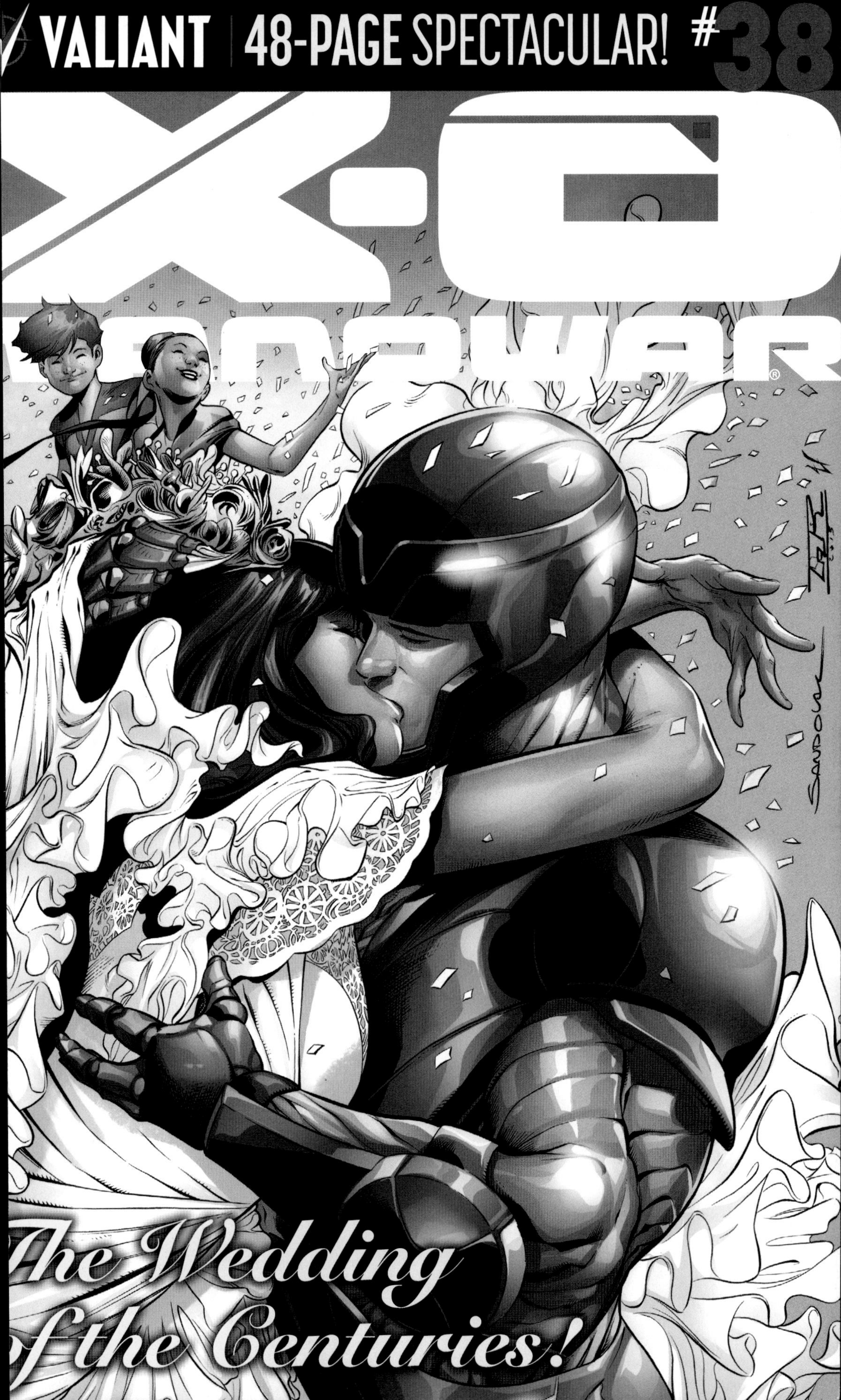
VALIANT
48-PAGE SPECTACULAR!
#38
The Wedding
of the Centuries!

The noble Visigoth warrior Aric of Dacia was kidnapped by the alien race known as the Vine and thrust into slavery. He rebelled and captured the sentient power suit Shanhara, a being worshipped as a deity by the Vine, and returned to Earth - only to discover centuries had passed and the world he knew was gone. Bonded to Shanhara, Aric has lost his home but found a new purpose as the protector of Earth...

The story so far...

Aric of Dacia recently returned to Earth after leading an army of Armor Wearers against DEAD HAND, a relentless robotic army that threatened life on Earth - and countless more worlds.

Back on Earth, his fellow time-displaced Visigoths have managed to create their own homeland in western Nebraska under supervision of Colonel Ja Capshaw of the United St Army and G.A.T.E.

Since his return to Earth, he has been romantically linked to the Lady Saana. Their relationship has been full of love and tension as Aric's duties as X-O Manowar put life at risk and as both struggle to find identity in this world. Before they move forv to the future, they must put the past behind them.

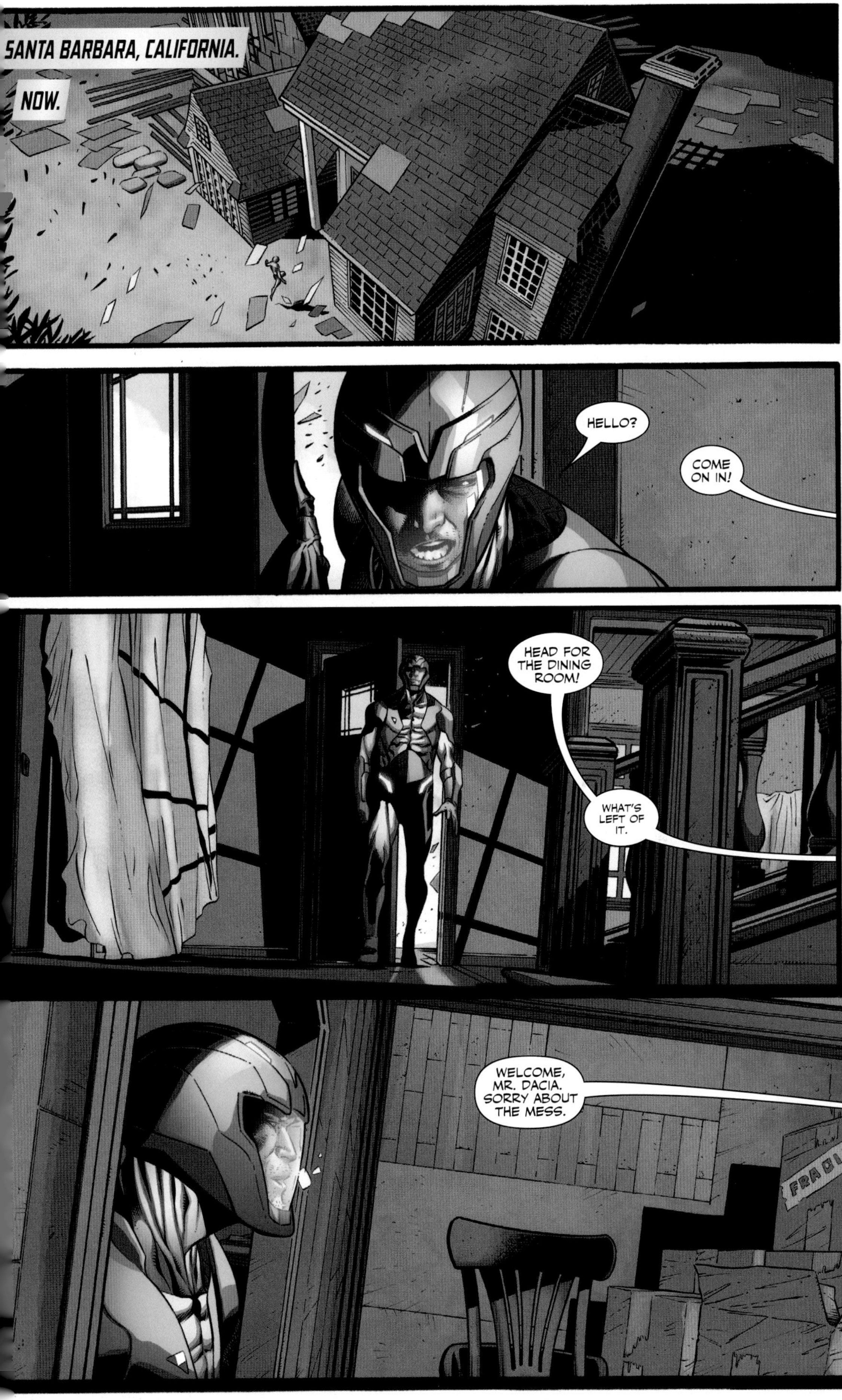
SANTA BARBARA, CALIFORNIA.
NOW.
HELLO?
COME ON IN!
HEAD FOR THE DINING ROOM!
WHAT'S LEFT OF IT.
WELCOME, MR. DACIA. SORRY ABOUT THE MESS.
FRAGIL

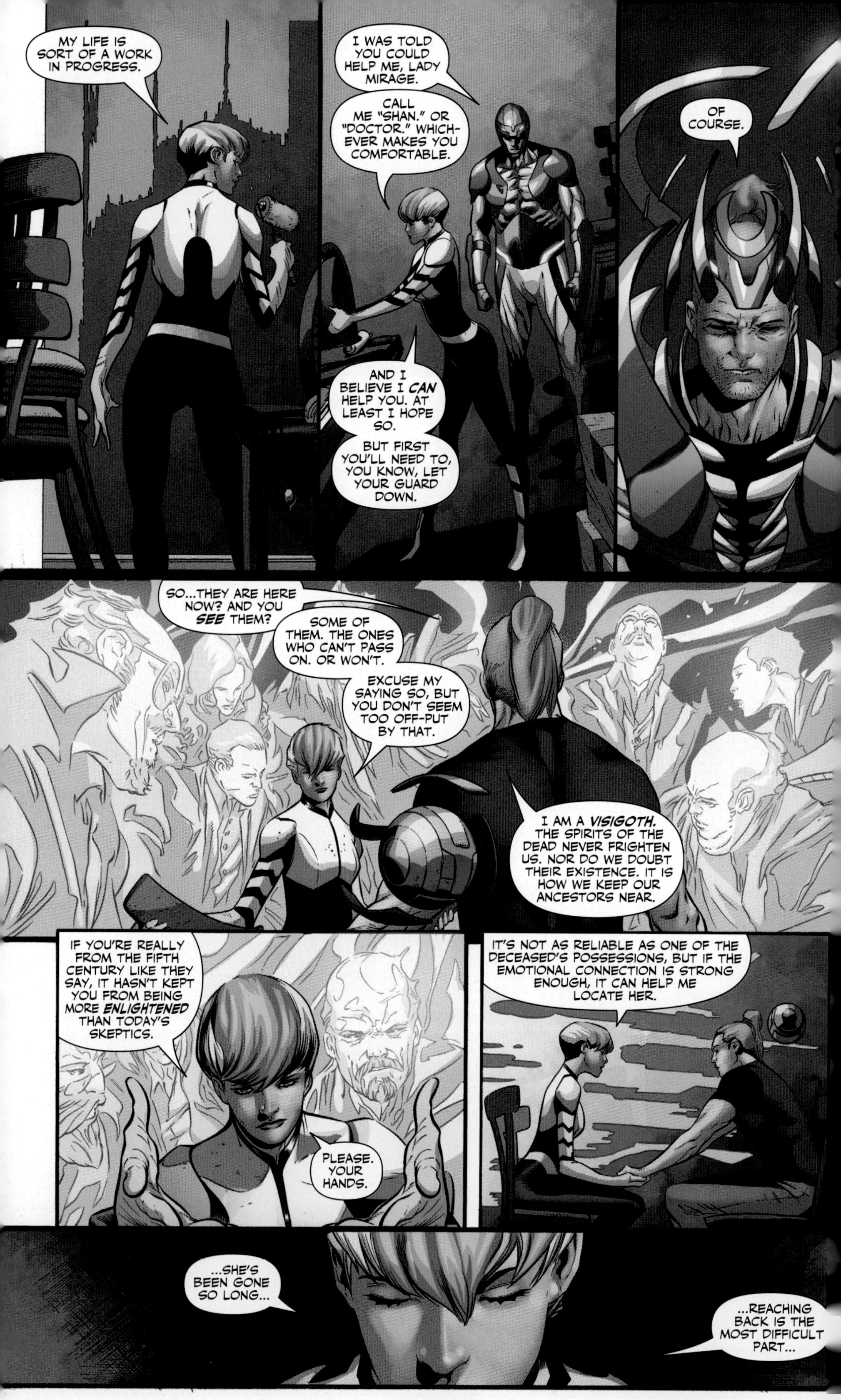
MY LIFE IS SORT OF A WORK IN PROGRESS.
I WAS TOLD YOU COULD HELP ME, LADY MIRAGE.
CALL ME "SHAN." OR "DOCTOR." WHICH-EVER MAKES YOU COMFORTABLE.
AND I BELIEVE I CAN HELP YOU. AT LEAST I HOPE SO.
BUT FIRST YOU'LL NEED TO, YOU KNOW, LET YOUR GUARD DOWN.
OF COURSE.
SO...THEY ARE HERE NOW? AND YOU SEE THEM?
SOME OF THEM. THE ONES WHO CAN'T PASS ON. OR WON'T.
EXCUSE MY SAYING SO, BUT YOU DON'T SEEM TOO OFF-PUT BY THAT.
I AM A VISIGOTH. THE SPIRITS OF THE DEAD NEVER FRIGHTEN US. NOR DO WE DOUBT THEIR EXISTENCE. IT IS HOW WE KEEP OUR ANCESTORS NEAR.
IF YOU'RE REALLY FROM THE FIFTH CENTURY LIKE THEY SAY, IT HASN'T KEPT YOU FROM BEING MORE ENLIGHTENED THAN TODAY'S SKEPTICS.
PLEASE. YOUR HANDS.
IT'S NOT AS RELIABLE AS ONE OF THE DECEASED'S POSSESSIONS, BUT IF THE EMOTIONAL CONNECTION IS STRONG ENOUGH, IT CAN HELP ME LOCATE HER.
...SHE'S BEEN GONE SO LONG...
...REACHING BACK IS THE MOST DIFFICULT PART...

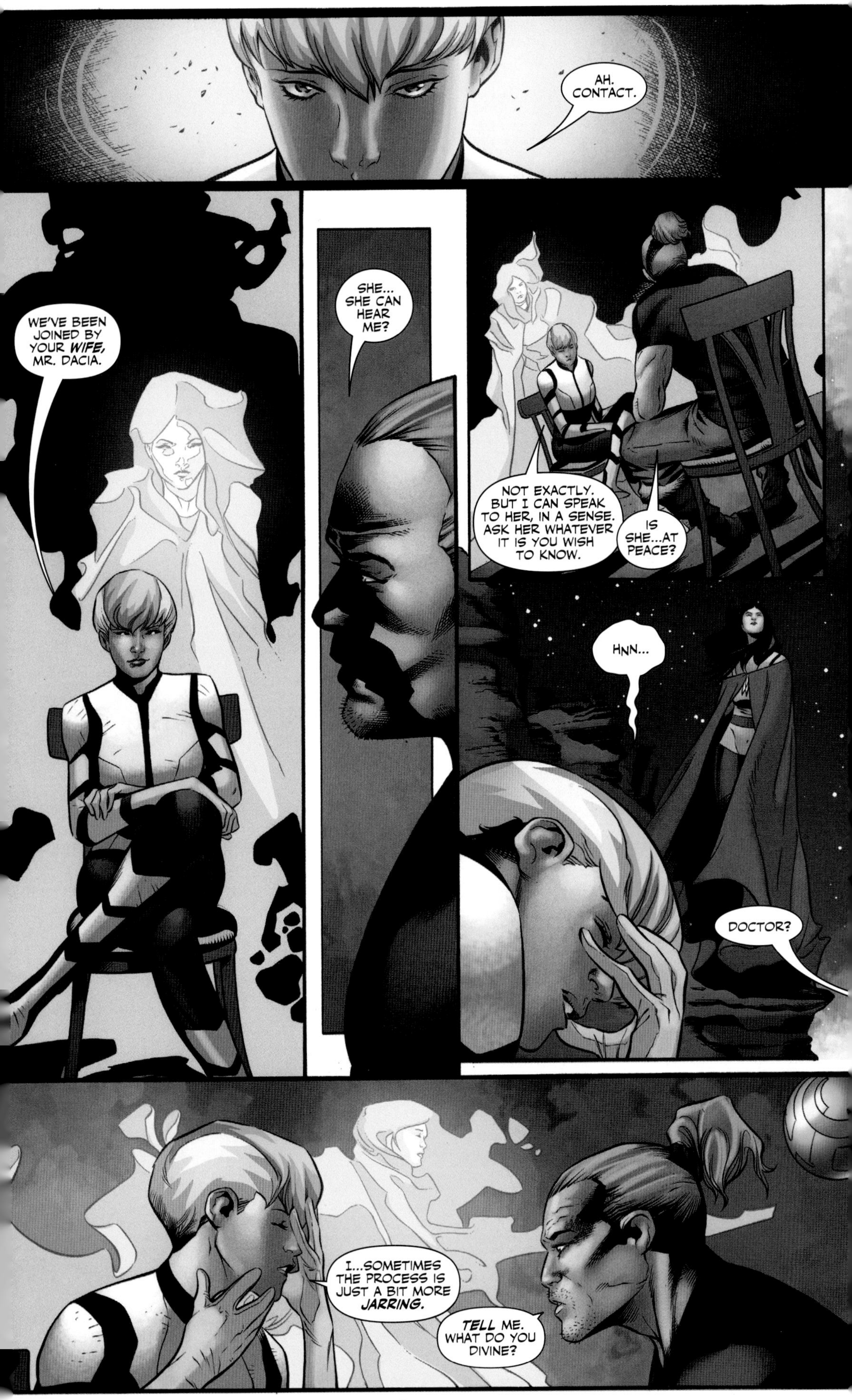
AH. CONTACT.
WE'VE BEEN JOINED BY YOUR WIFE, MR. DACIA.
SHE... SHE CAN HEAR ME?
NOT EXACTLY. BUT I CAN SPEAK TO HER, IN A SENSE. ASK HER WHATEVER IT IS YOU WISH TO KNOW.
IS SHE...AT PEACE?
HNN...
DOCTOR?
I...SOMETIMES THE PROCESS IS JUST A BIT MORE JARRING.
TELL ME. WHAT DO YOU DIVINE?

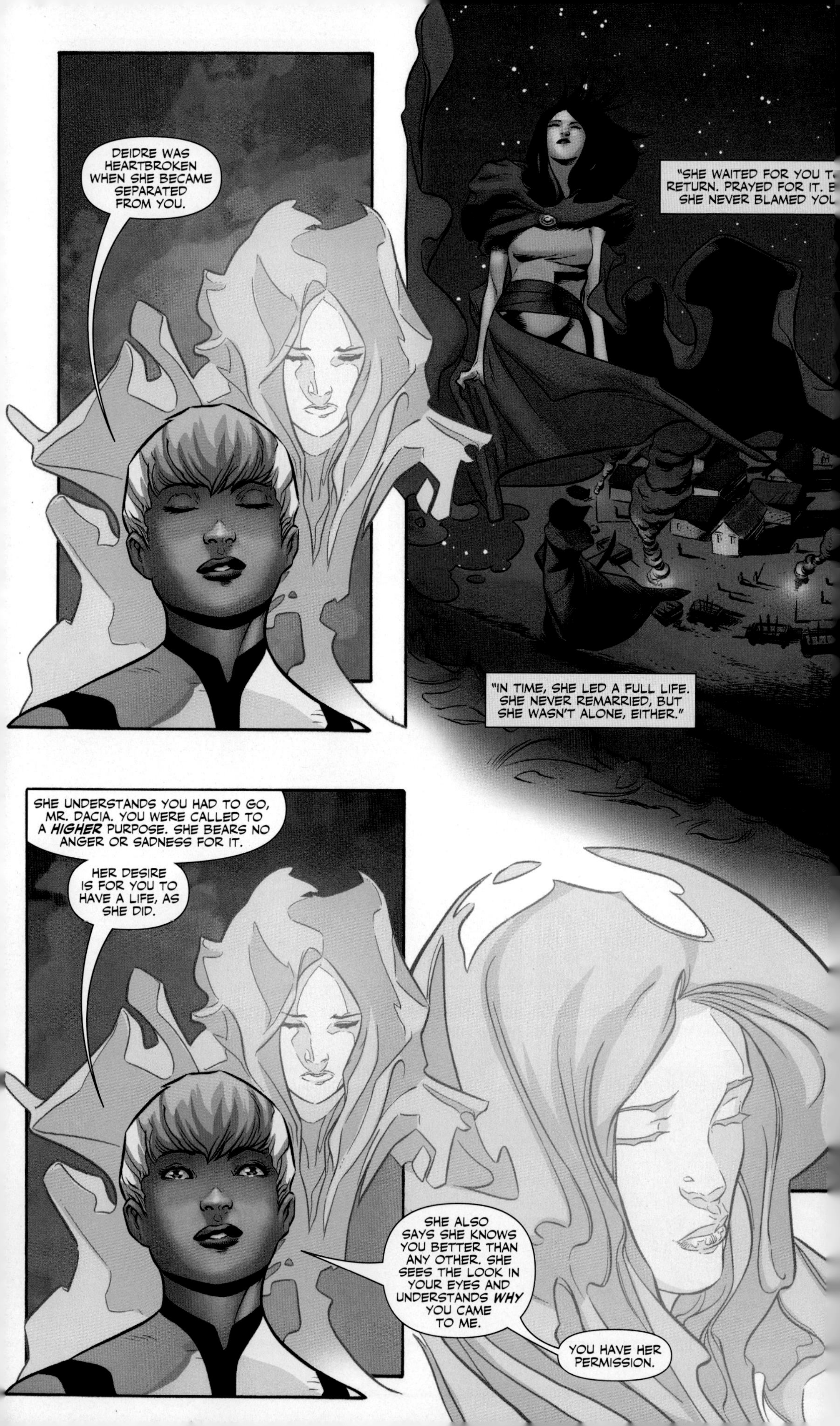
DEIDRE WAS HEARTBROKEN WHEN SHE BECAME SEPARATED FROM YOU.
"SHE WAITED FOR YOU T RETURN. PRAYED FOR IT. B SHE NEVER BLAMED YOU
"IN TIME, SHE LED A FULL LIFE. SHE NEVER REMARRIED, BUT SHE WASN'T ALONE, EITHER."
SHE UNDERSTANDS YOU HAD TO GO, MR. DACIA. YOU WERE CALLED TO A ***HIGHER*** PURPOSE. SHE BEARS NO ANGER OR SADNESS FOR IT.
HER DESIRE IS FOR YOU TO HAVE A LIFE, AS SHE DID.
SHE ALSO SAYS SHE KNOWS YOU BETTER THAN ANY OTHER. SHE SEES THE LOOK IN YOUR EYES AND UNDERSTANDS ***WHY*** YOU CAME TO ME.
YOU HAVE HER PERMISSION.

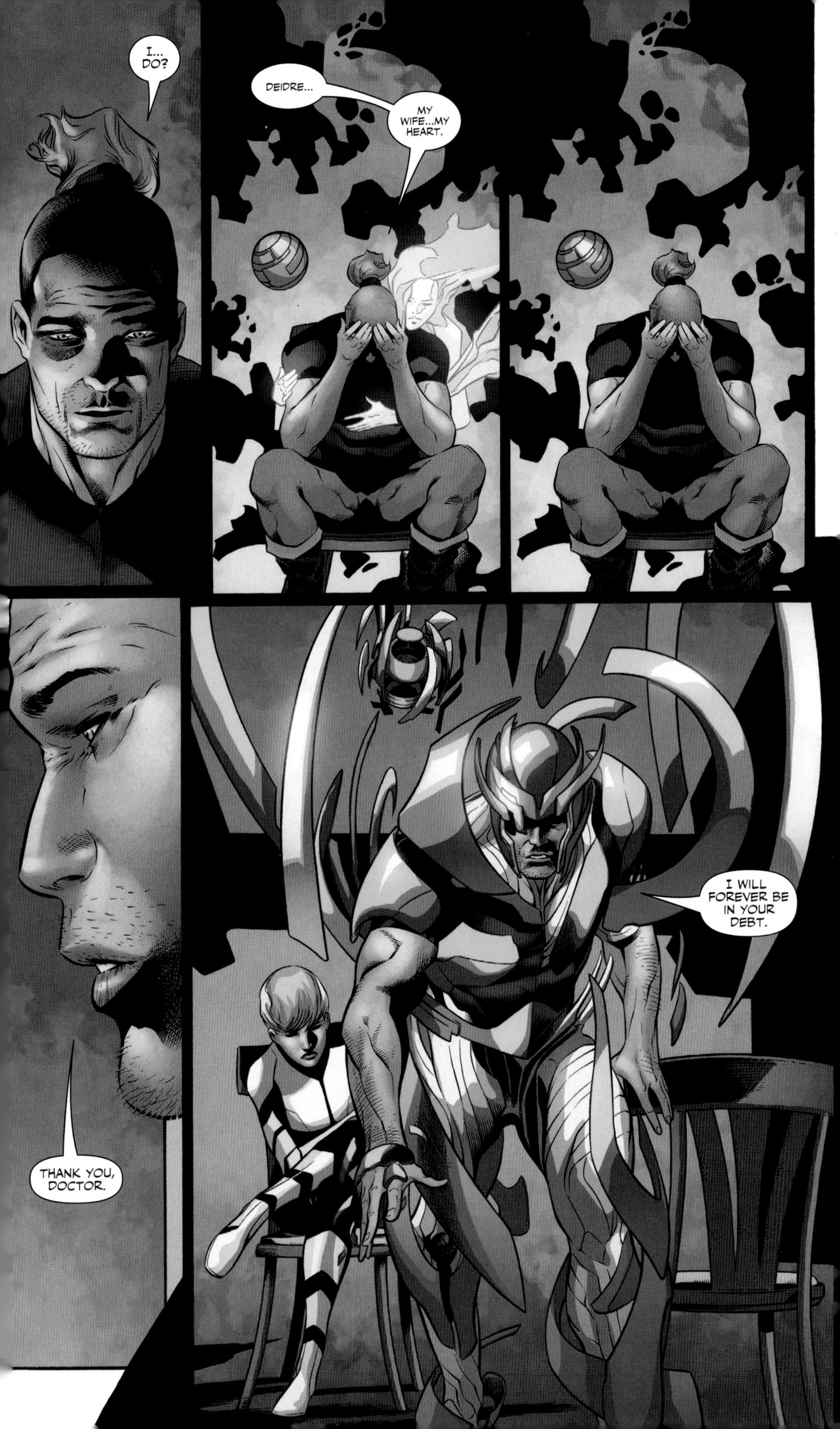
I... DO?
DEIDRE...
MY WIFE...MY HEART.
THANK YOU, DOCTOR.
I WILL FOREVER BE IN YOUR DEBT.

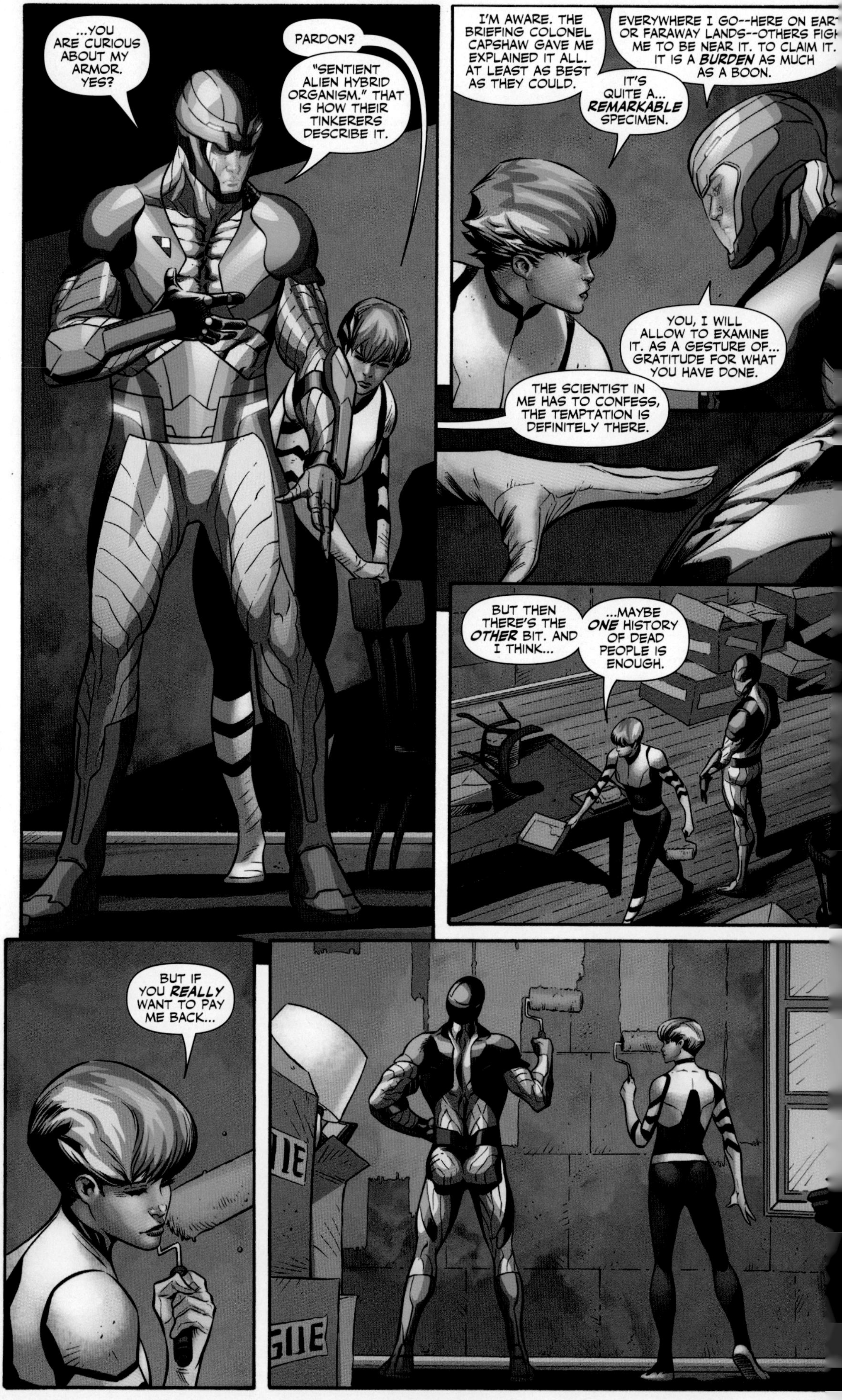
...YOU ARE CURIOUS ABOUT MY ARMOR. YES?
PARDON?
"SENTIENT ALIEN HYBRID ORGANISM." THAT IS HOW THEIR TINKERERS DESCRIBE IT.
I'M AWARE. THE BRIEFING COLONEL CAPSHAW GAVE ME EXPLAINED IT ALL. AT LEAST AS BEST AS THEY COULD.
IT'S QUITE A... REMARKABLE SPECIMEN.
EVERYWHERE I GO--HERE ON EART OR FARAWAY LANDS--OTHERS FIGH ME TO BE NEAR IT. TO CLAIM IT. IT IS A BURDEN AS MUCH AS A BOON.
YOU, I WILL ALLOW TO EXAMINE IT. AS A GESTURE OF... GRATITUDE FOR WHAT YOU HAVE DONE.
THE SCIENTIST IN ME HAS TO CONFESS, THE TEMPTATION IS DEFINITELY THERE.
BUT THEN THERE'S THE OTHER BIT. AND I THINK...
...MAYBE ONE HISTORY OF DEAD PEOPLE IS ENOUGH.
BUT IF YOU REALLY WANT TO PAY ME BACK...

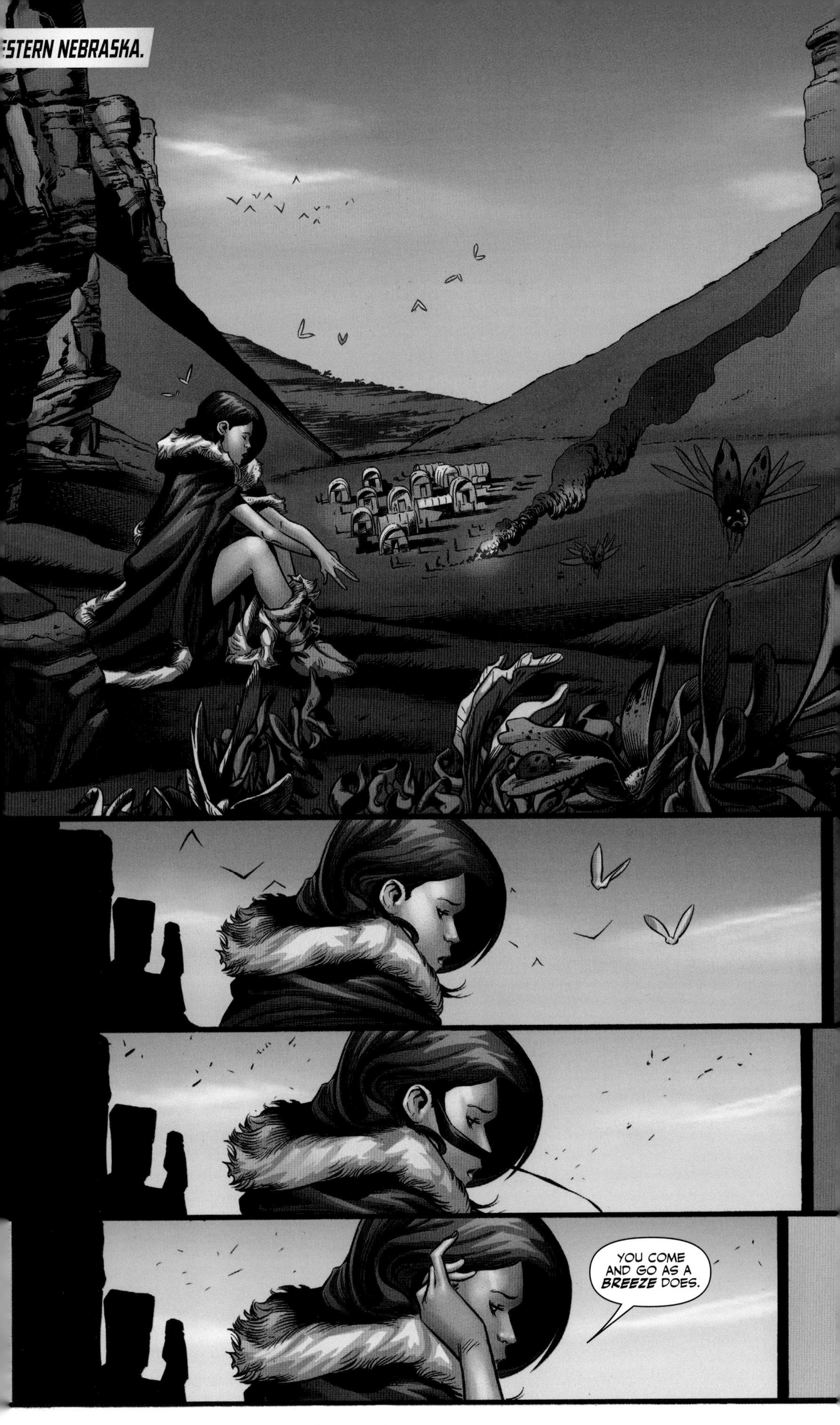
ESTERN NEBRASKA.
YOU COME AND GO AS A BREEZE DOES.

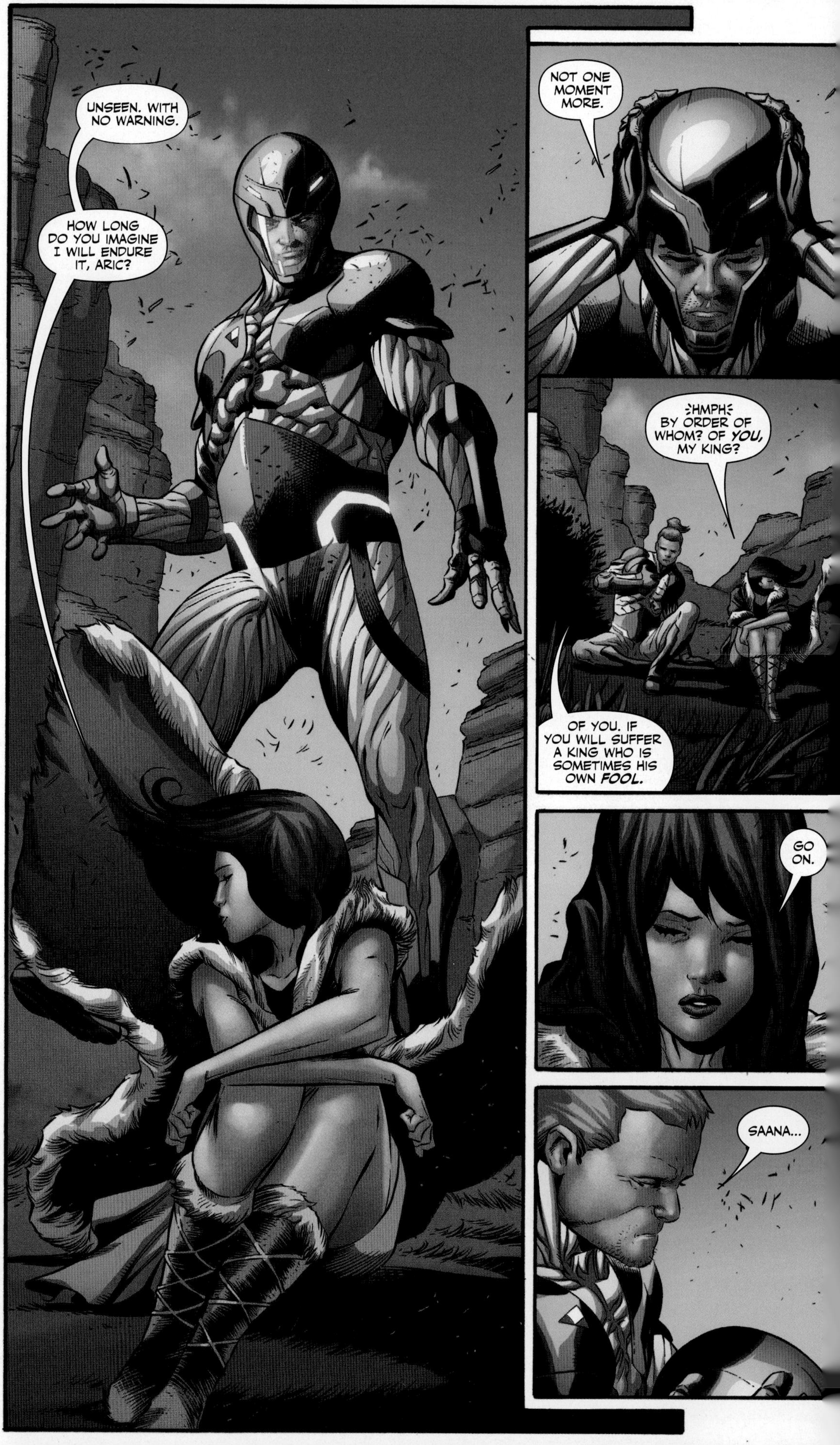
UNSEEN. WITH NO WARNING.
HOW LONG DO YOU IMAGINE I WILL ENDURE IT, ARIC?
NOT ONE MOMENT MORE.
HMPH
BY ORDER OF WHOM? OF *YOU,* MY KING?
OF YOU. IF YOU WILL SUFFER A KING WHO IS SOMETIMES HIS OWN *FOOL.*
GO ON.
SAANA...

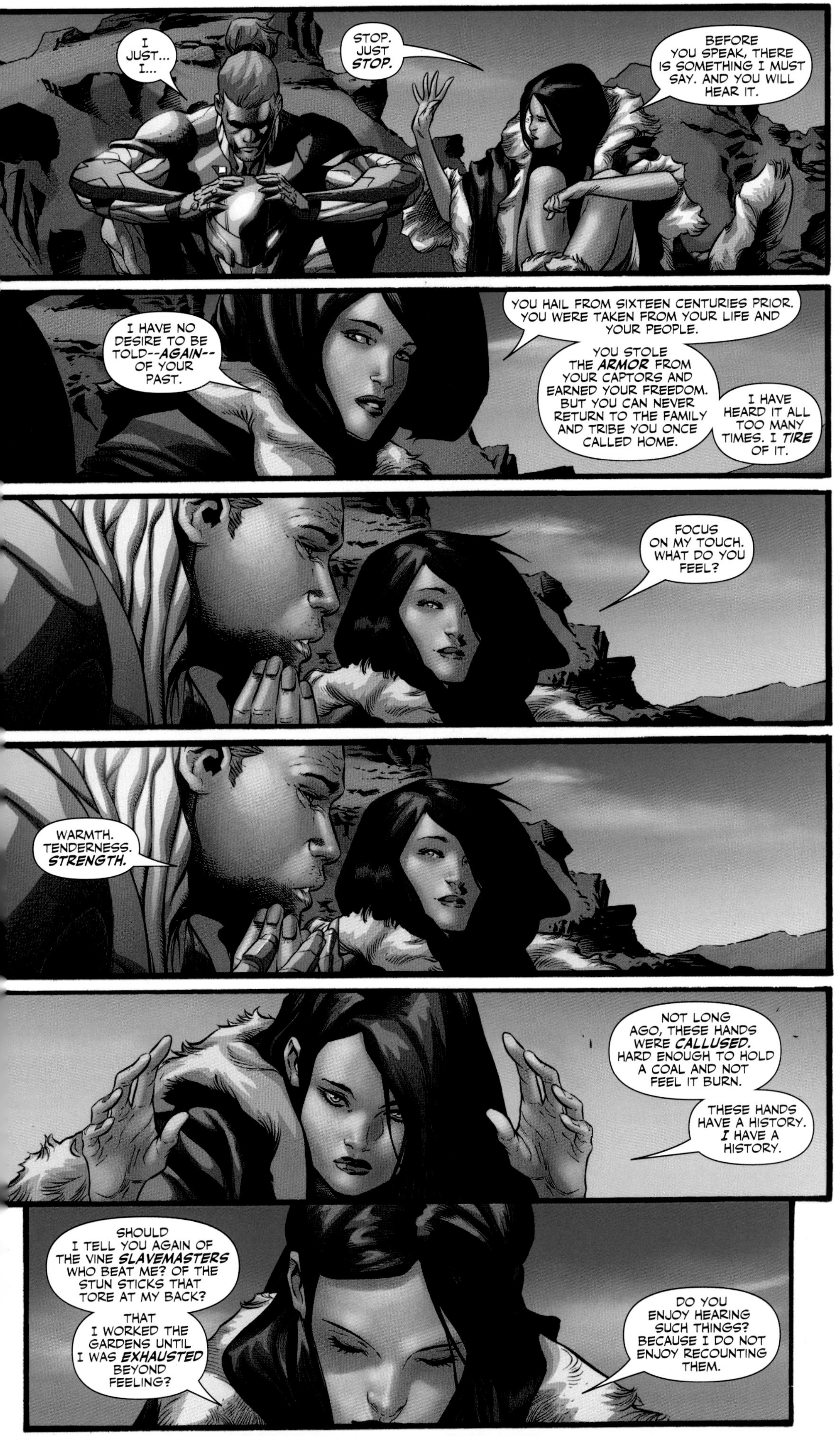

I JUST... I...
STOP. JUST STOP.
BEFORE YOU SPEAK, THERE IS SOMETHING I MUST SAY. AND YOU WILL HEAR IT.
I HAVE NO DESIRE TO BE TOLD--AGAIN--OF YOUR PAST.
YOU HAIL FROM SIXTEEN CENTURIES PRIOR. YOU WERE TAKEN FROM YOUR LIFE AND YOUR PEOPLE.
YOU STOLE THE ARMOR FROM YOUR CAPTORS AND EARNED YOUR FREEDOM. BUT YOU CAN NEVER RETURN TO THE FAMILY AND TRIBE YOU ONCE CALLED HOME.
I HAVE HEARD IT ALL TOO MANY TIMES. I TIRE OF IT.
FOCUS ON MY TOUCH. WHAT DO YOU FEEL?
WARMTH. TENDERNESS. STRENGTH.
NOT LONG AGO, THESE HANDS WERE CALLUSED. HARD ENOUGH TO HOLD A COAL AND NOT FEEL IT BURN.
THESE HANDS HAVE A HISTORY. I HAVE A HISTORY.
SHOULD I TELL YOU AGAIN OF THE VINE SLAVEMASTERS WHO BEAT ME? OF THE STUN STICKS THAT TORE AT MY BACK?
THAT I WORKED THE GARDENS UNTIL I WAS EXHAUSTED BEYOND FEELING?
DO YOU ENJOY HEARING SUCH THINGS? BECAUSE I DO NOT ENJOY RECOUNTING THEM.

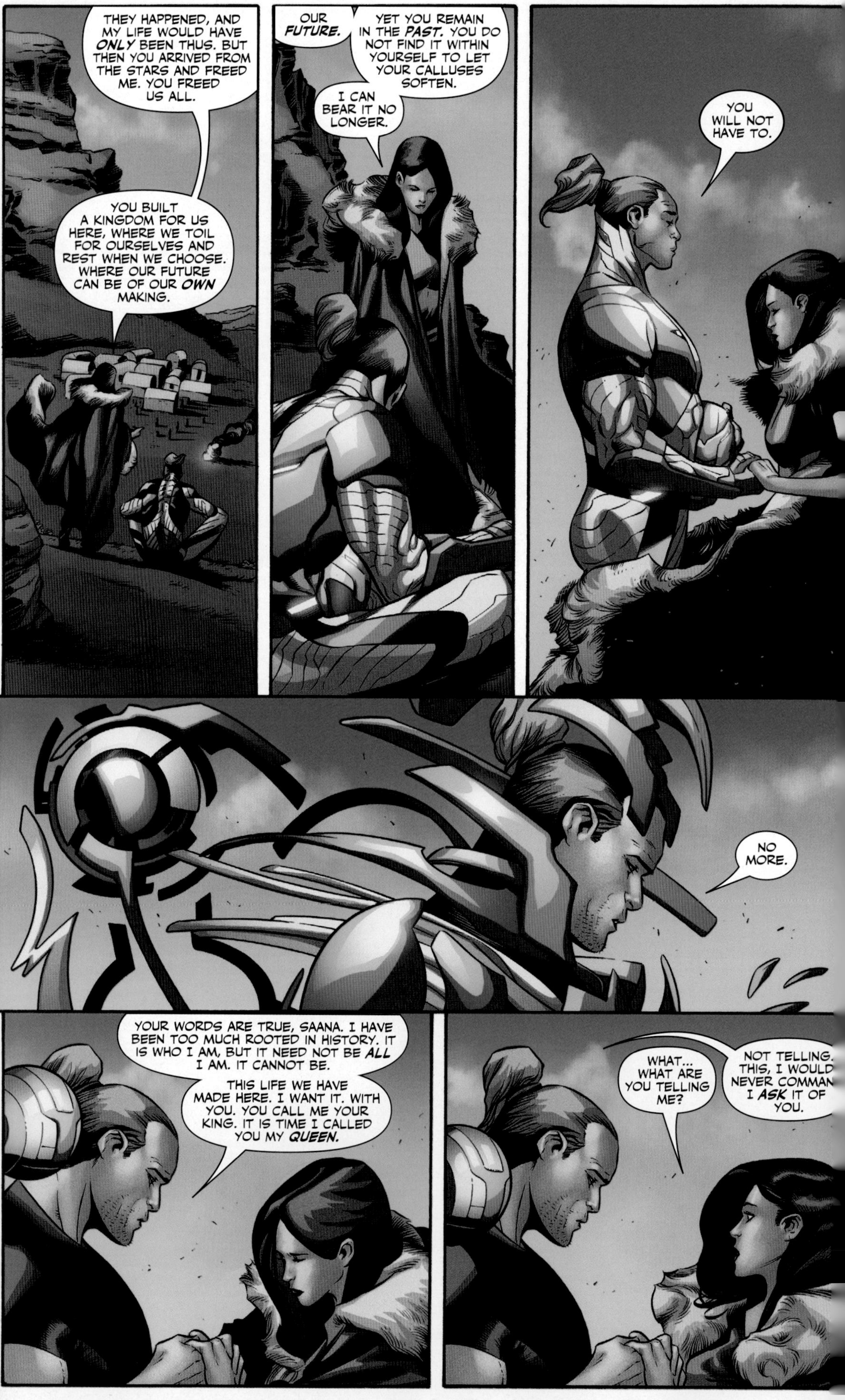
THEY HAPPENED, AND MY LIFE WOULD HAVE ONLY BEEN THUS. BUT THEN YOU ARRIVED FROM THE STARS AND FREED ME. YOU FREED US ALL.
YOU BUILT A KINGDOM FOR US HERE, WHERE WE TOIL FOR OURSELVES AND REST WHEN WE CHOOSE. WHERE OUR FUTURE CAN BE OF OUR OWN MAKING.
OUR FUTURE.
YET YOU REMAIN IN THE PAST. YOU DO NOT FIND IT WITHIN YOURSELF TO LET YOUR CALLUSES SOFTEN.
I CAN BEAR IT NO LONGER.
YOU WILL NOT HAVE TO.
NO MORE.
YOUR WORDS ARE TRUE, SAANA. I HAVE BEEN TOO MUCH ROOTED IN HISTORY. IT IS WHO I AM, BUT IT NEED NOT BE ALL I AM. IT CANNOT BE.
THIS LIFE WE HAVE MADE HERE. I WANT IT. WITH YOU. YOU CALL ME YOUR KING. IT IS TIME I CALLED YOU MY QUEEN.
WHAT... WHAT ARE YOU TELLING ME?
NOT TELLING. THIS, I WOULD NEVER COMMAN I ASK IT OF YOU.

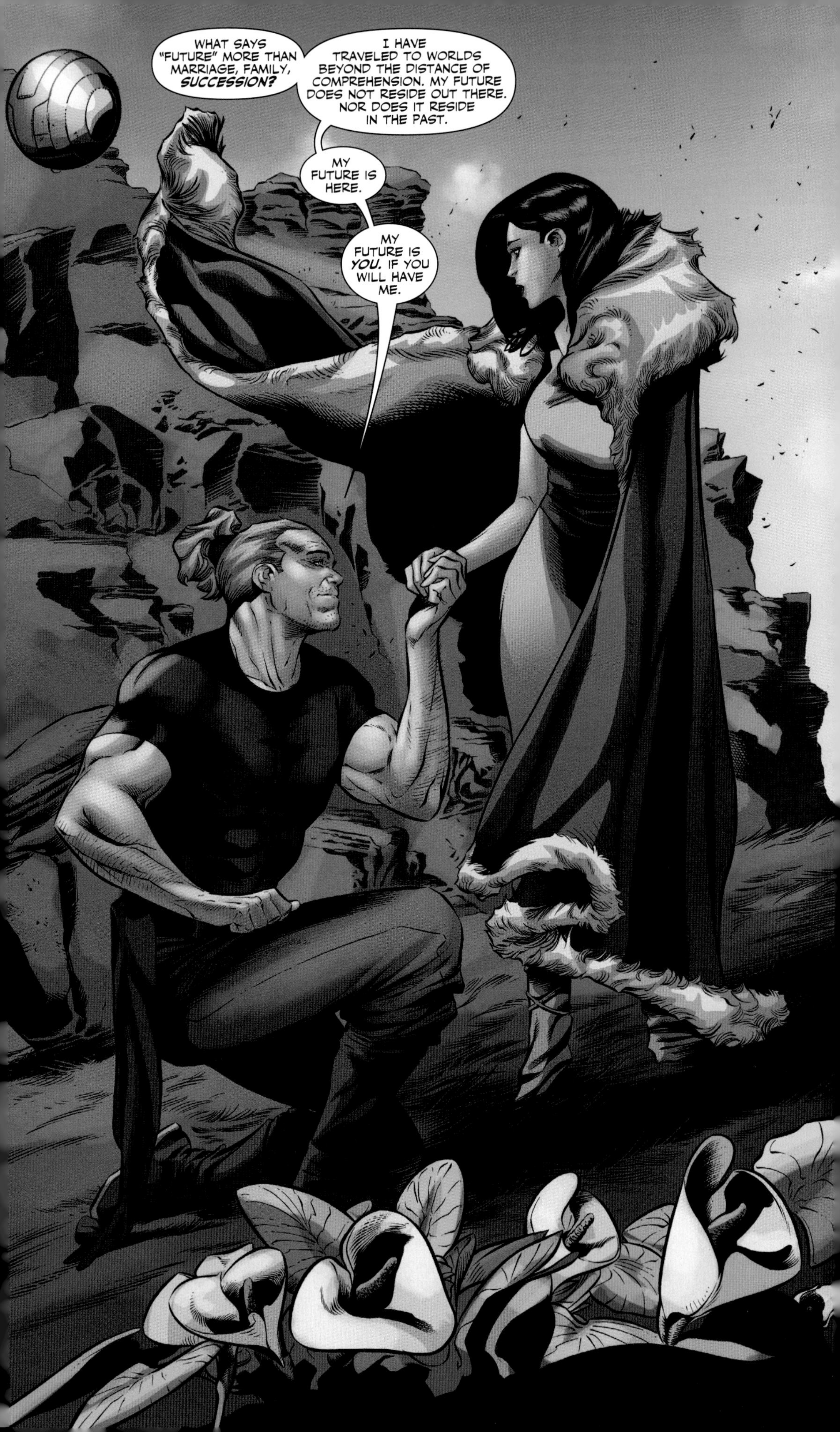
WHAT SAYS "FUTURE" MORE THAN MARRIAGE, FAMILY, *SUCCESSION?*
I HAVE TRAVELED TO WORLDS BEYOND THE DISTANCE OF COMPREHENSION. MY FUTURE DOES NOT RESIDE OUT THERE. NOR DOES IT RESIDE IN THE PAST.
MY FUTURE IS HERE.
MY FUTURE IS *YOU.* IF YOU WILL HAVE ME.

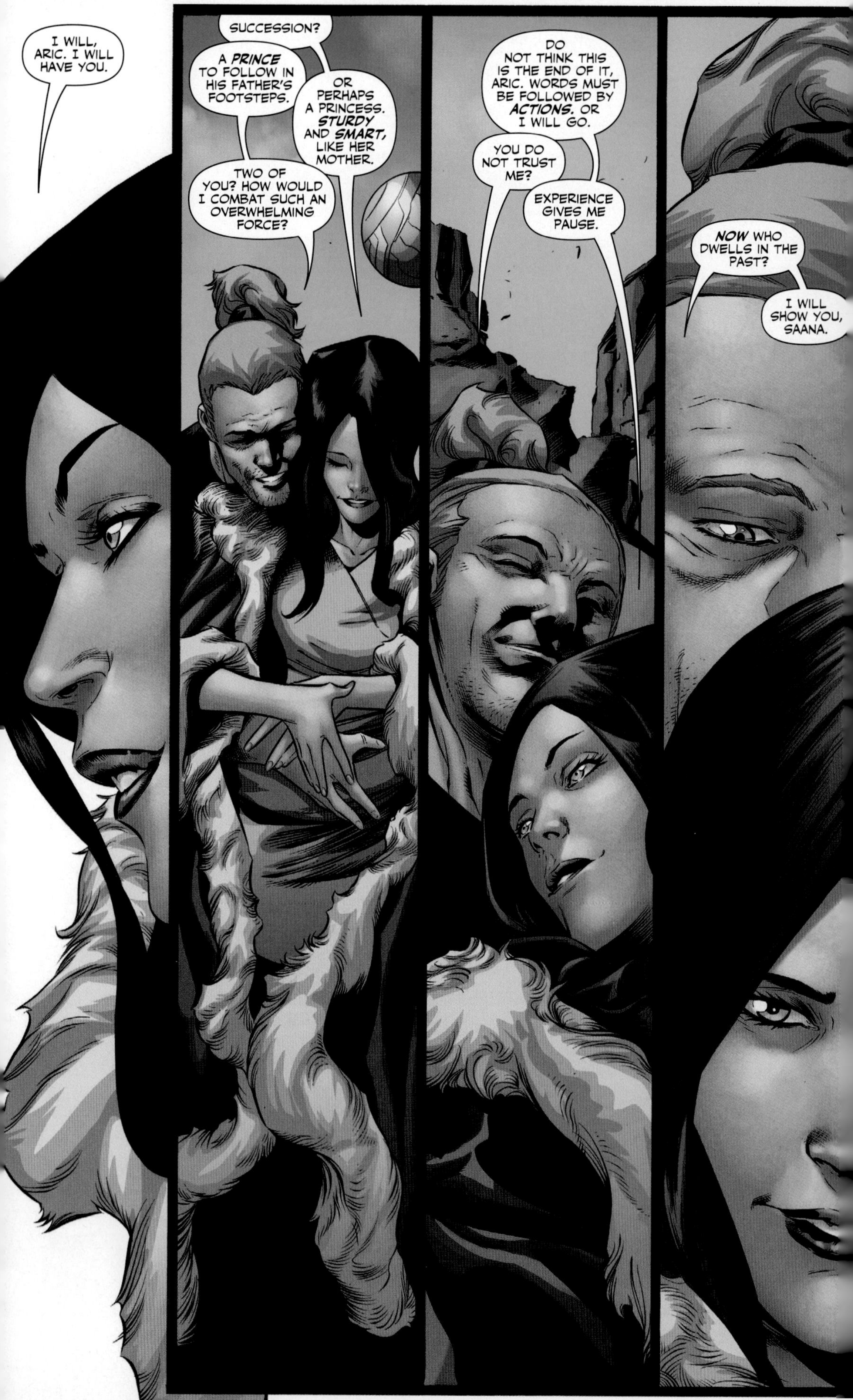
I WILL, ARIC. I WILL HAVE YOU.
SUCCESSION?
A PRINCE TO FOLLOW IN HIS FATHER'S FOOTSTEPS.
OR PERHAPS A PRINCESS. STURDY AND SMART, LIKE HER MOTHER.
TWO OF YOU? HOW WOULD I COMBAT SUCH AN OVERWHELMING FORCE?
DO NOT THINK THIS IS THE END OF IT, ARIC. WORDS MUST BE FOLLOWED BY ACTIONS. OR I WILL GO.
YOU DO NOT TRUST ME?
EXPERIENCE GIVES ME PAUSE.
NOW WHO DWELLS IN THE PAST?
I WILL SHOW YOU, SAANA.

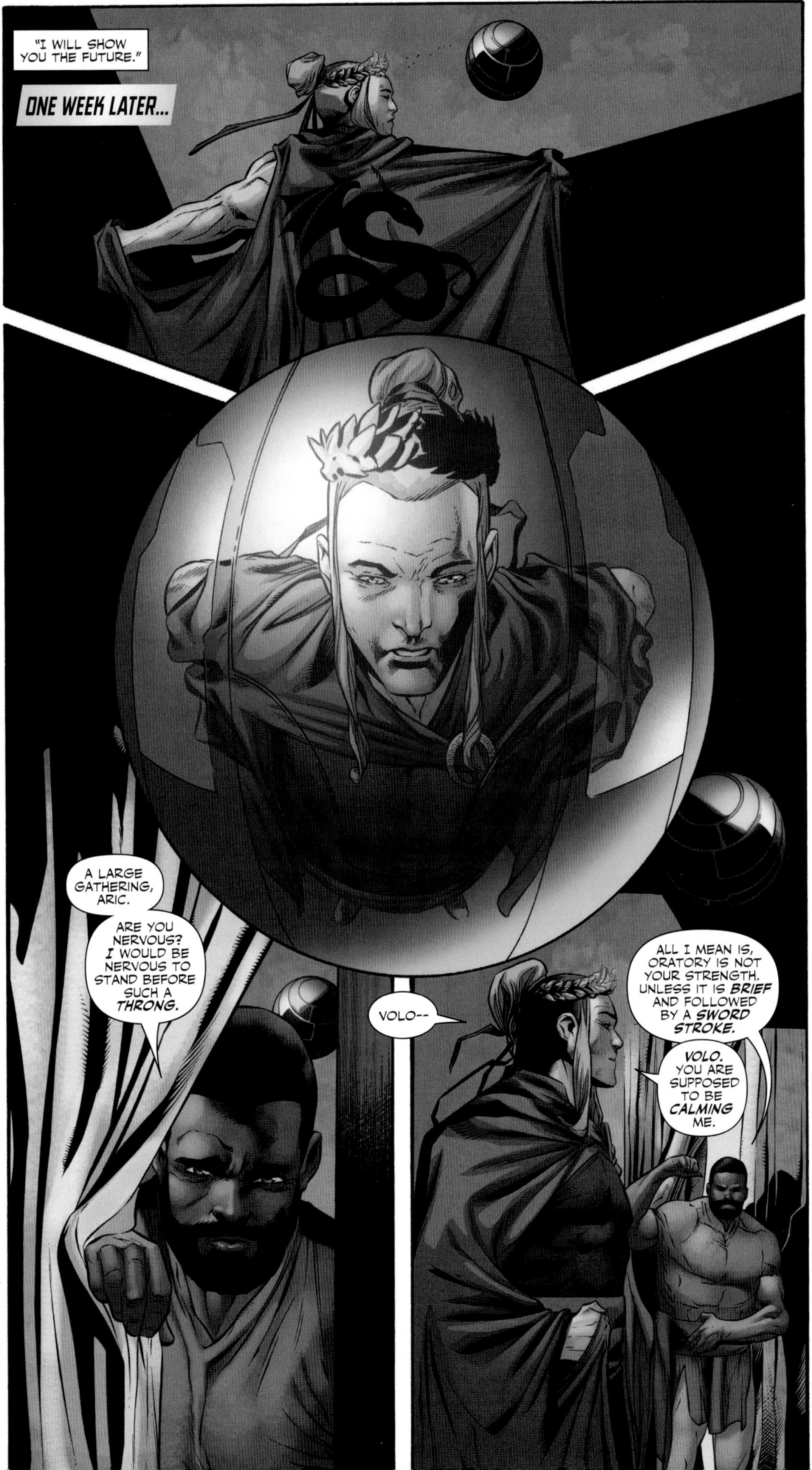
"I WILL SHOW YOU THE FUTURE."
ONE WEEK LATER...
A LARGE GATHERING, ARIC.
ARE YOU NERVOUS? I WOULD BE NERVOUS TO STAND BEFORE SUCH A THRONG.
VOLO--
ALL I MEAN IS, ORATORY IS NOT YOUR STRENGTH. UNLESS IT IS BRIEF AND FOLLOWED BY A SWORD STROKE.
VOLO. YOU ARE SUPPOSED TO BE CALMING ME.

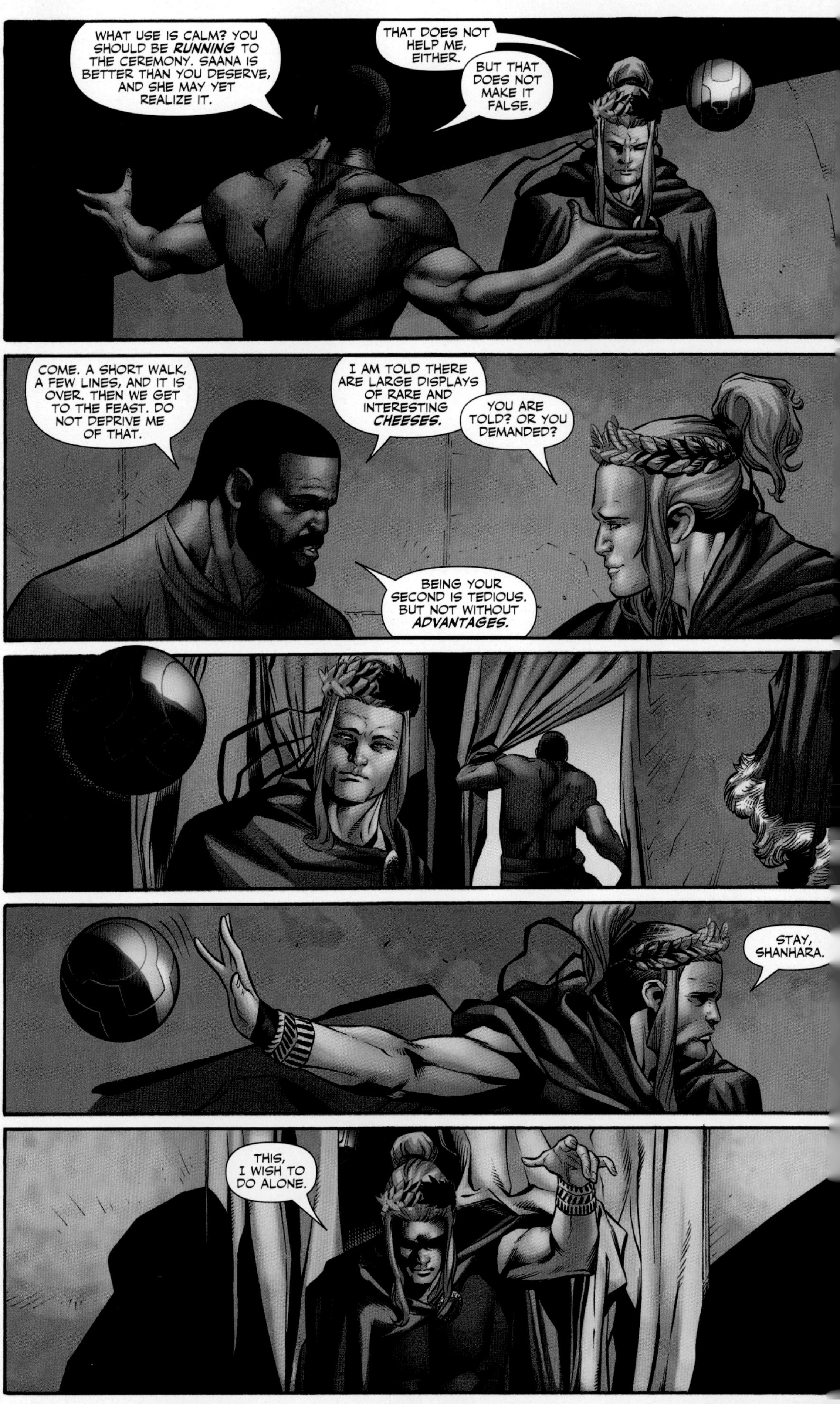
WHAT USE IS CALM? YOU SHOULD BE RUNNING TO THE CEREMONY. SAANA IS BETTER THAN YOU DESERVE, AND SHE MAY YET REALIZE IT.
THAT DOES NOT HELP ME, EITHER.
BUT THAT DOES NOT MAKE IT FALSE.
COME. A SHORT WALK, A FEW LINES, AND IT IS OVER. THEN WE GET TO THE FEAST. DO NOT DEPRIVE ME OF THAT.
I AM TOLD THERE ARE LARGE DISPLAYS OF RARE AND INTERESTING CHEESES.
YOU ARE TOLD? OR YOU DEMANDED?
BEING YOUR SECOND IS TEDIOUS. BUT NOT WITHOUT ADVANTAGES.
STAY, SHANHARA.
THIS, I WISH TO DO ALONE.

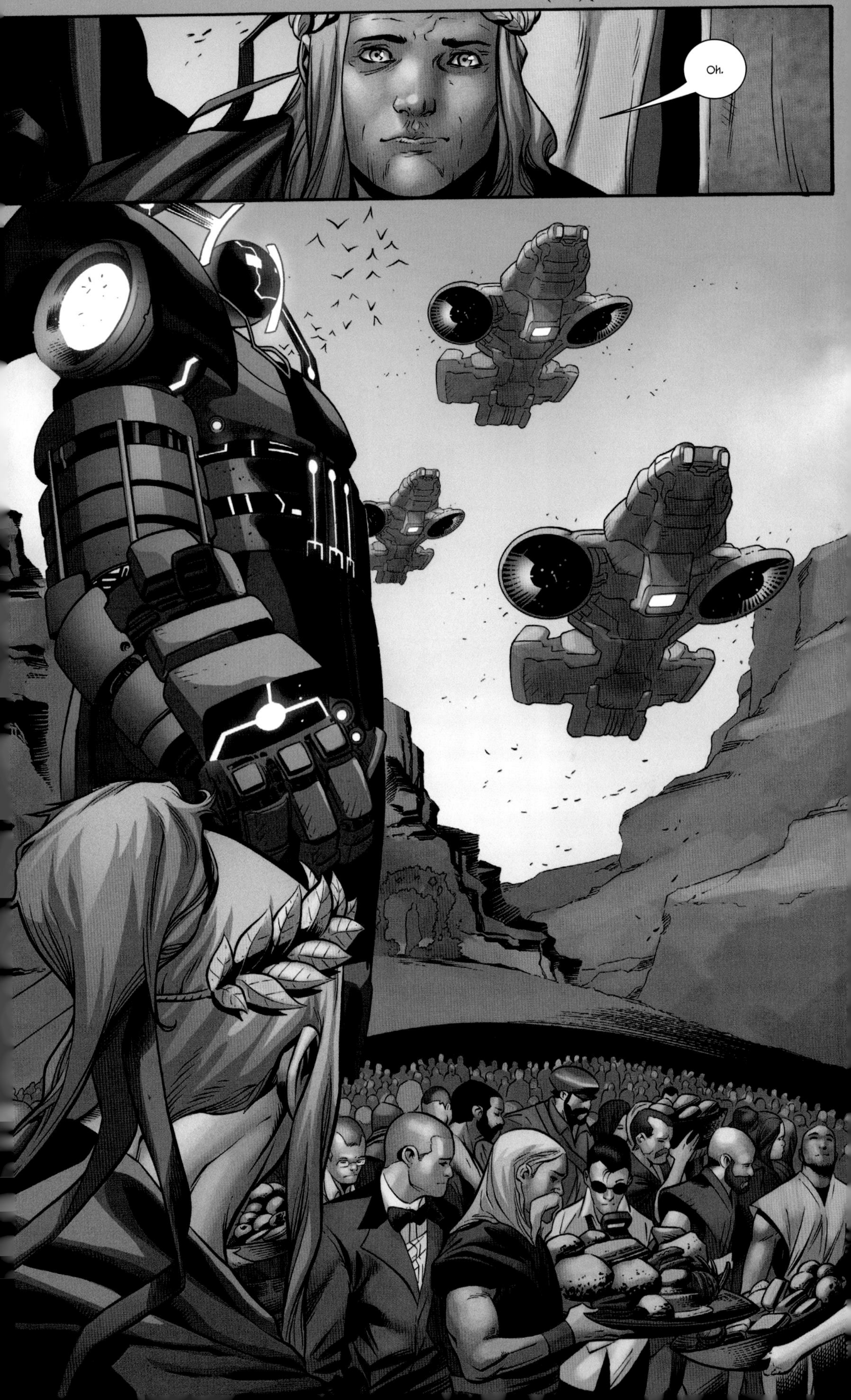
Oh.

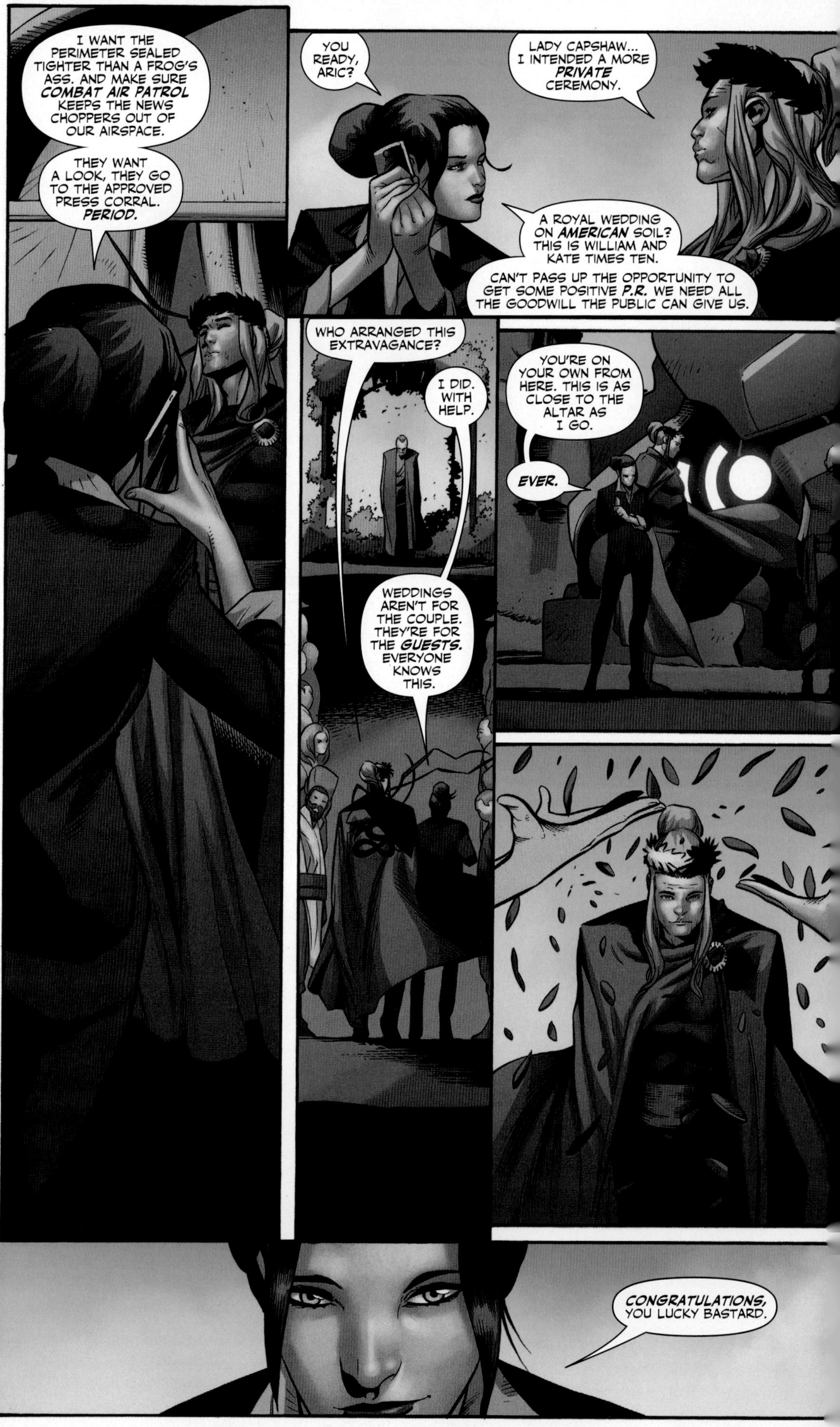
I WANT THE PERIMETER SEALED TIGHTER THAN A FROG'S ASS. AND MAKE SURE COMBAT AIR PATROL KEEPS THE NEWS CHOPPERS OUT OF OUR AIRSPACE.
THEY WANT A LOOK, THEY GO TO THE APPROVED PRESS CORRAL. PERIOD.
YOU READY, ARIC?
LADY CAPSHAW... I INTENDED A MORE PRIVATE CEREMONY.
A ROYAL WEDDING ON AMERICAN SOIL? THIS IS WILLIAM AND KATE TIMES TEN.
CAN'T PASS UP THE OPPORTUNITY TO GET SOME POSITIVE P.R. WE NEED ALL THE GOODWILL THE PUBLIC CAN GIVE US.
WHO ARRANGED THIS EXTRAVAGANCE?
I DID. WITH HELP.
WEDDINGS AREN'T FOR THE COUPLE. THEY'RE FOR THE GUESTS. EVERYONE KNOWS THIS.
YOU'RE ON YOUR OWN FROM HERE. THIS IS AS CLOSE TO THE ALTAR AS I GO.
EVER.
CONGRATULATIONS, YOU LUCKY BASTARD.

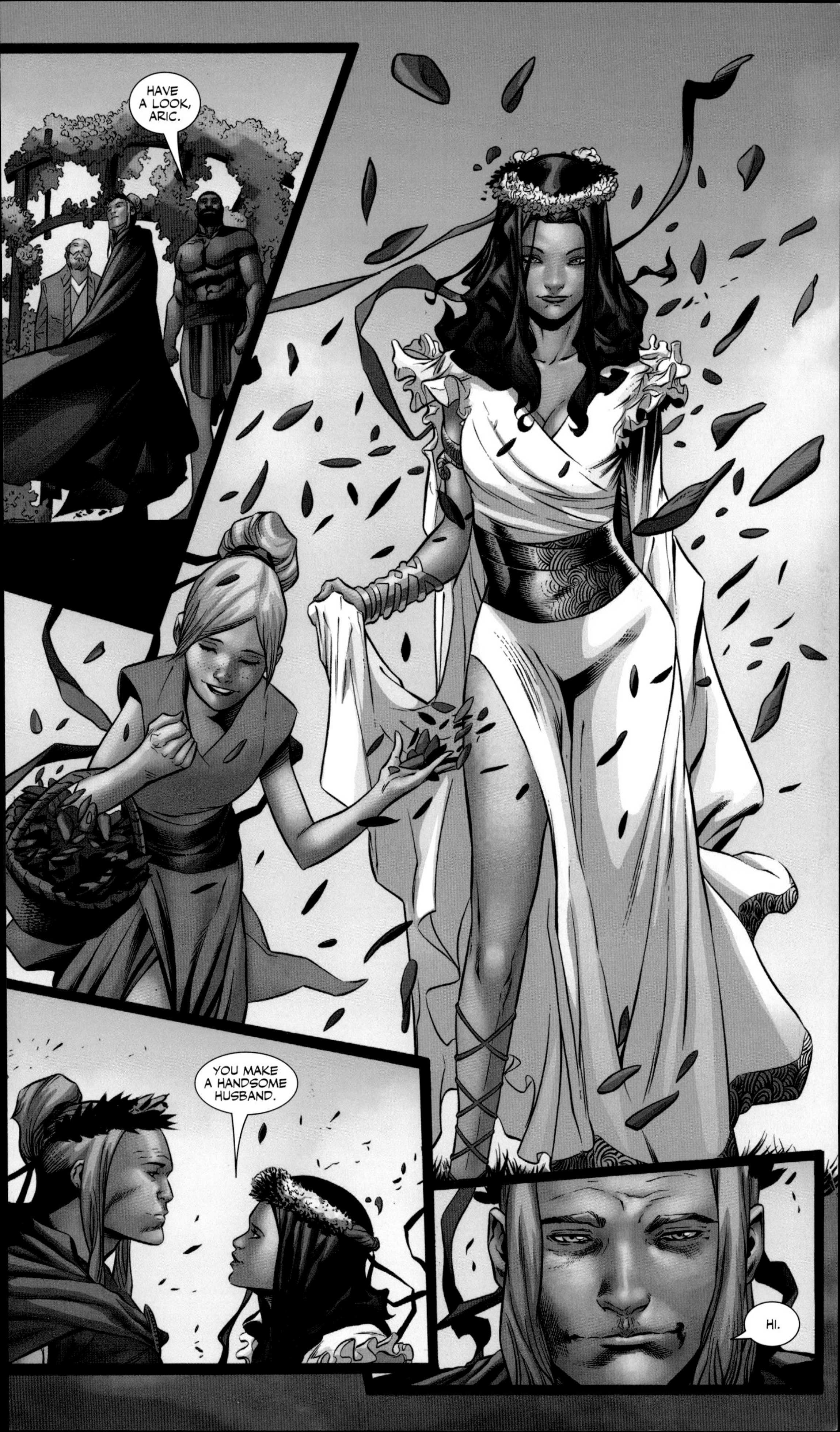
HAVE A LOOK, ARIC.
YOU MAKE A HANDSOME HUSBAND.
HI.

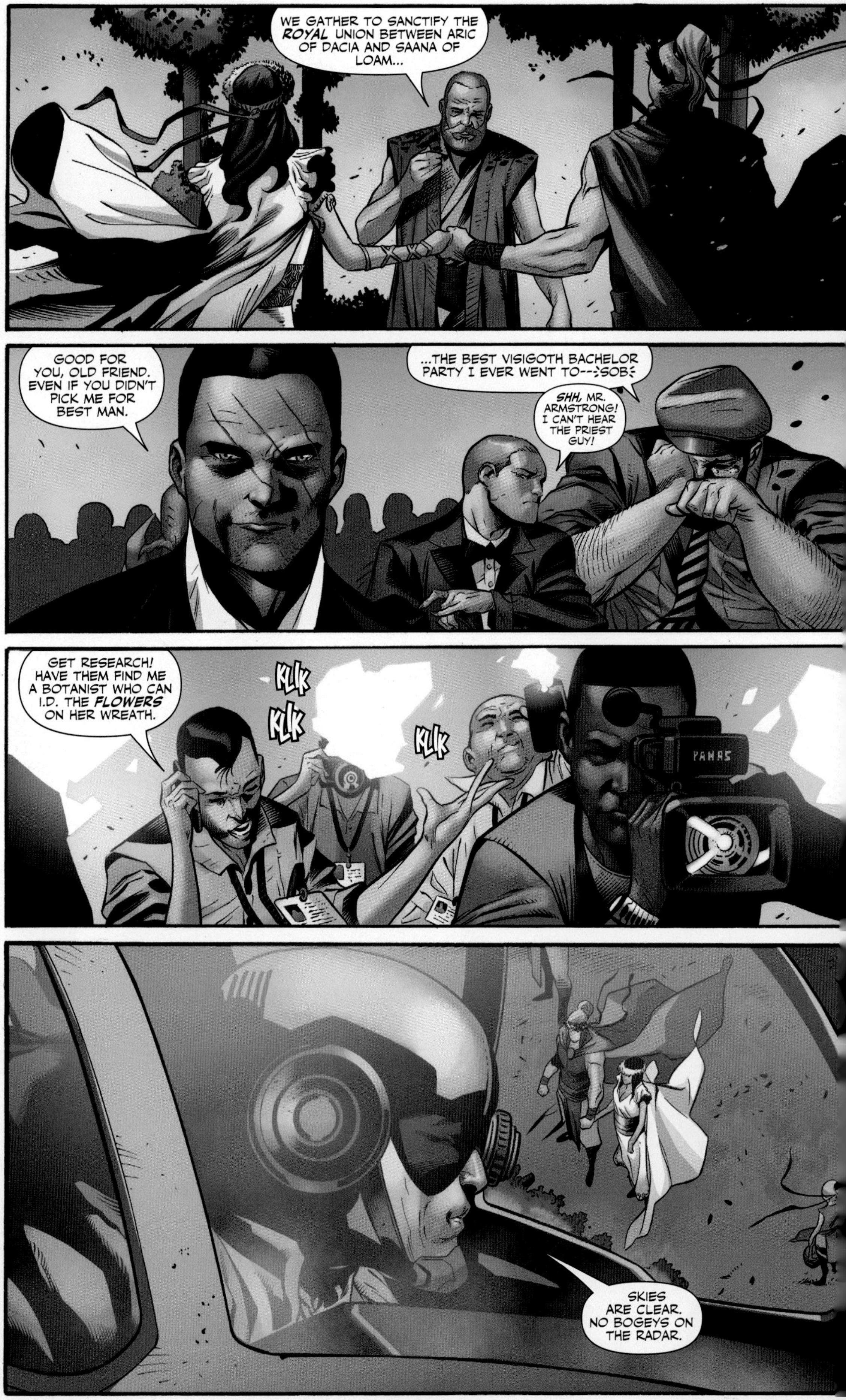
WE GATHER TO SANCTIFY THE ROYAL UNION BETWEEN ARIC OF DACIA AND SAANA OF LOAM...
GOOD FOR YOU, OLD FRIEND. EVEN IF YOU DIDN'T PICK ME FOR BEST MAN.
...THE BEST VISIGOTH BACHELOR PARTY I EVER WENT TO--SOB
SHH, MR. ARMSTRONG! I CAN'T HEAR THE PRIEST GUY!
GET RESEARCH! HAVE THEM FIND ME A BOTANIST WHO CAN I.D. THE FLOWERS ON HER WREATH.
KLIK
KLIK
KLIK
PAMAS
SKIES ARE CLEAR. NO BOGEYS ON THE RADAR.

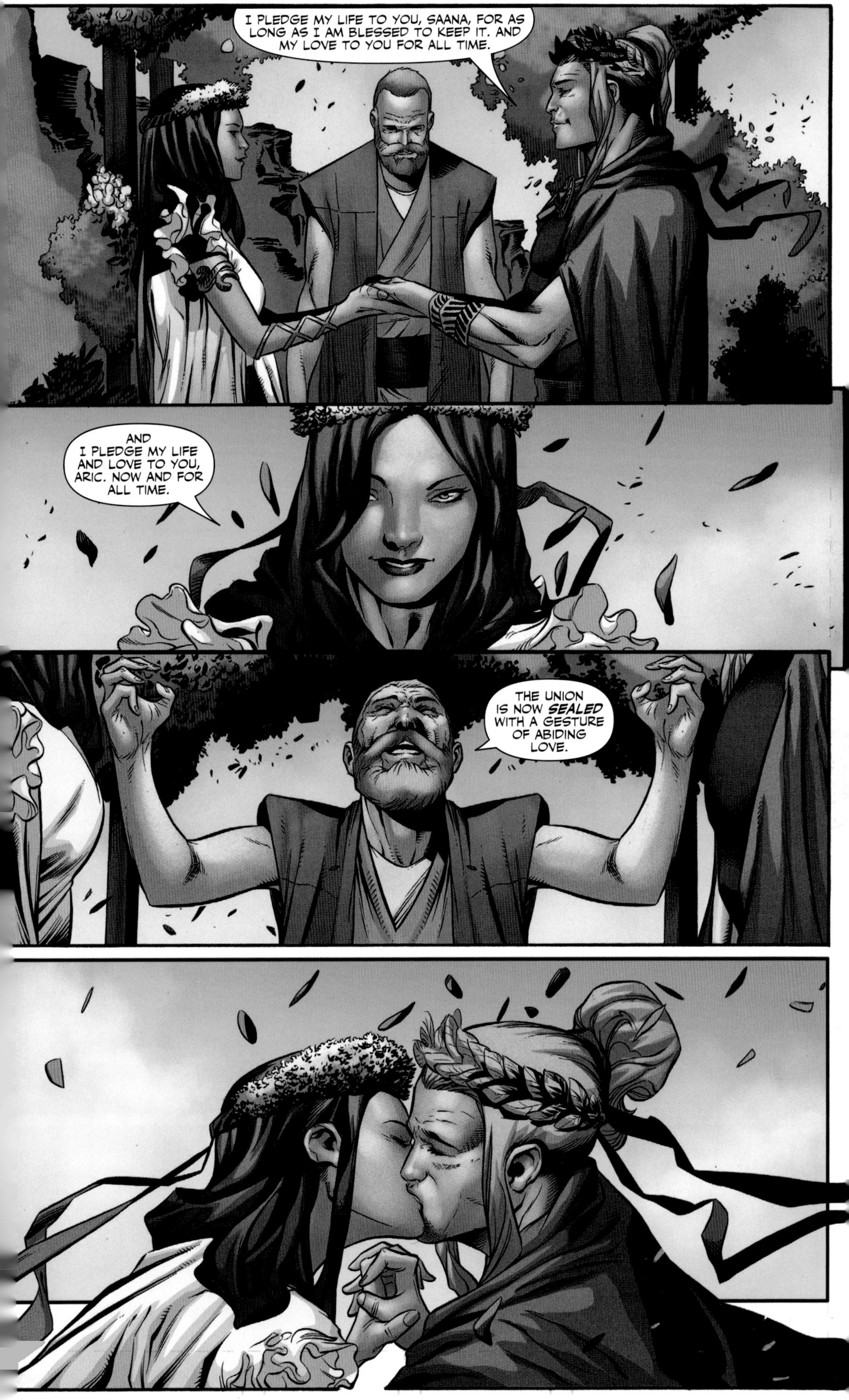
I PLEDGE MY LIFE TO YOU, SAANA, FOR AS LONG AS I AM BLESSED TO KEEP IT. AND MY LOVE TO YOU FOR ALL TIME.
AND I PLEDGE MY LIFE AND LOVE TO YOU, ARIC. NOW AND FOR ALL TIME.
THE UNION IS NOW SEALED WITH A GESTURE OF ABIDING LOVE.

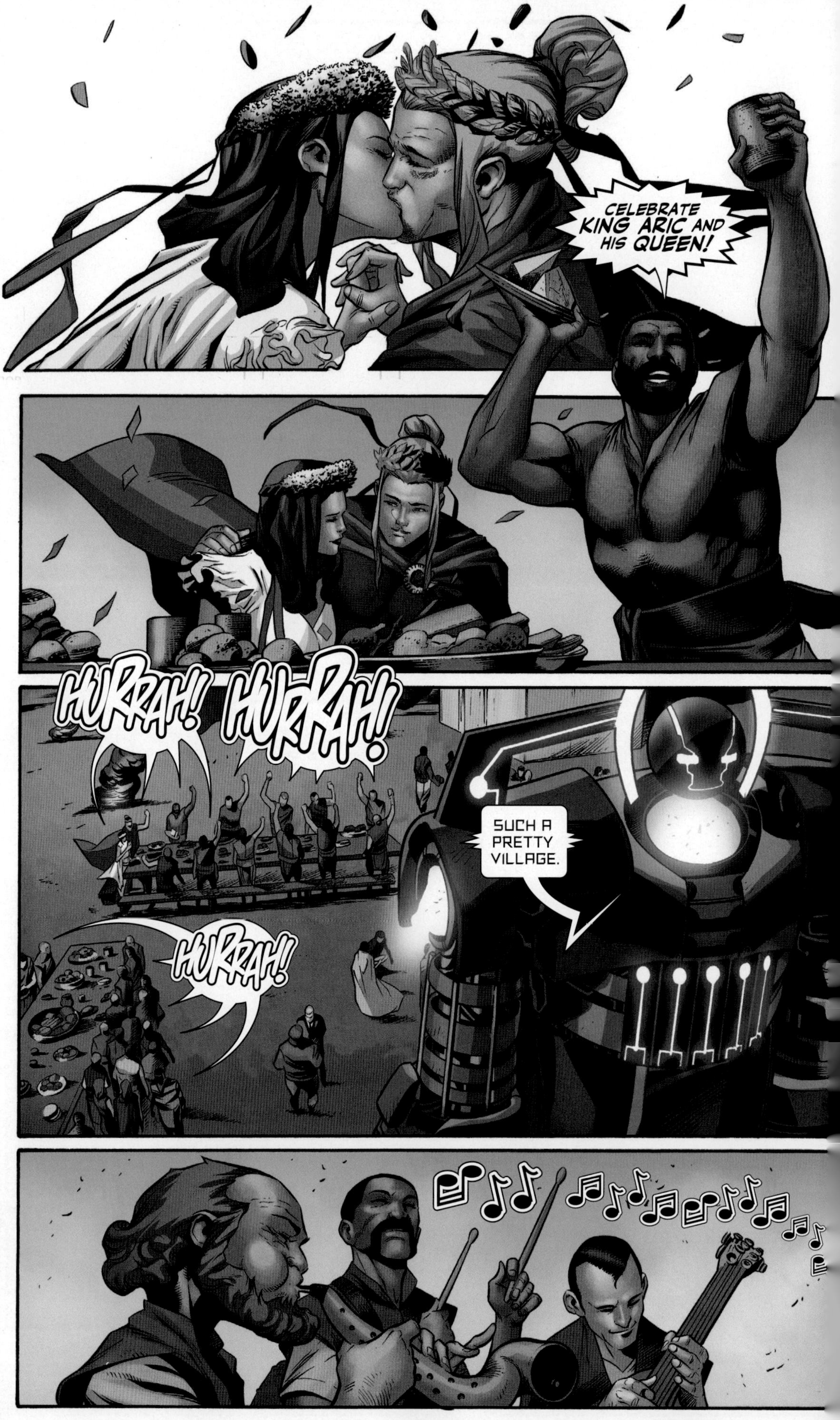
CELEBRATE KING ARIC AND HIS QUEEN!
HURRAH! HURRAH!
SUCH A PRETTY VILLAGE.
HURRAH!

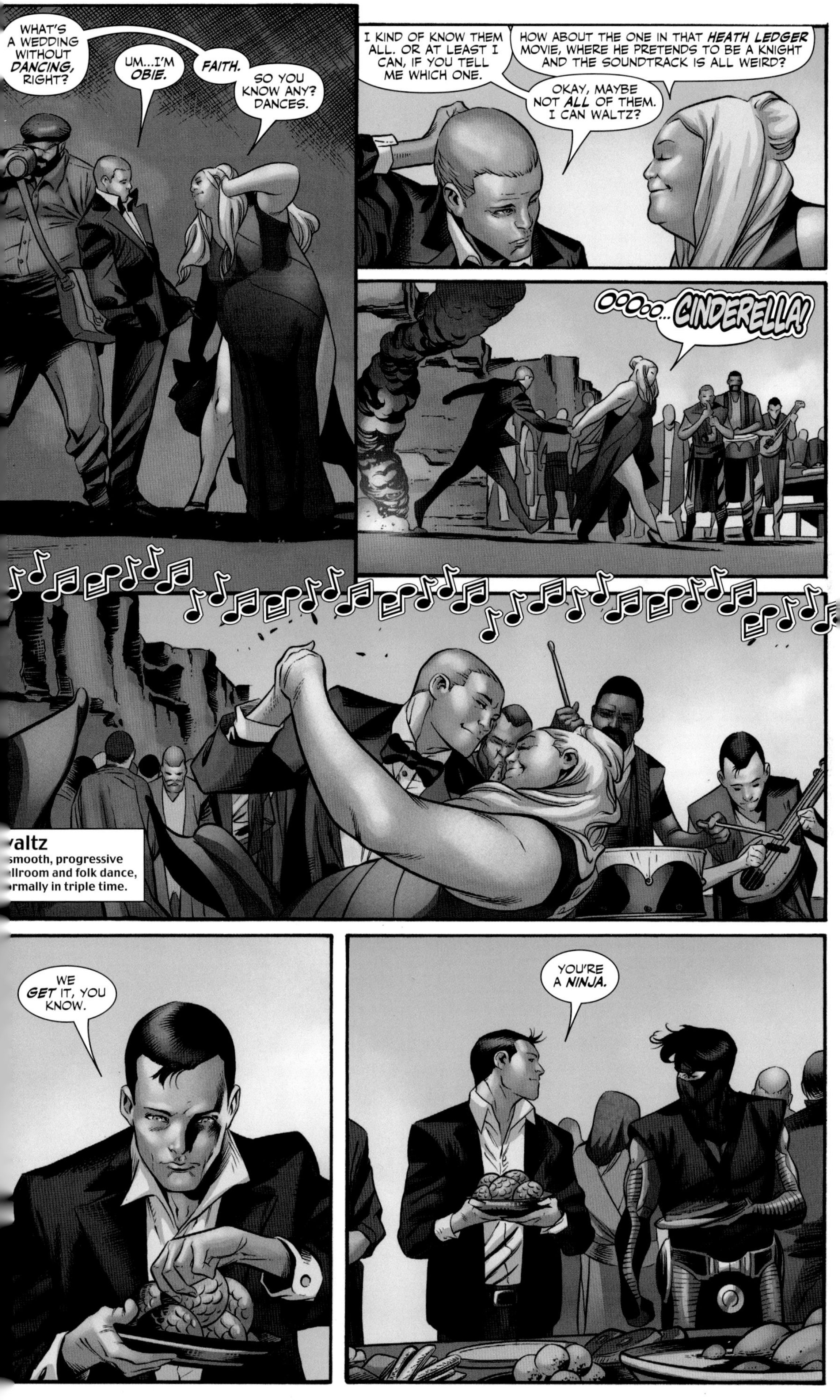
WHAT'S A WEDDING WITHOUT DANCING, RIGHT?
UM...I'M OBIE.
FAITH.
SO YOU KNOW ANY? DANCES.
I KIND OF KNOW THEM ALL. OR AT LEAST I CAN, IF YOU TELL ME WHICH ONE.
HOW ABOUT THE ONE IN THAT HEATH LEDGER MOVIE, WHERE HE PRETENDS TO BE A KNIGHT AND THE SOUNDTRACK IS ALL WEIRD?
OKAY, MAYBE NOT ALL OF THEM. I CAN WALTZ?
OOOoo...CINDERELLA!
waltz
smooth, progressive
ballroom and folk dance,
normally in triple time.
WE GET IT, YOU KNOW.
YOU'RE A NINJA.

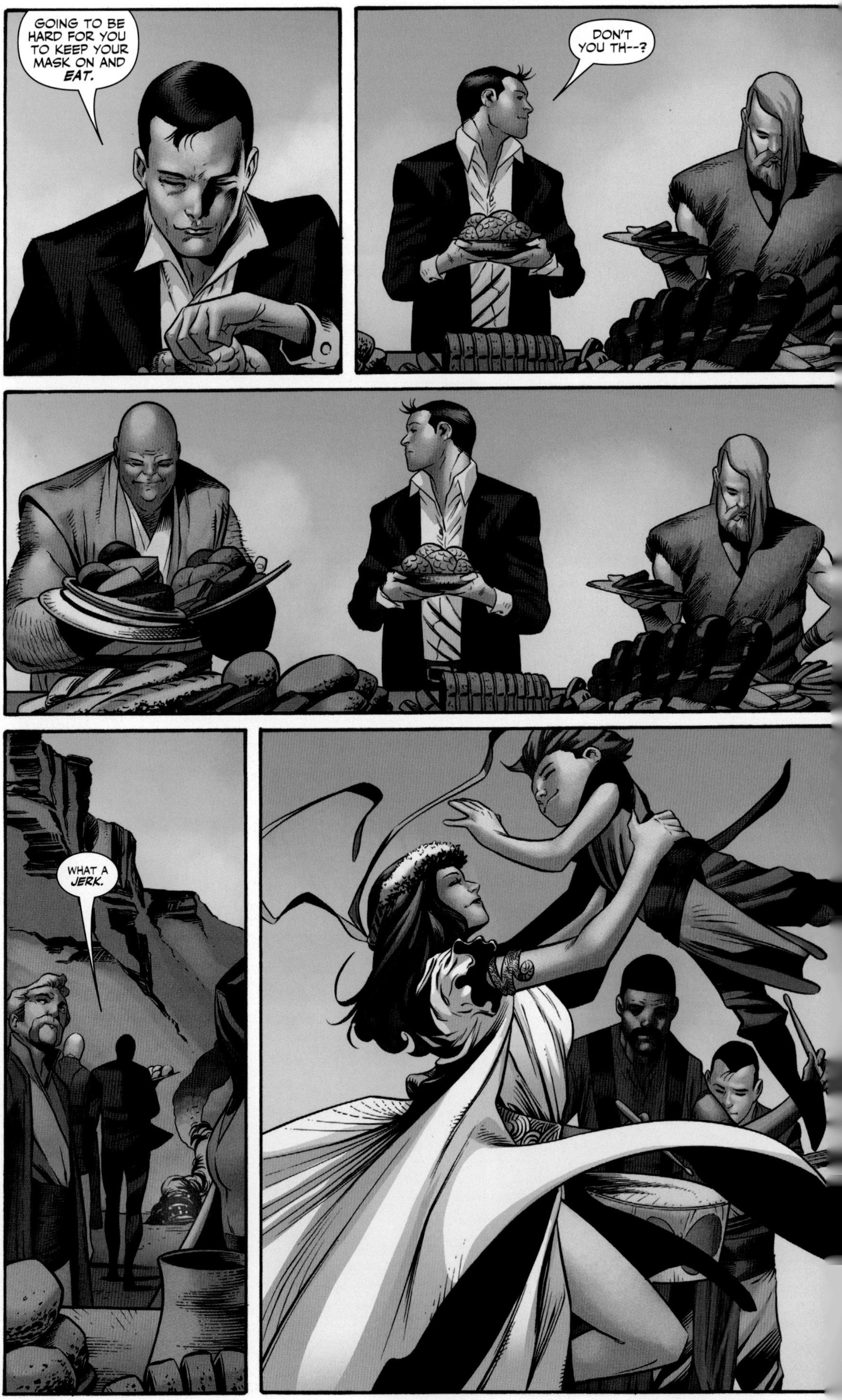
GOING TO BE HARD FOR YOU TO KEEP YOUR MASK ON AND *EAT.*
DON'T YOU TH--?
WHAT A *JERK.*

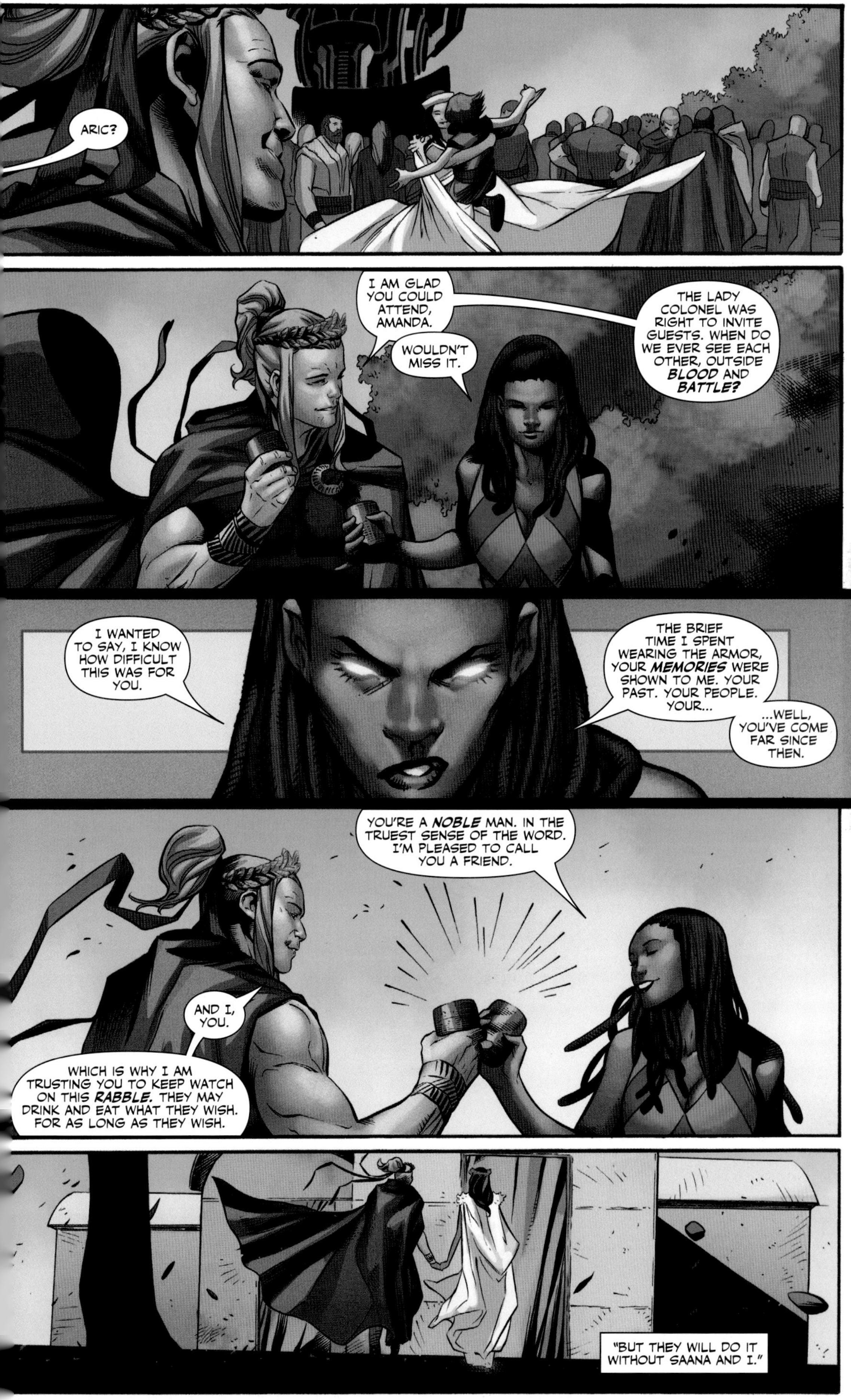
ARIC?
I AM GLAD YOU COULD ATTEND, AMANDA.
WOULDN'T MISS IT.
THE LADY COLONEL WAS RIGHT TO INVITE GUESTS. WHEN DO WE EVER SEE EACH OTHER, OUTSIDE BLOOD AND BATTLE?
I WANTED TO SAY, I KNOW HOW DIFFICULT THIS WAS FOR YOU.
THE BRIEF TIME I SPENT WEARING THE ARMOR, YOUR MEMORIES WERE SHOWN TO ME. YOUR PAST. YOUR PEOPLE. YOUR...
...WELL, YOU'VE COME FAR SINCE THEN.
YOU'RE A NOBLE MAN. IN THE TRUEST SENSE OF THE WORD. I'M PLEASED TO CALL YOU A FRIEND.
AND I, YOU.
WHICH IS WHY I AM TRUSTING YOU TO KEEP WATCH ON THIS RABBLE. THEY MAY DRINK AND EAT WHAT THEY WISH. FOR AS LONG AS THEY WISH.
"BUT THEY WILL DO IT WITHOUT SAANA AND I."

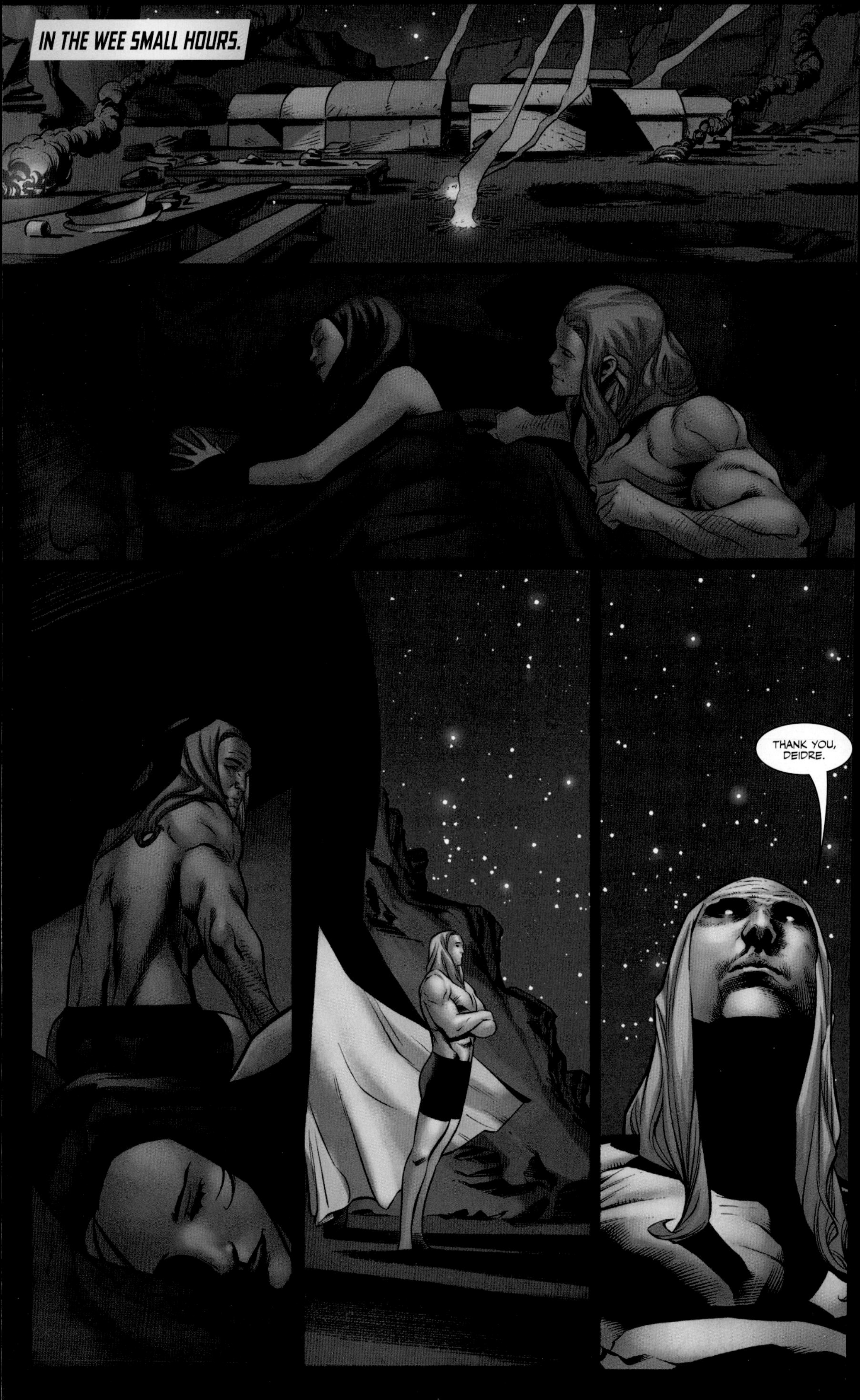
IN THE WEE SMALL HOURS.
THANK YOU, DEIDRE.

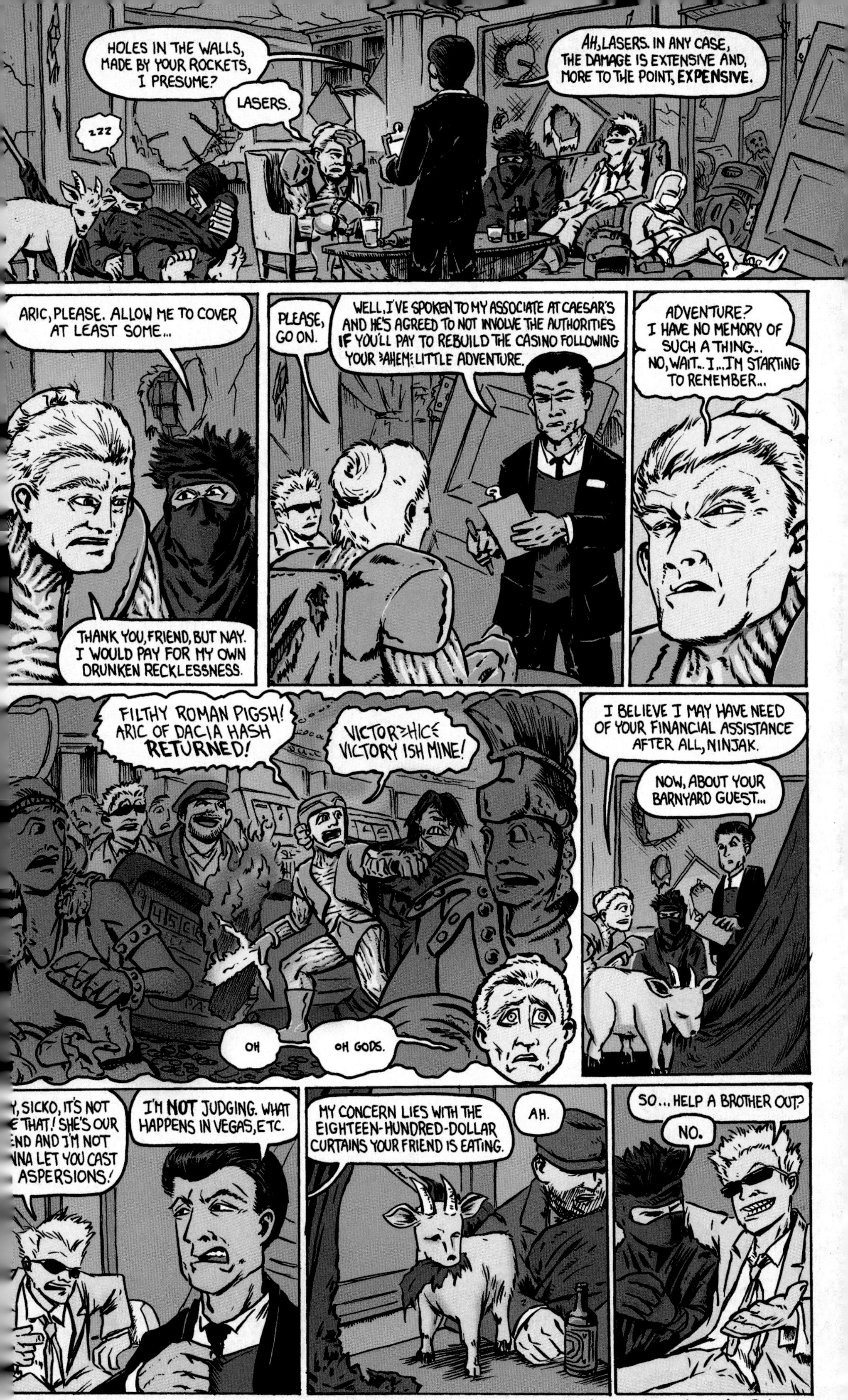
HOLES IN THE WALLS, MADE BY YOUR ROCKETS, I PRESUME?
ZZZ
LASERS.
AH, LASERS. IN ANY CASE, THE DAMAGE IS EXTENSIVE AND, MORE TO THE POINT, EXPENSIVE.
ARIC, PLEASE. ALLOW ME TO COVER AT LEAST SOME...
THANK YOU, FRIEND, BUT NAY. I WOULD PAY FOR MY OWN DRUNKEN RECKLESSNESS.
PLEASE, GO ON.
WELL, I'VE SPOKEN TO MY ASSOCIATE AT CAESAR'S AND HE'S AGREED TO NOT INVOLVE THE AUTHORITIES IF YOU'LL PAY TO REBUILD THE CASINO FOLLOWING YOUR AHEM LITTLE ADVENTURE.
ADVENTURE? I HAVE NO MEMORY OF SUCH A THING.. NO, WAIT.. I...I'M STARTING TO REMEMBER...
FILTHY ROMAN PIGSH! ARIC OF DACIA HASH RETURNED!
VICTOR HIC VICTORY ISH MINE!
OH
OH GODS.
I BELIEVE I MAY HAVE NEED OF YOUR FINANCIAL ASSISTANCE AFTER ALL, NINJAK.
NOW, ABOUT YOUR BARNYARD GUEST...
Y, SICKO, IT'S NOT E THAT! SHE'S OUR END AND I'M NOT NNA LET YOU CAST ASPERSIONS!
I'M NOT JUDGING. WHAT HAPPENS IN VEGAS, ETC.
MY CONCERN LIES WITH THE EIGHTEEN-HUNDRED-DOLLAR CURTAINS YOUR FRIEND IS EATING.
AH.
SO... HELP A BROTHER OUT?
NO.

Written and drawn by Rafer Roberts

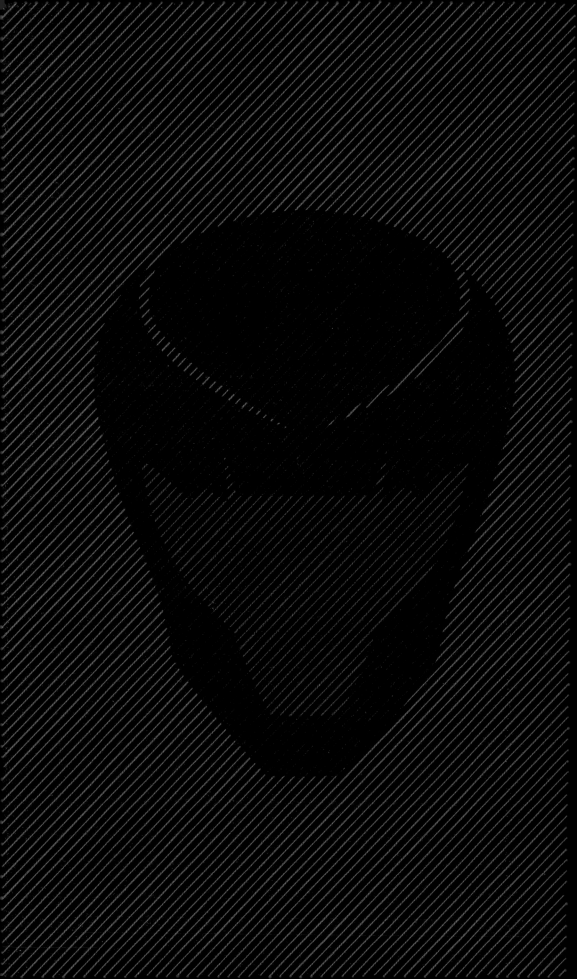

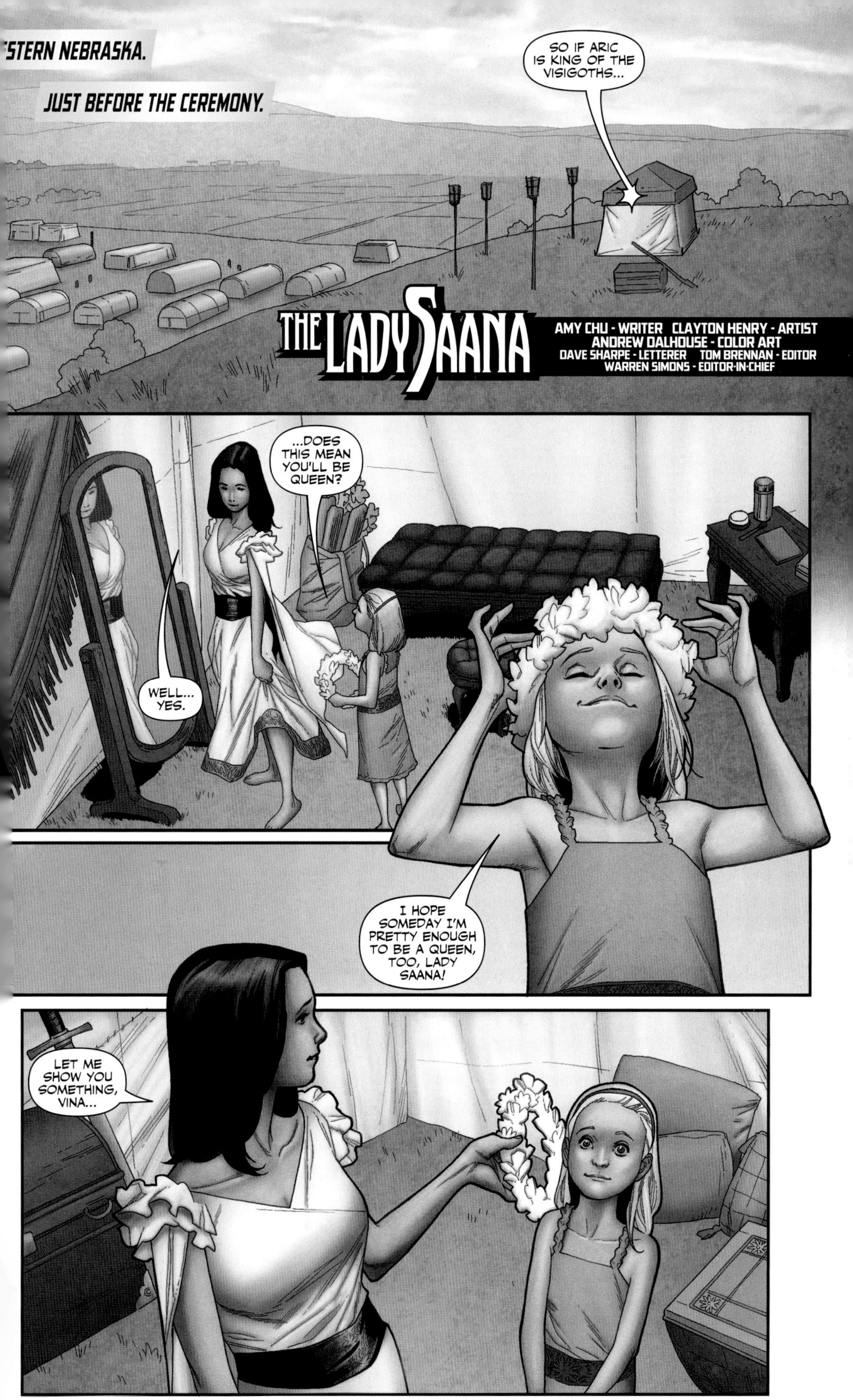
STERN NEBRASKA.
JUST BEFORE THE CEREMONY.
SO IF ARIC IS KING OF THE VISIGOTHS...
THE LADY SAANA
AMY CHU - WRITER CLAYTON HENRY - ARTIST
ANDREW DALHOUSE - COLOR ART
DAVE SHARPE - LETTERER TOM BRENNAN - EDITOR
WARREN SIMONS - EDITOR-IN-CHIEF
...DOES THIS MEAN YOU'LL BE QUEEN?
WELL... YES.
I HOPE SOMEDAY I'M PRETTY ENOUGH TO BE A QUEEN, TOO, LADY SAANA!
LET ME SHOW YOU SOMETHING, VINA...

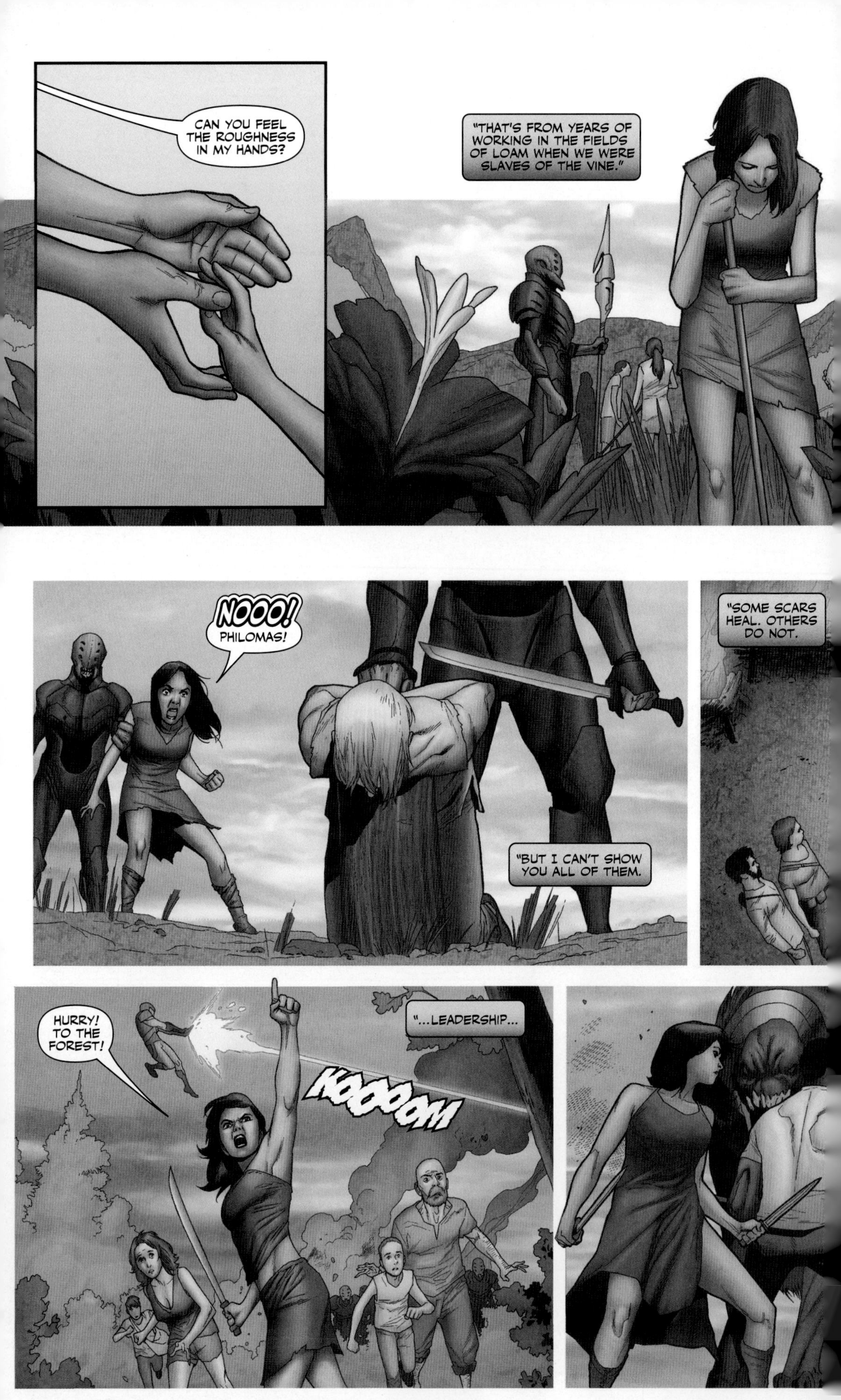
CAN YOU FEEL THE ROUGHNESS IN MY HANDS?
"THAT'S FROM YEARS OF WORKING IN THE FIELDS OF LOAM WHEN WE WERE SLAVES OF THE VINE."
NOOO! PHILOMAS!
"BUT I CAN'T SHOW YOU ALL OF THEM.
"SOME SCARS HEAL. OTHERS DO NOT.
HURRY! TO THE FOREST!
"...LEADERSHIP...
KOOOOM

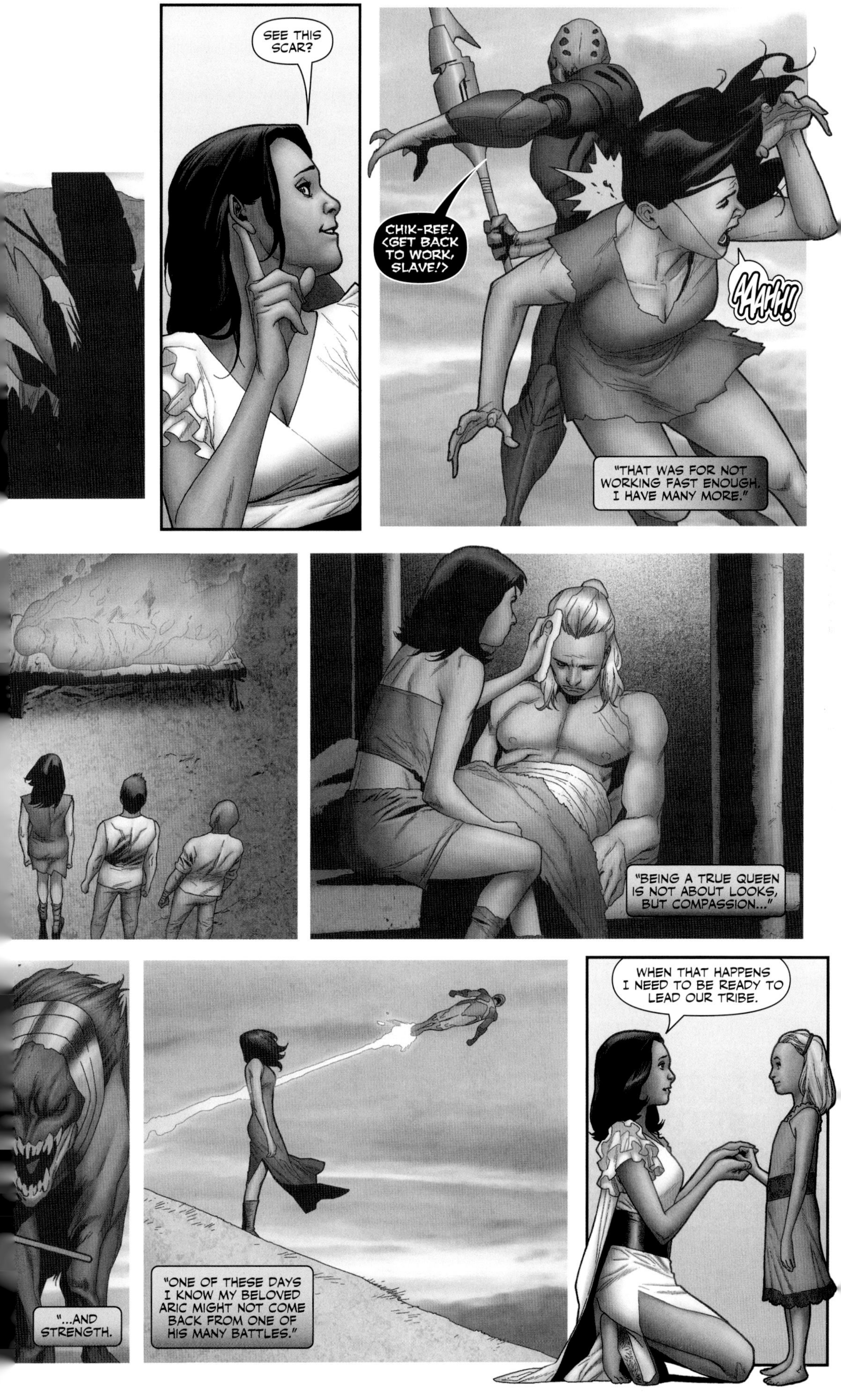
SEE THIS SCAR?
CHIK-REE! <GET BACK TO WORK, SLAVE!>
AAAHH!
"THAT WAS FOR NOT WORKING FAST ENOUGH. I HAVE MANY MORE."
"BEING A TRUE QUEEN IS NOT ABOUT LOOKS, BUT COMPASSION..."
"...AND STRENGTH.
"ONE OF THESE DAYS I KNOW MY BELOVED ARIC MIGHT NOT COME BACK FROM ONE OF HIS MANY BATTLES."
WHEN THAT HAPPENS I NEED TO BE READY TO LEAD OUR TRIBE.

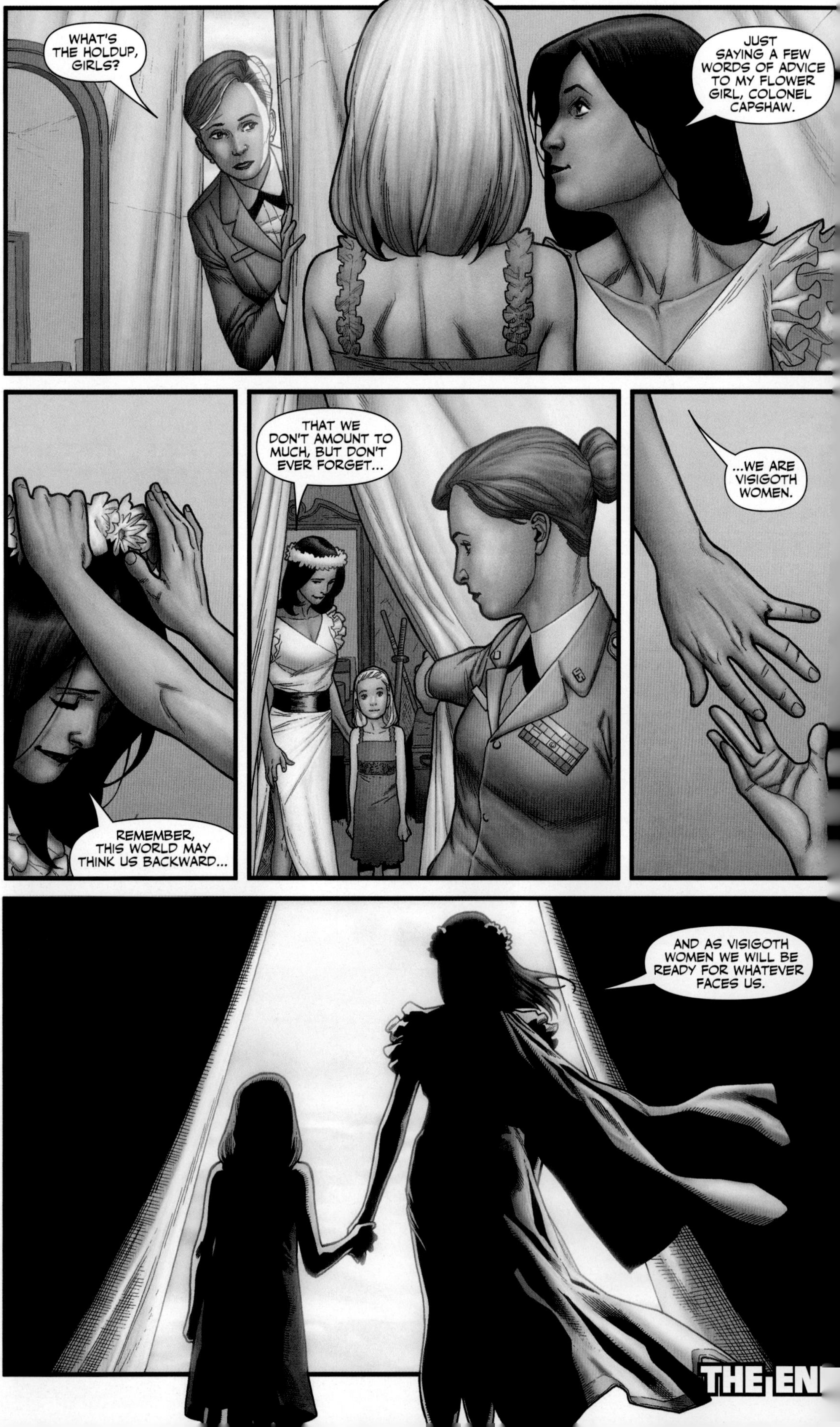
WHAT'S THE HOLDUP, GIRLS?
JUST SAYING A FEW WORDS OF ADVICE TO MY FLOWER GIRL, COLONEL CAPSHAW.
REMEMBER, THIS WORLD MAY THINK US BACKWARD...
THAT WE DON'T AMOUNT TO MUCH, BUT DON'T EVER FORGET...
...WE ARE VISIGOTH WOMEN.
AND AS VISIGOTH WOMEN WE WILL BE READY FOR WHATEVER FACES US.
THE EN

RACE.

391 A.D.

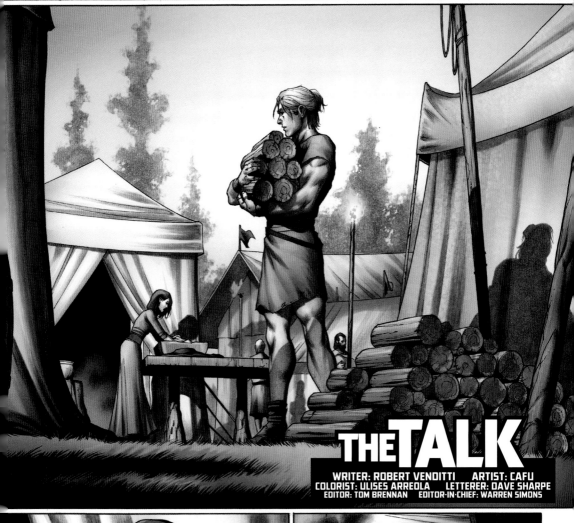

THE TALK

WRITER: ROBERT VENDITTI   ARTIST: CAFU
COLORIST: ULISES ARREOLA   LETTERER: DAVE SHARPE
EDITOR: TOM BRENNAN   EDITOR-IN-CHIEF: WARREN SIMONS

HURRY, BOY! BRING WOOD FOR THE FIRE!

YES, FATHER!

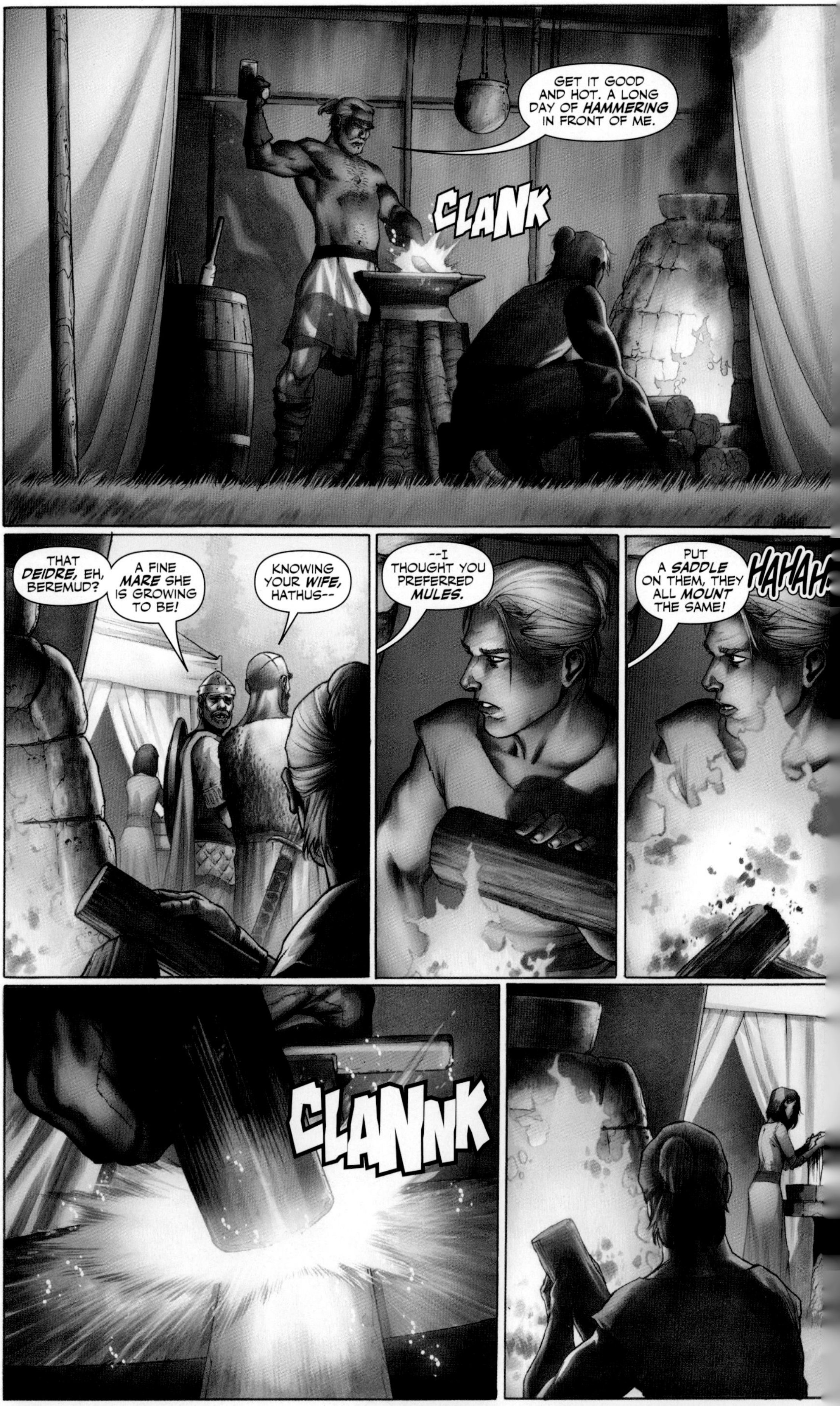
GET IT GOOD AND HOT. A LONG DAY OF *HAMMERING* IN FRONT OF ME.
CLANK
THAT *DEIDRE,* EH, BEREMUD?
A FINE *MARE* SHE IS GROWING TO BE!
KNOWING YOUR *WIFE,* HATHUS--
--I THOUGHT YOU PREFERRED *MULES.*
PUT A *SADDLE* ON THEM, THEY ALL *MOUNT* THE SAME!
HAHAH
CLANNK

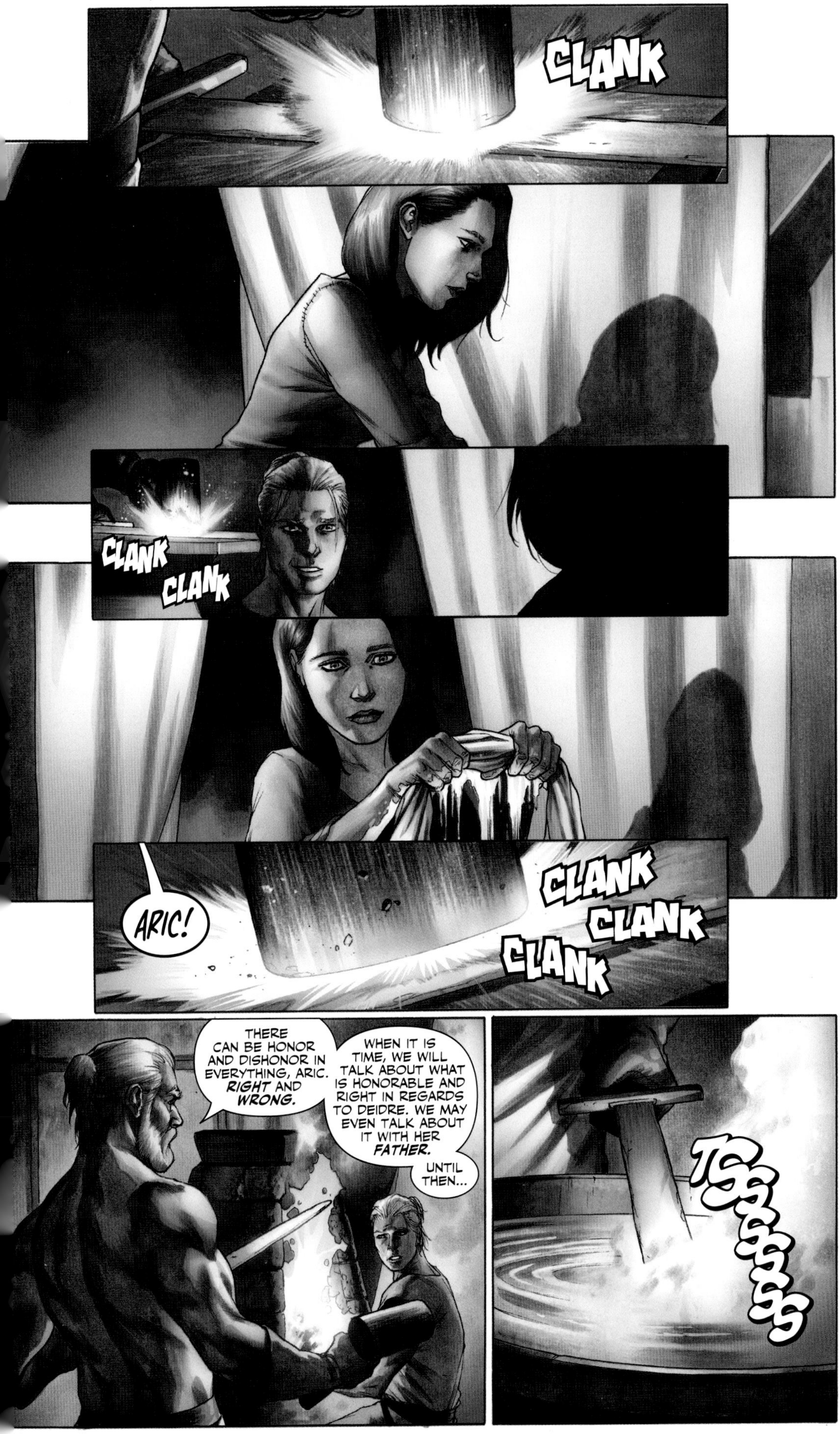
CLANK
CLANK
CLANK
ARIC!
CLANK
CLANK
CLANK
THERE CAN BE HONOR AND DISHONOR IN EVERYTHING, ARIC. RIGHT AND WRONG.
WHEN IT IS TIME, WE WILL TALK ABOUT WHAT IS HONORABLE AND RIGHT IN REGARDS TO DEIDRE. WE MAY EVEN TALK ABOUT IT WITH HER FATHER.
UNTIL THEN...
TSSSSSS

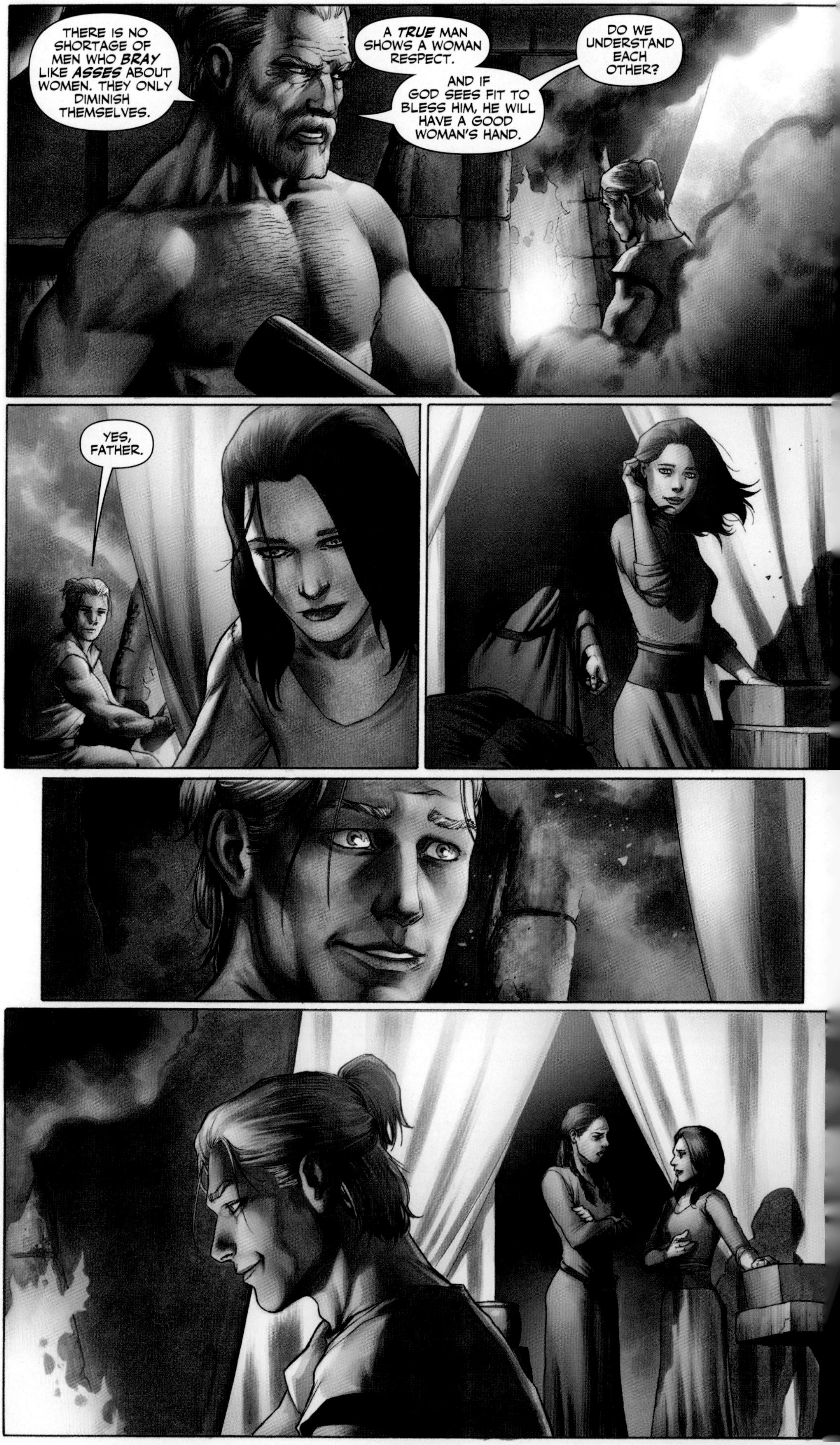
THERE IS NO SHORTAGE OF MEN WHO *BRAY* LIKE *ASSES* ABOUT WOMEN. THEY ONLY DIMINISH THEMSELVES.
A *TRUE* MAN SHOWS A WOMAN RESPECT.
AND IF GOD SEES FIT TO BLESS HIM, HE WILL HAVE A GOOD WOMAN'S HAND.
DO WE UNDERSTAND EACH OTHER?
YES, FATHER.

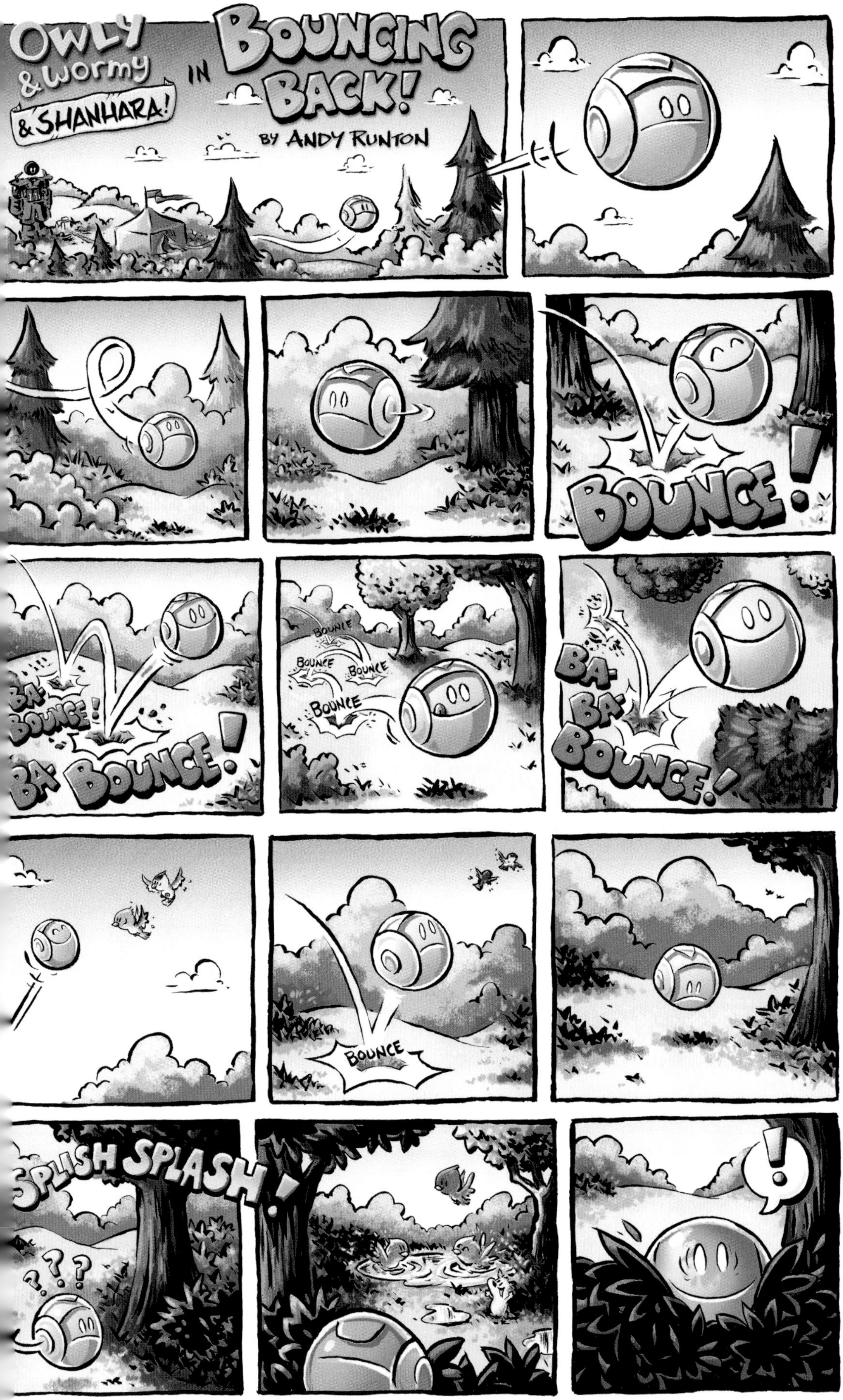

OWLY & WORMY & SHANHARA! IN
BOUNCING BACK!
BY ANDY RUNTON
BOUNCE!
BA-BOUNCE!
BA-BOUNCE!
BOUNCE
BOUNCE
BOUNCE
BOUNCE
BA-BA-BOUNCE!
BOUNCE
SPLISH SPLASH!
???
!

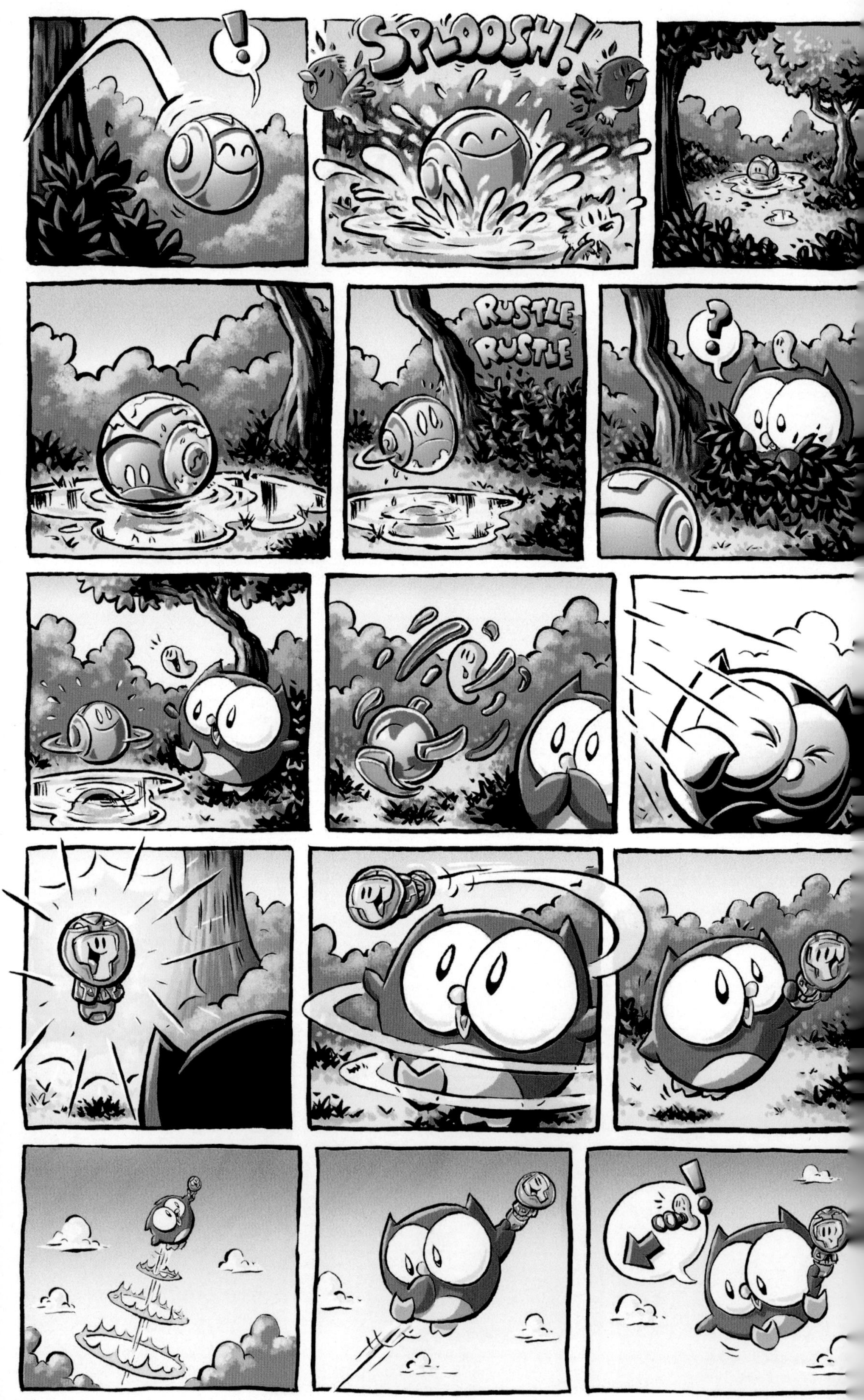
SPLOOSH!
RUSTLE
RUSTLE

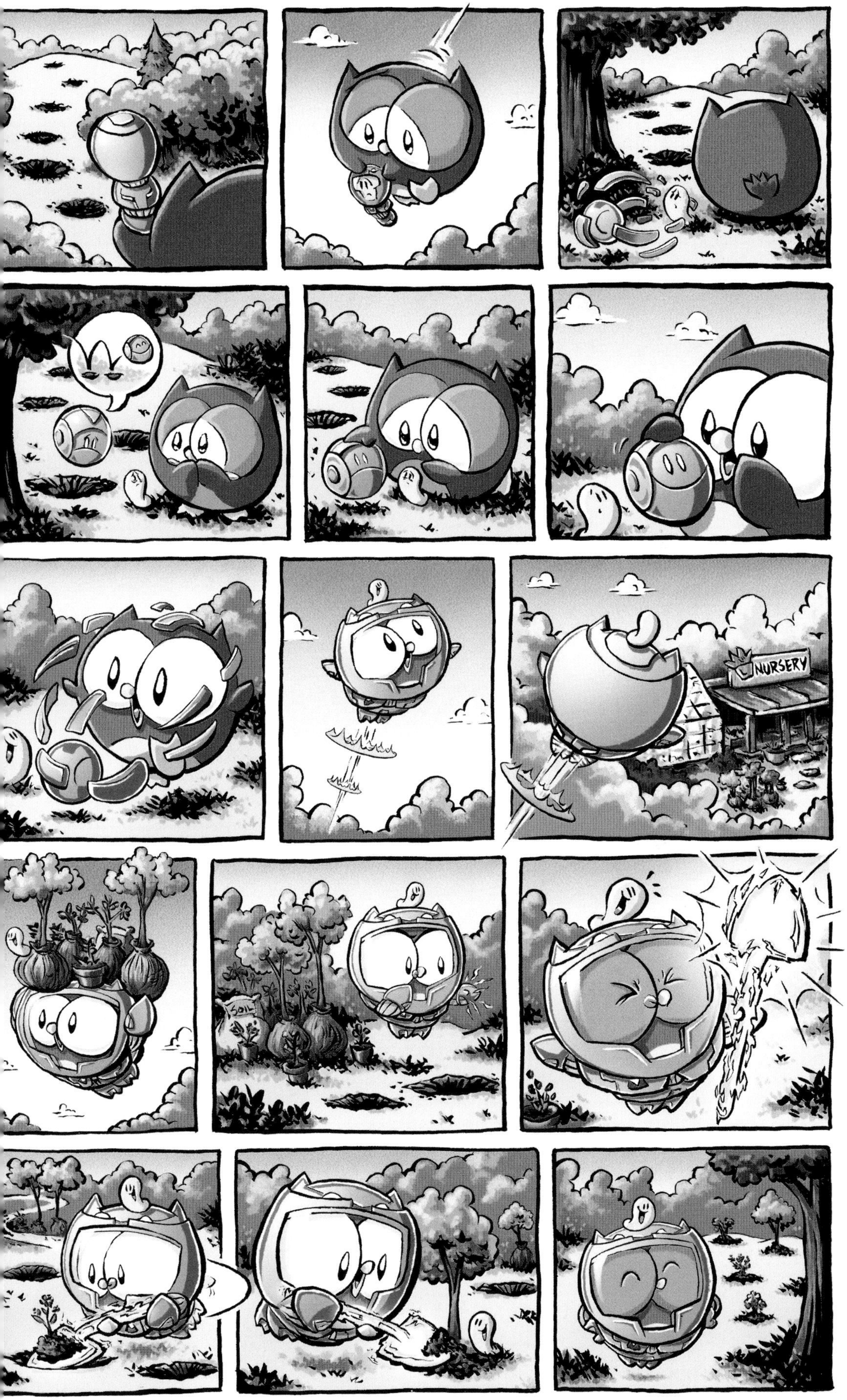
NURSERY
SOIL

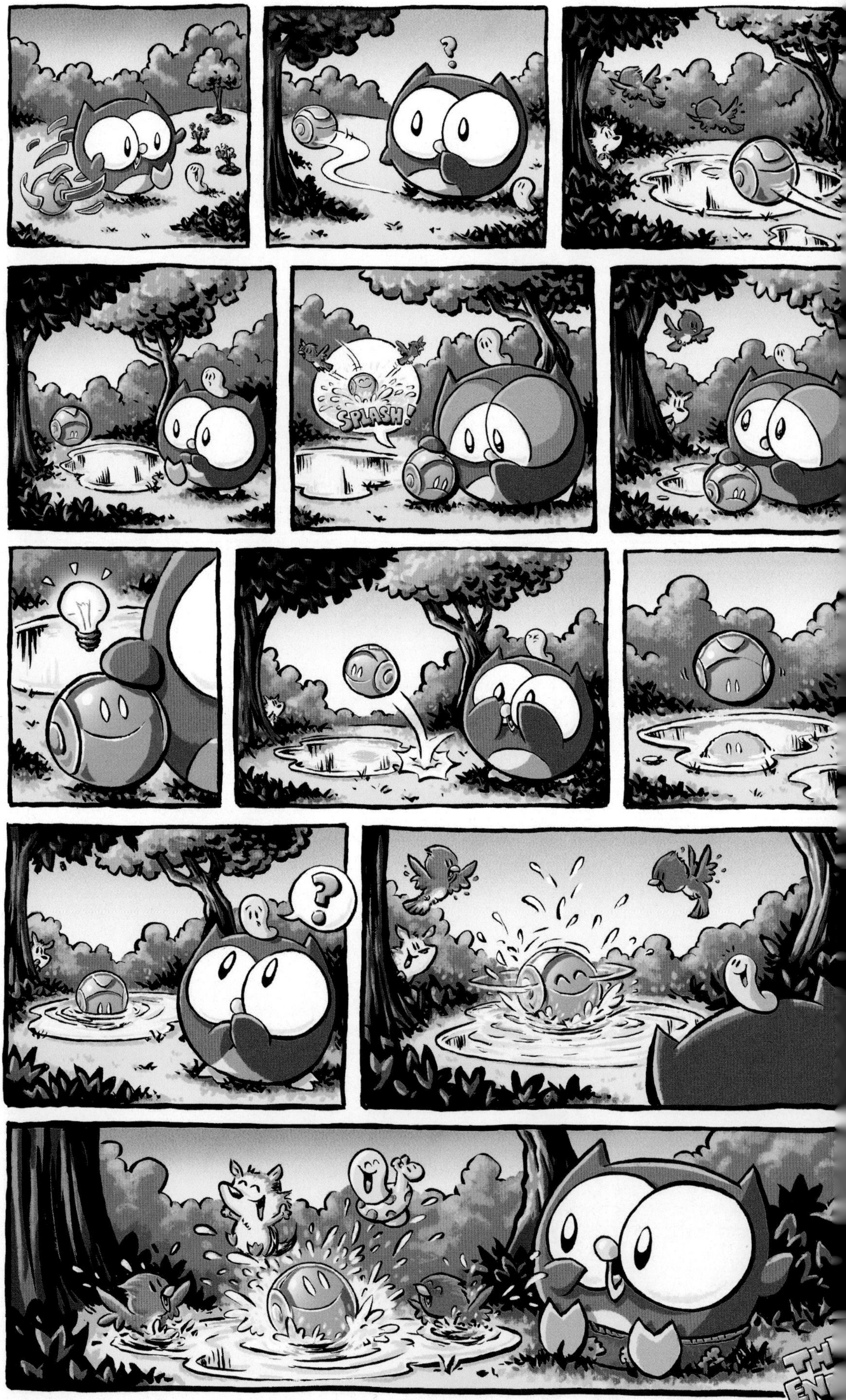
?
SPLASH!
?

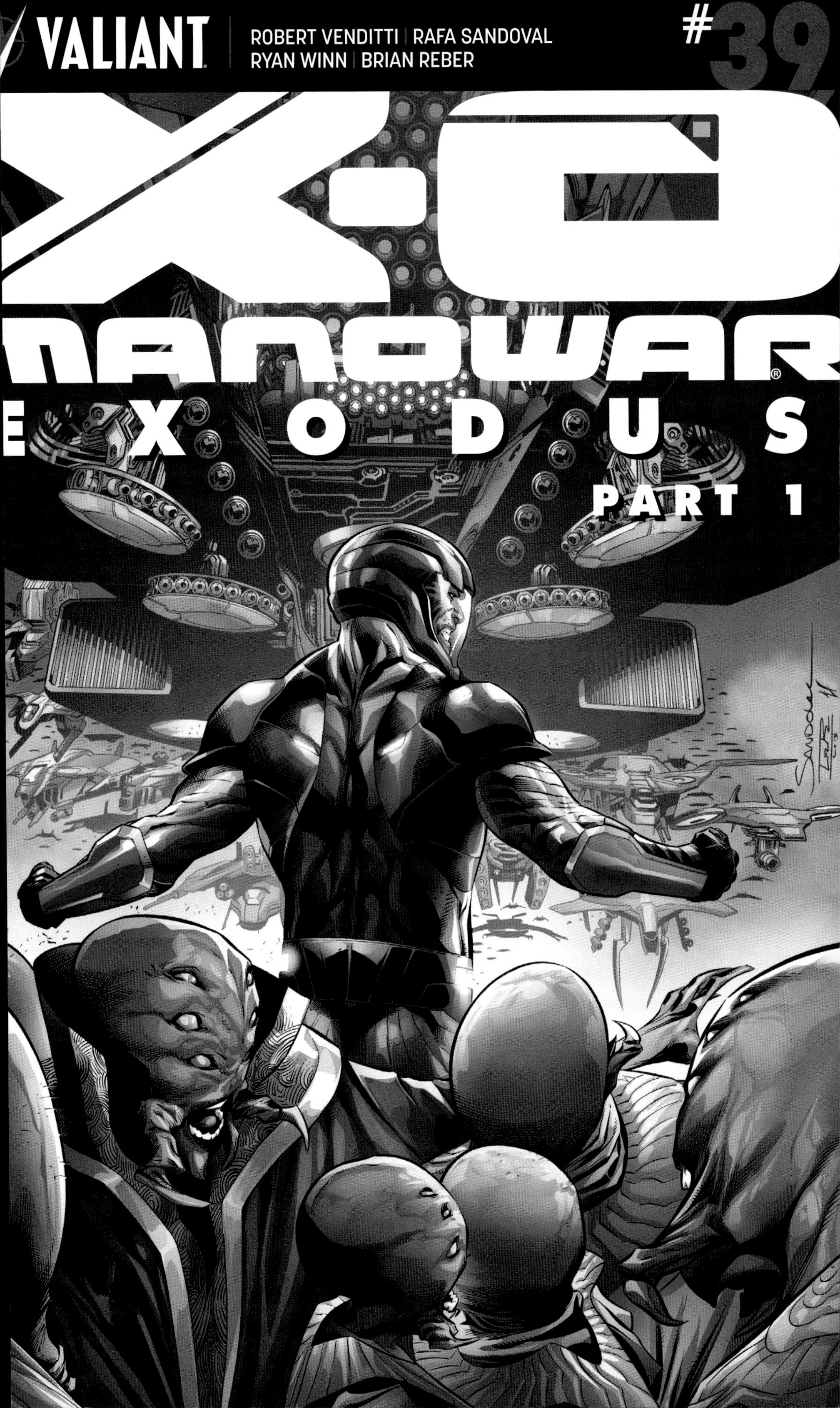
VALIANT
ROBERT VENDITTI | RAFA SANDOVAL
RYAN WINN | BRIAN REBER
#39
X-O MANOWAR®
EXODUS
PART 1

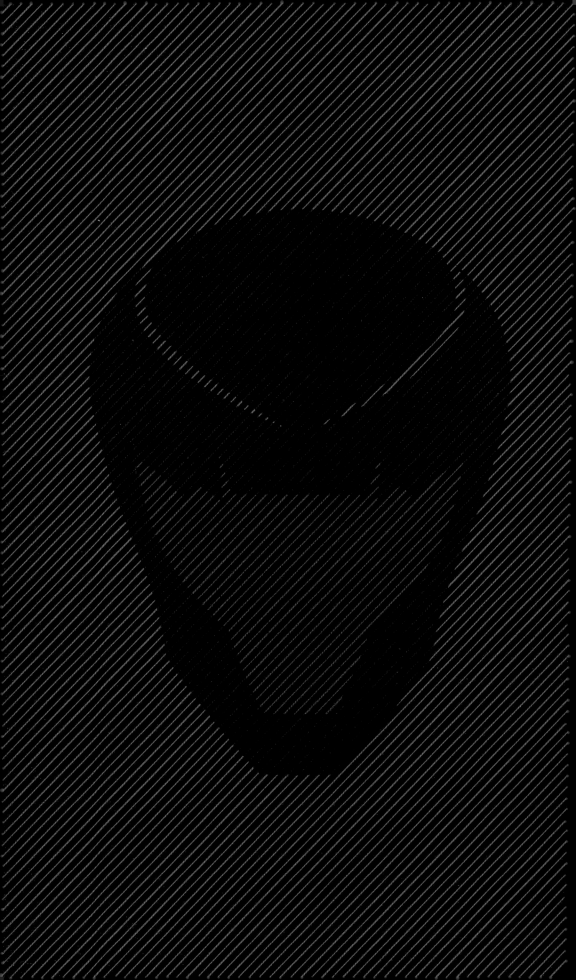

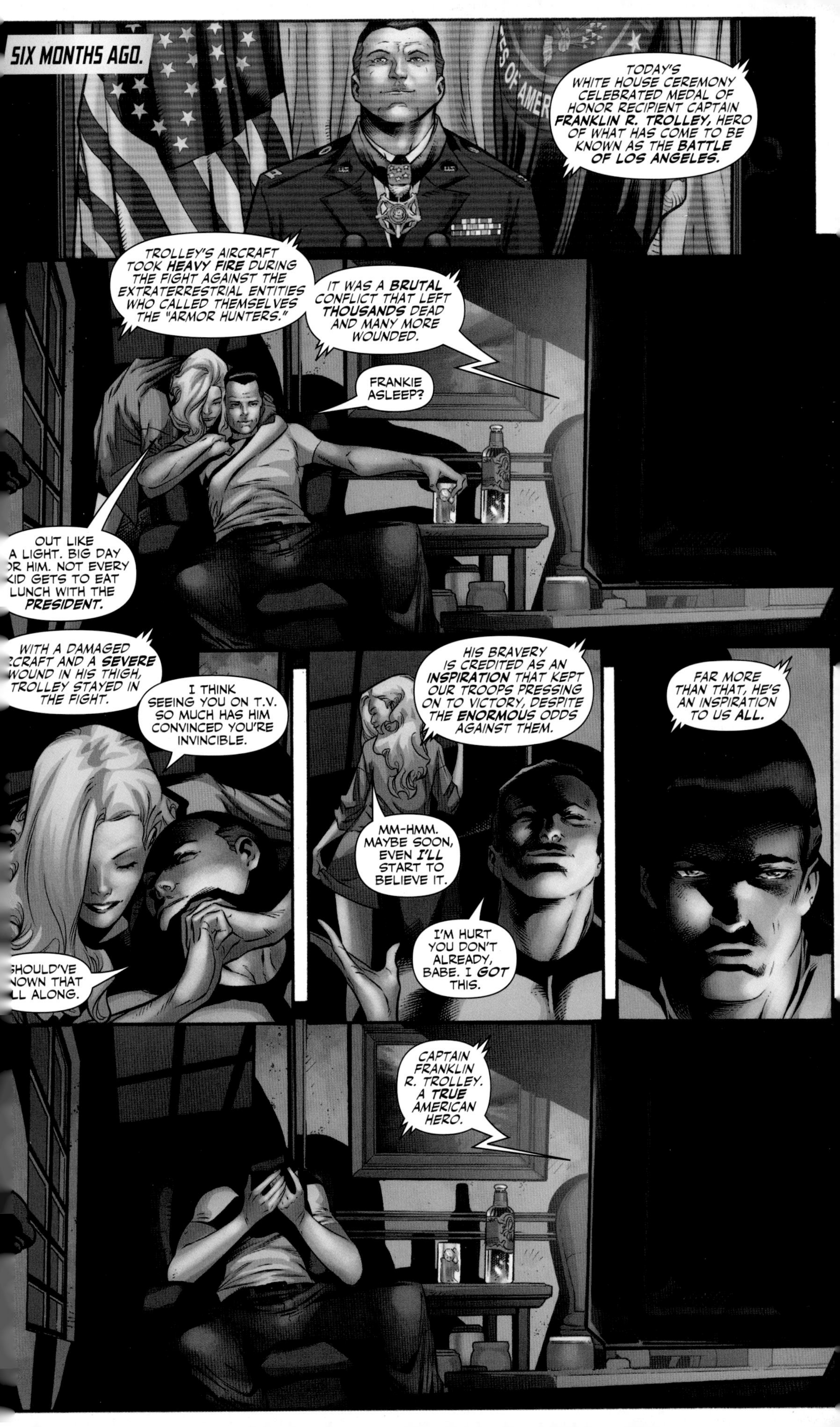
SIX MONTHS AGO.
TODAY'S WHITE HOUSE CEREMONY CELEBRATED MEDAL OF HONOR RECIPIENT CAPTAIN FRANKLIN R. TROLLEY, HERO OF WHAT HAS COME TO BE KNOWN AS THE BATTLE OF LOS ANGELES.
TROLLEY'S AIRCRAFT TOOK HEAVY FIRE DURING THE FIGHT AGAINST THE EXTRATERRESTRIAL ENTITIES WHO CALLED THEMSELVES THE "ARMOR HUNTERS."
IT WAS A BRUTAL CONFLICT THAT LEFT THOUSANDS DEAD AND MANY MORE WOUNDED.
FRANKIE ASLEEP?
OUT LIKE A LIGHT. BIG DAY OR HIM. NOT EVERY KID GETS TO EAT LUNCH WITH THE PRESIDENT.
WITH A DAMAGED RCRAFT AND A SEVERE WOUND IN HIS THIGH, TROLLEY STAYED IN THE FIGHT.
I THINK SEEING YOU ON T.V. SO MUCH HAS HIM CONVINCED YOU'RE INVINCIBLE.
SHOULD'VE NOWN THAT LL ALONG.
HIS BRAVERY IS CREDITED AS AN INSPIRATION THAT KEPT OUR TROOPS PRESSING ON TO VICTORY, DESPITE THE ENORMOUS ODDS AGAINST THEM.
MM-HMM. MAYBE SOON, EVEN I'LL START TO BELIEVE IT.
I'M HURT YOU DON'T ALREADY, BABE. I GOT THIS.
FAR MORE THAN THAT, HE'S AN INSPIRATION TO US ALL.
CAPTAIN FRANKLIN R. TROLLEY. A TRUE AMERICAN HERO.

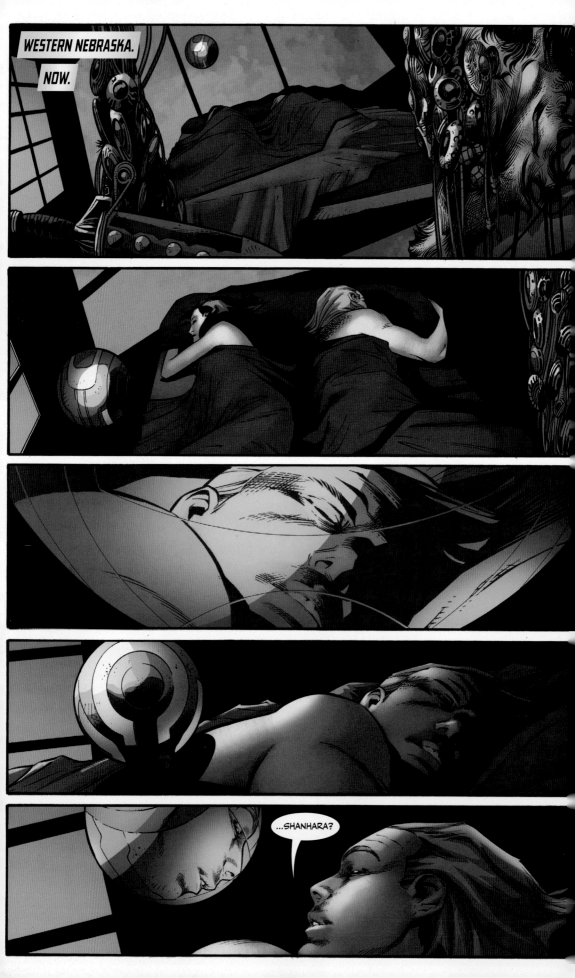

WESTERN NEBRASKA.

NOW.

...SHANHARA?

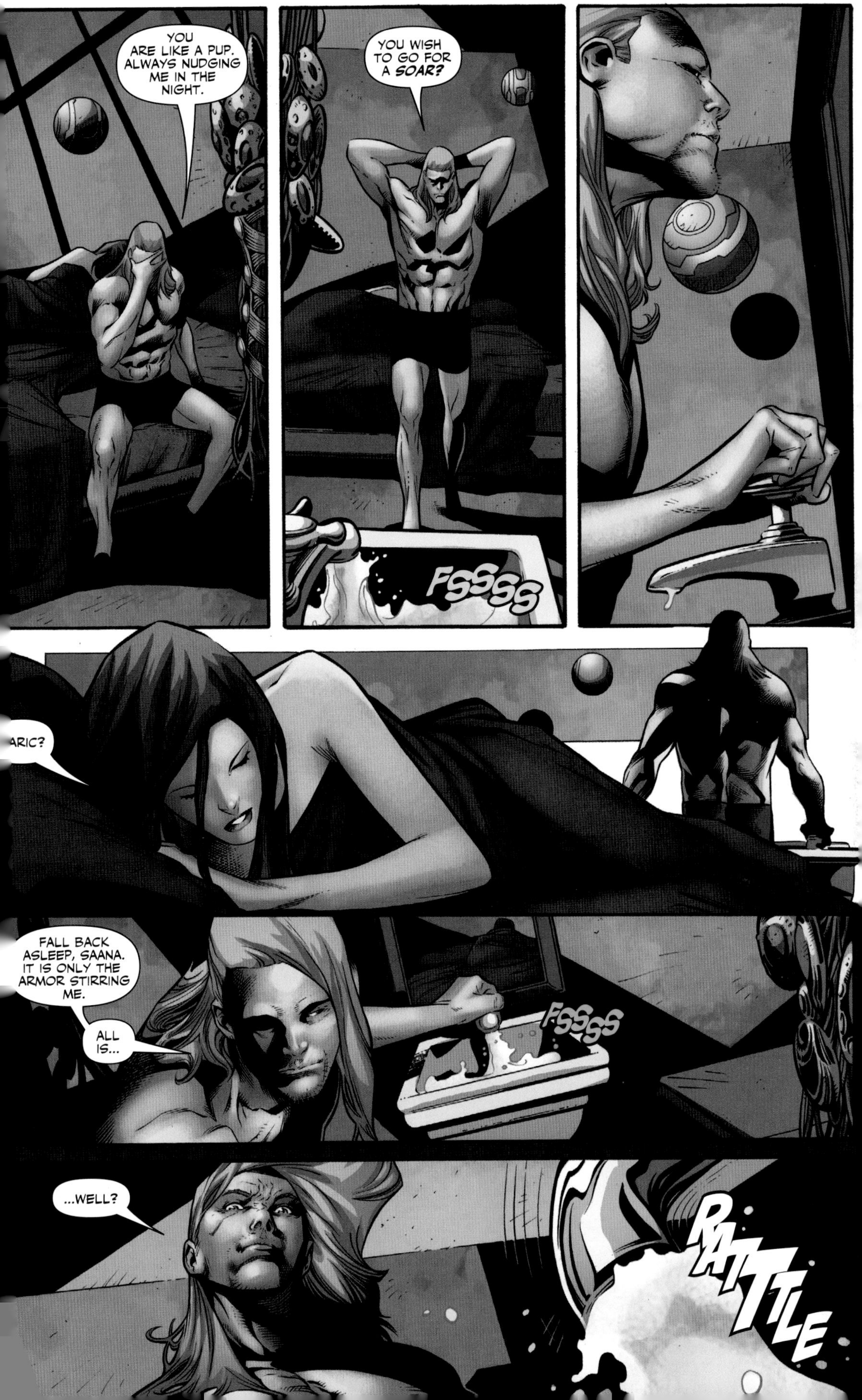
YOU ARE LIKE A PUP. ALWAYS NUDGING ME IN THE NIGHT.
YOU WISH TO GO FOR A SOAR?
FSSSS
ARIC?
FALL BACK ASLEEP, SAANA. IT IS ONLY THE ARMOR STIRRING ME.
ALL IS...
FSSSS
...WELL?
RATTLE

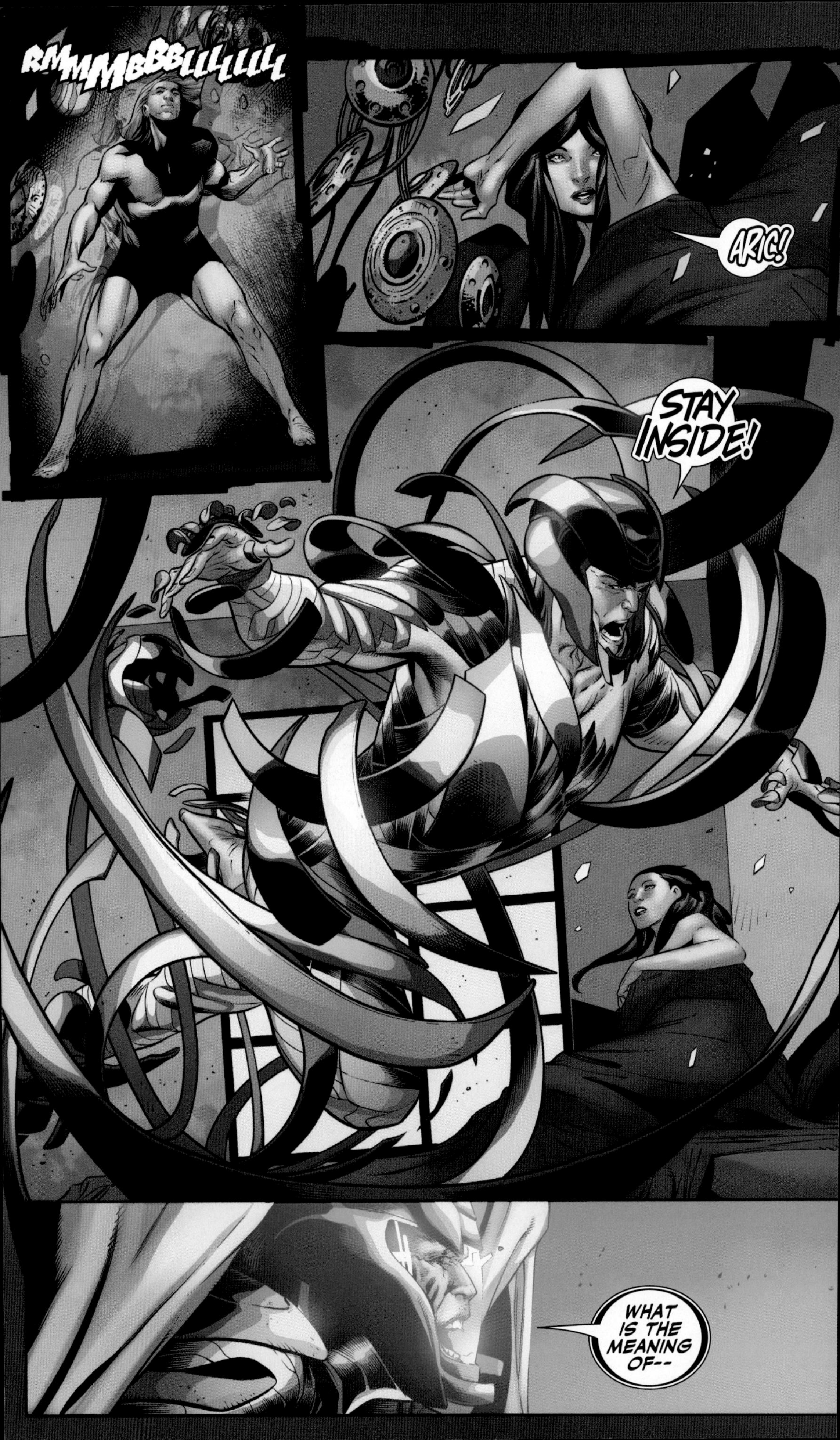
RMMMBBBLLLLLLL
ARIC!
STAY INSIDE!
WHAT IS THE MEANING OF--

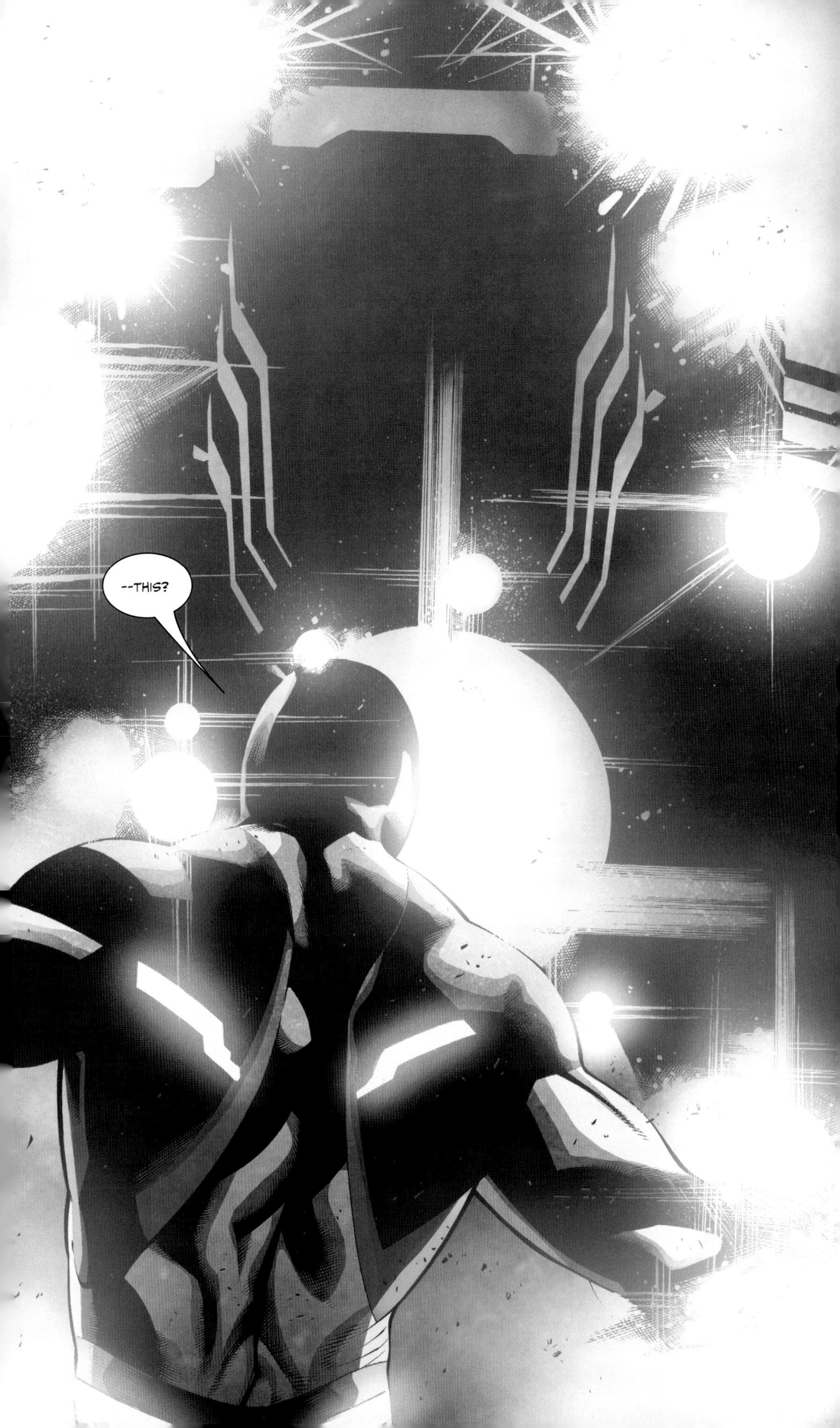
--THIS?

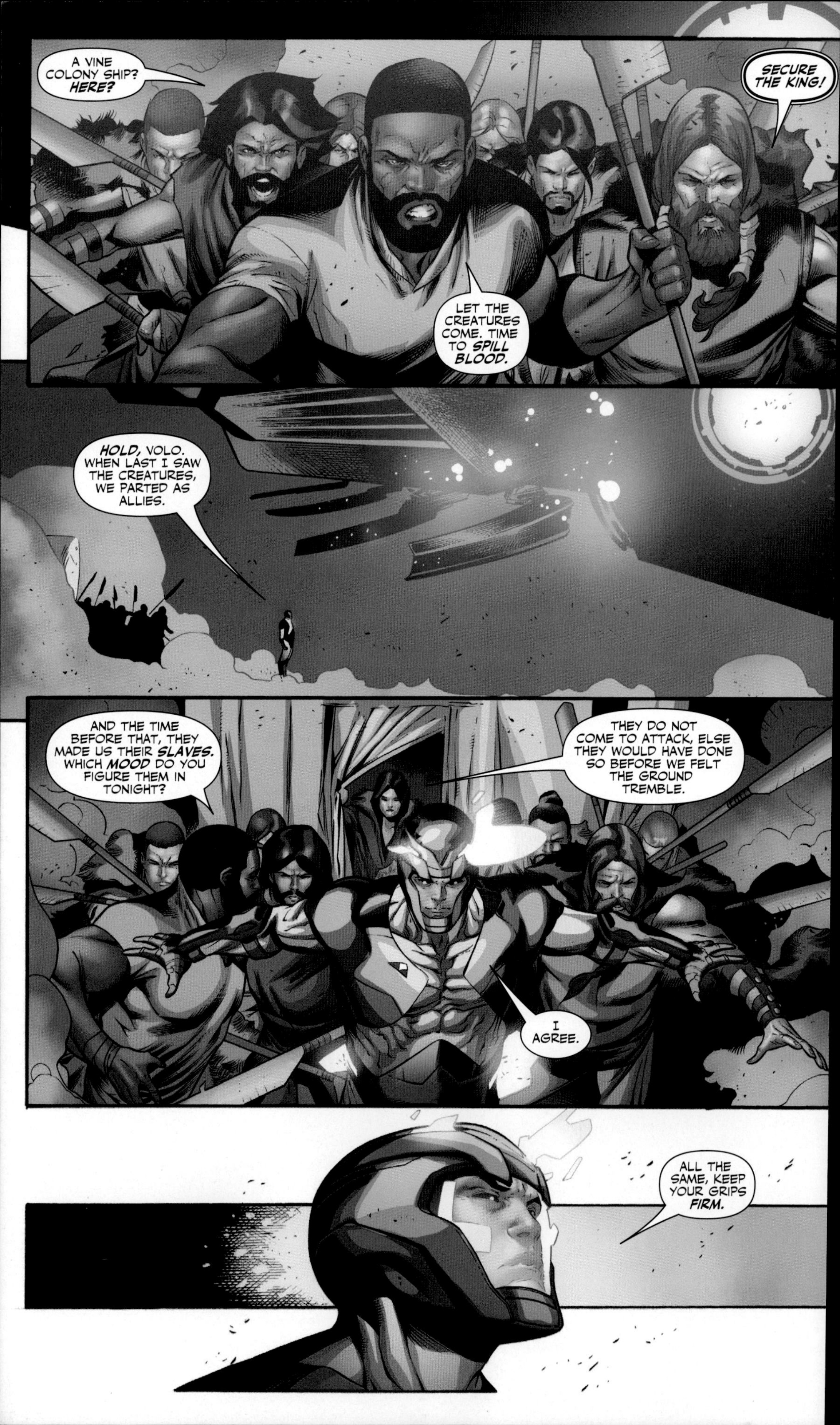
A VINE COLONY SHIP? HERE?
SECURE THE KING!
LET THE CREATURES COME. TIME TO SPILL BLOOD.
HOLD, VOLO. WHEN LAST I SAW THE CREATURES, WE PARTED AS ALLIES.
AND THE TIME BEFORE THAT, THEY MADE US THEIR SLAVES. WHICH MOOD DO YOU FIGURE THEM IN TONIGHT?
THEY DO NOT COME TO ATTACK, ELSE THEY WOULD HAVE DONE SO BEFORE WE FELT THE GROUND TREMBLE.
I AGREE.
ALL THE SAME, KEEP YOUR GRIPS FIRM.

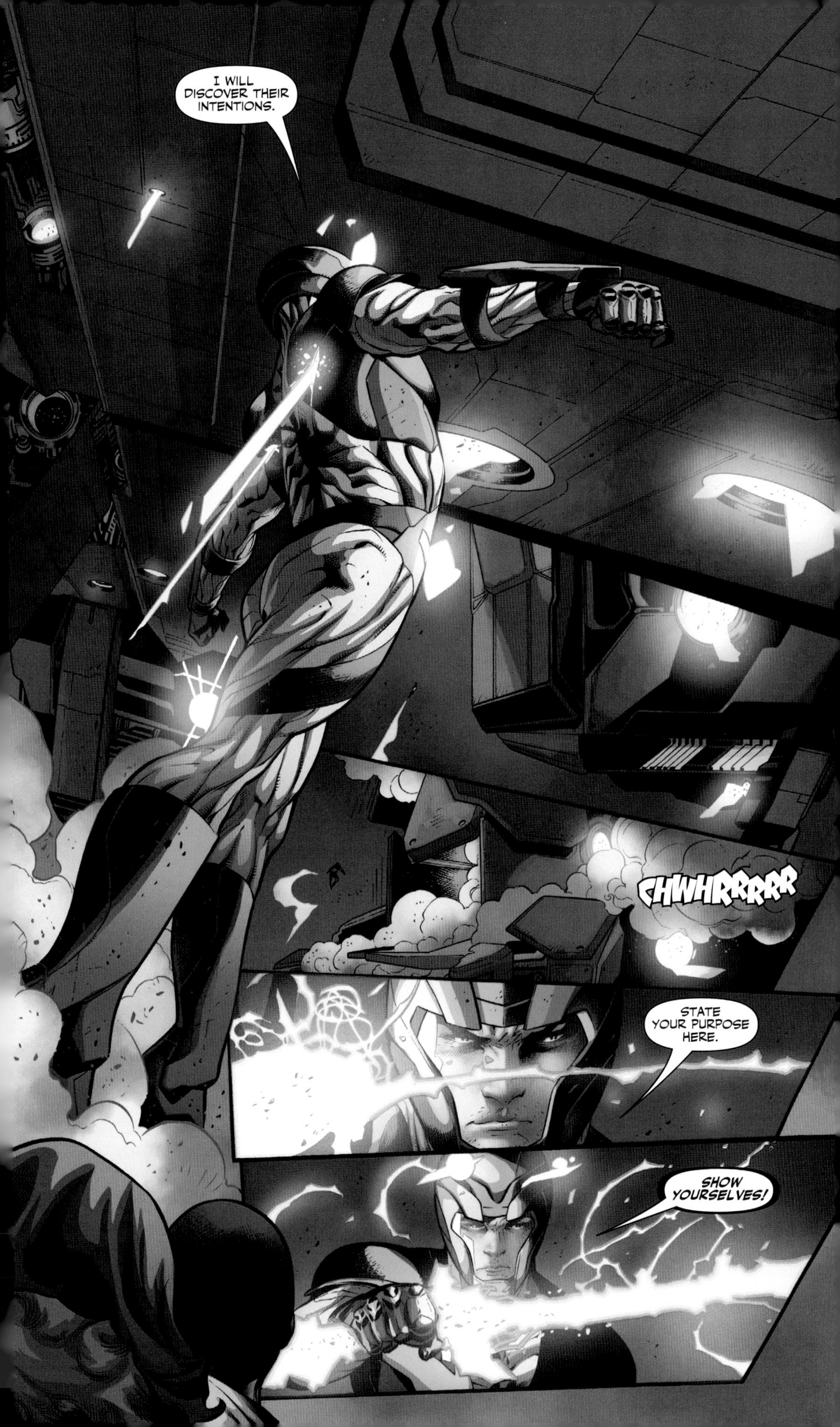
I WILL DISCOVER THEIR INTENTIONS.
CHWHRRRRR
STATE YOUR PURPOSE HERE.
SHOW YOURSELVES!

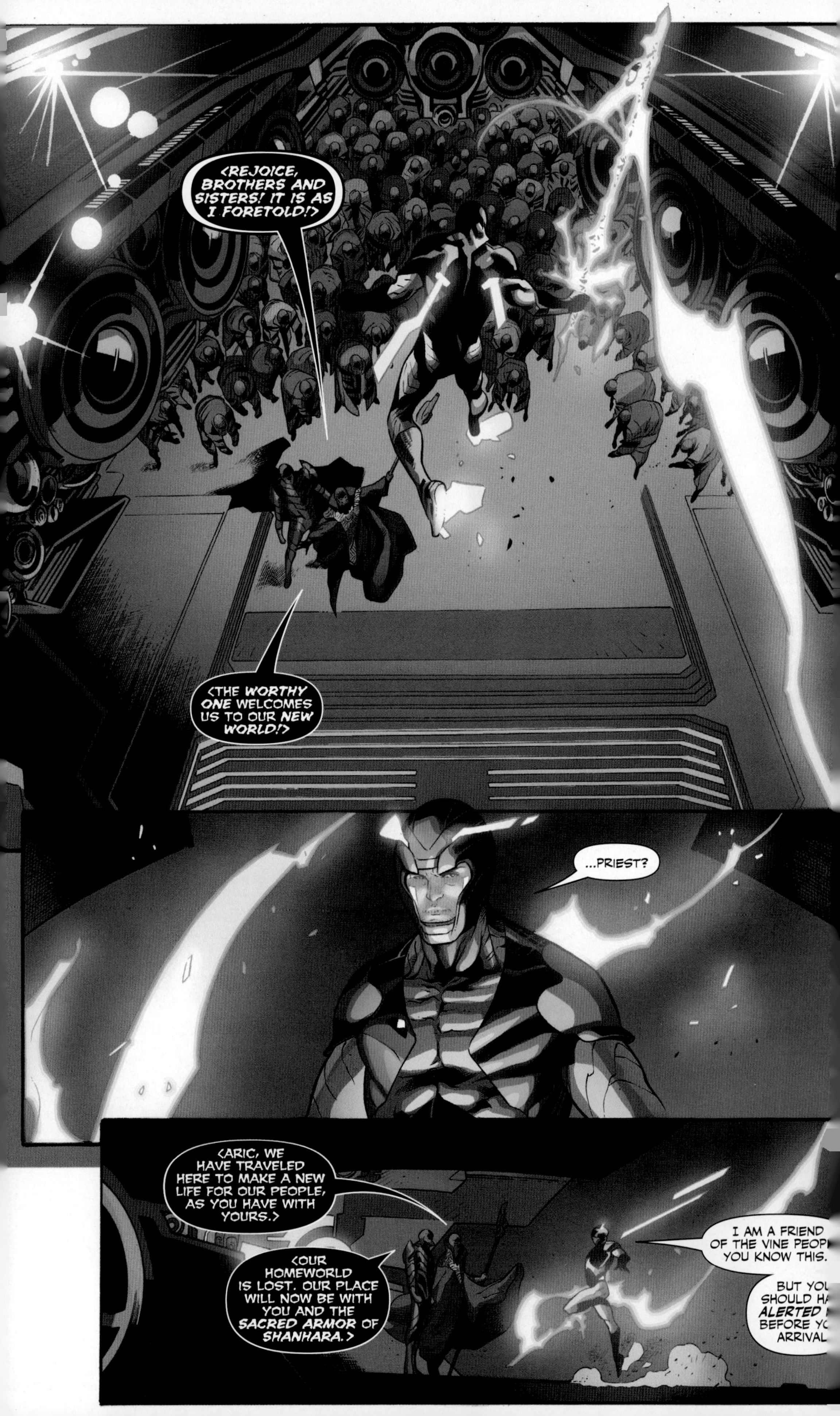
<REJOICE, BROTHERS AND SISTERS! IT IS AS I FORETOLD!>
<THE WORTHY ONE WELCOMES US TO OUR NEW WORLD!>
...PRIEST?
<ARIC, WE HAVE TRAVELED HERE TO MAKE A NEW LIFE FOR OUR PEOPLE, AS YOU HAVE WITH YOURS.>
<OUR HOMEWORLD IS LOST. OUR PLACE WILL NOW BE WITH YOU AND THE SACRED ARMOR OF SHANHARA.>
I AM A FRIEND OF THE VINE PEOP YOU KNOW THIS.
BUT YOU SHOULD HA ALERTED BEFORE YO ARRIVAL

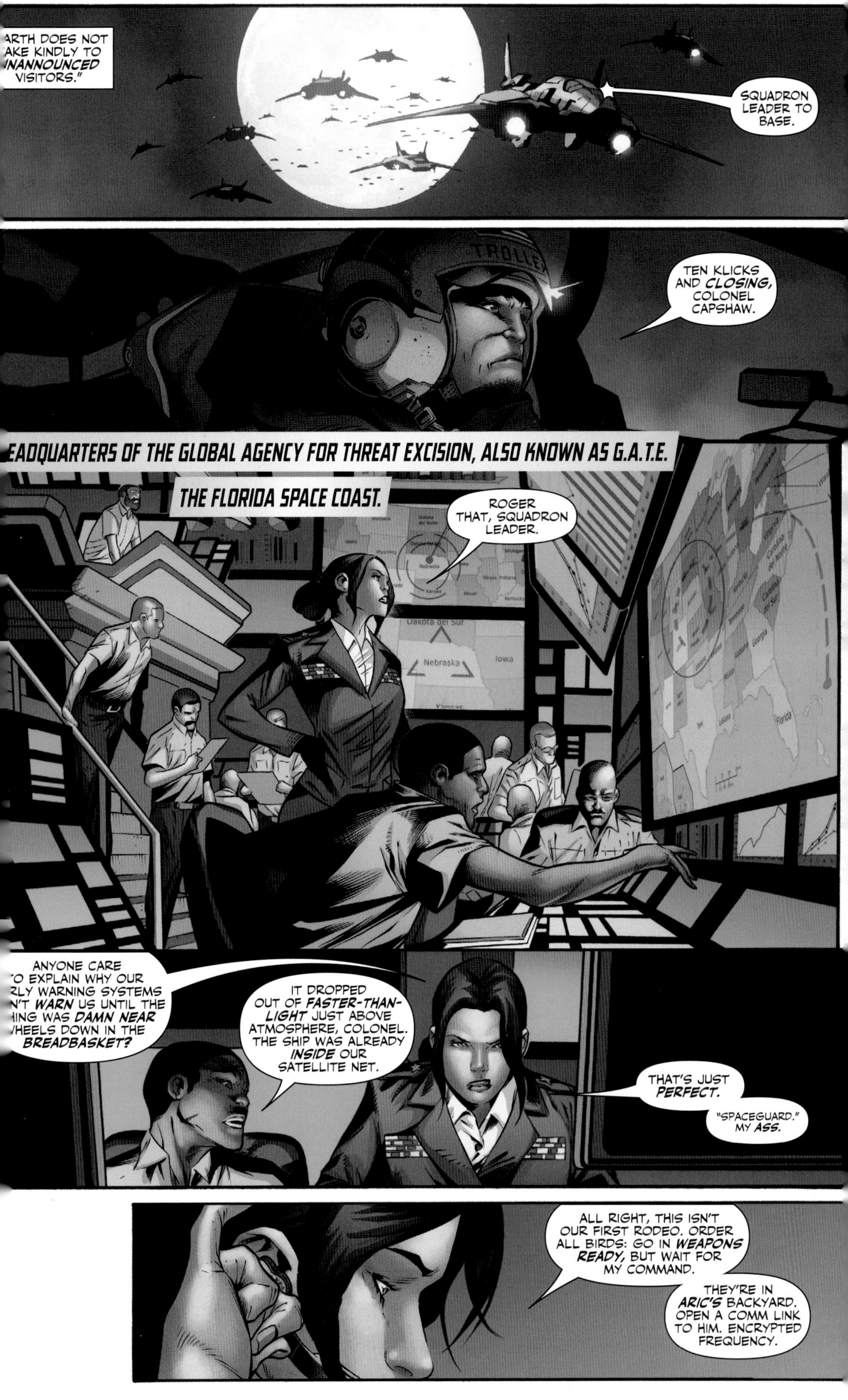
ARTH DOES NOT AKE KINDLY TO NANNOUNCED VISITORS."
SQUADRON LEADER TO BASE.
TEN KLICKS AND CLOSING, COLONEL CAPSHAW.
EADQUARTERS OF THE GLOBAL AGENCY FOR THREAT EXCISION, ALSO KNOWN AS G.A.T.E.
THE FLORIDA SPACE COAST.
ROGER THAT, SQUADRON LEADER.
ANYONE CARE O EXPLAIN WHY OUR RLY WARNING SYSTEMS N'T WARN US UNTIL THE HING WAS DAMN NEAR WHEELS DOWN IN THE BREADBASKET?
IT DROPPED OUT OF FASTER-THAN-LIGHT JUST ABOVE ATMOSPHERE, COLONEL. THE SHIP WAS ALREADY INSIDE OUR SATELLITE NET.
THAT'S JUST PERFECT.
"SPACEGUARD." MY ASS.
ALL RIGHT, THIS ISN'T OUR FIRST RODEO. ORDER ALL BIRDS: GO IN WEAPONS READY, BUT WAIT FOR MY COMMAND.
THEY'RE IN ARIC'S BACKYARD. OPEN A COMM LINK TO HIM. ENCRYPTED FREQUENCY.

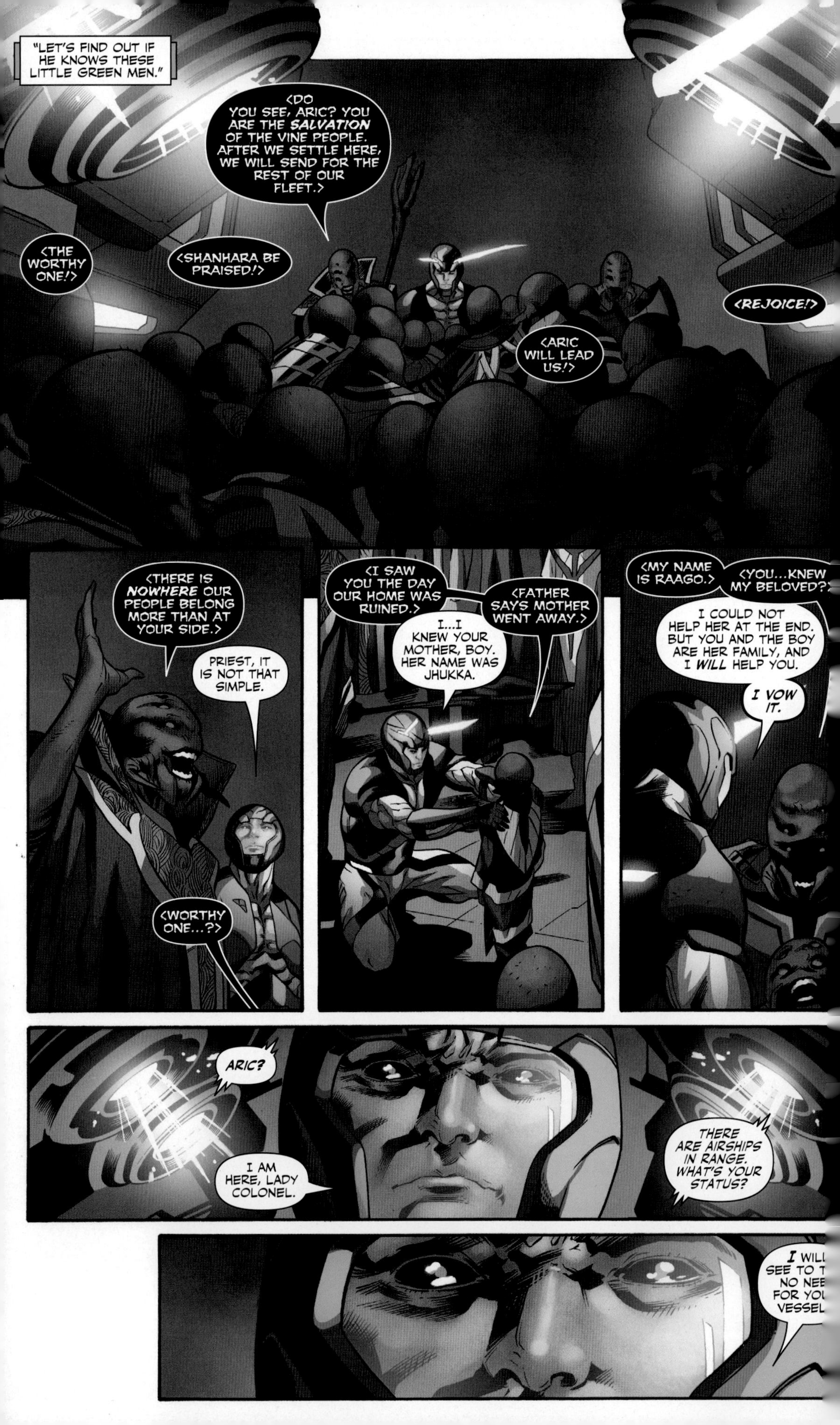
"LET'S FIND OUT IF HE KNOWS THESE LITTLE GREEN MEN."
<DO YOU SEE, ARIC? YOU ARE THE SALVATION OF THE VINE PEOPLE. AFTER WE SETTLE HERE, WE WILL SEND FOR THE REST OF OUR FLEET.>
<THE WORTHY ONE!>
<SHANHARA BE PRAISED!>
<REJOICE!>
<ARIC WILL LEAD US!>
<THERE IS NOWHERE OUR PEOPLE BELONG MORE THAN AT YOUR SIDE.>
PRIEST, IT IS NOT THAT SIMPLE.
<WORTHY ONE...?>
<I SAW YOU THE DAY OUR HOME WAS RUINED.>
<FATHER SAYS MOTHER WENT AWAY.>
I...I KNEW YOUR MOTHER, BOY. HER NAME WAS JHUKKA.
<MY NAME IS RAAGO.>
<YOU...KNEW MY BELOVED?>
I COULD NOT HELP HER AT THE END. BUT YOU AND THE BOY ARE HER FAMILY, AND I WILL HELP YOU.
I VOW IT.
ARIC?
I AM HERE, LADY COLONEL.
THERE ARE AIRSHIPS IN RANGE. WHAT'S YOUR STATUS?

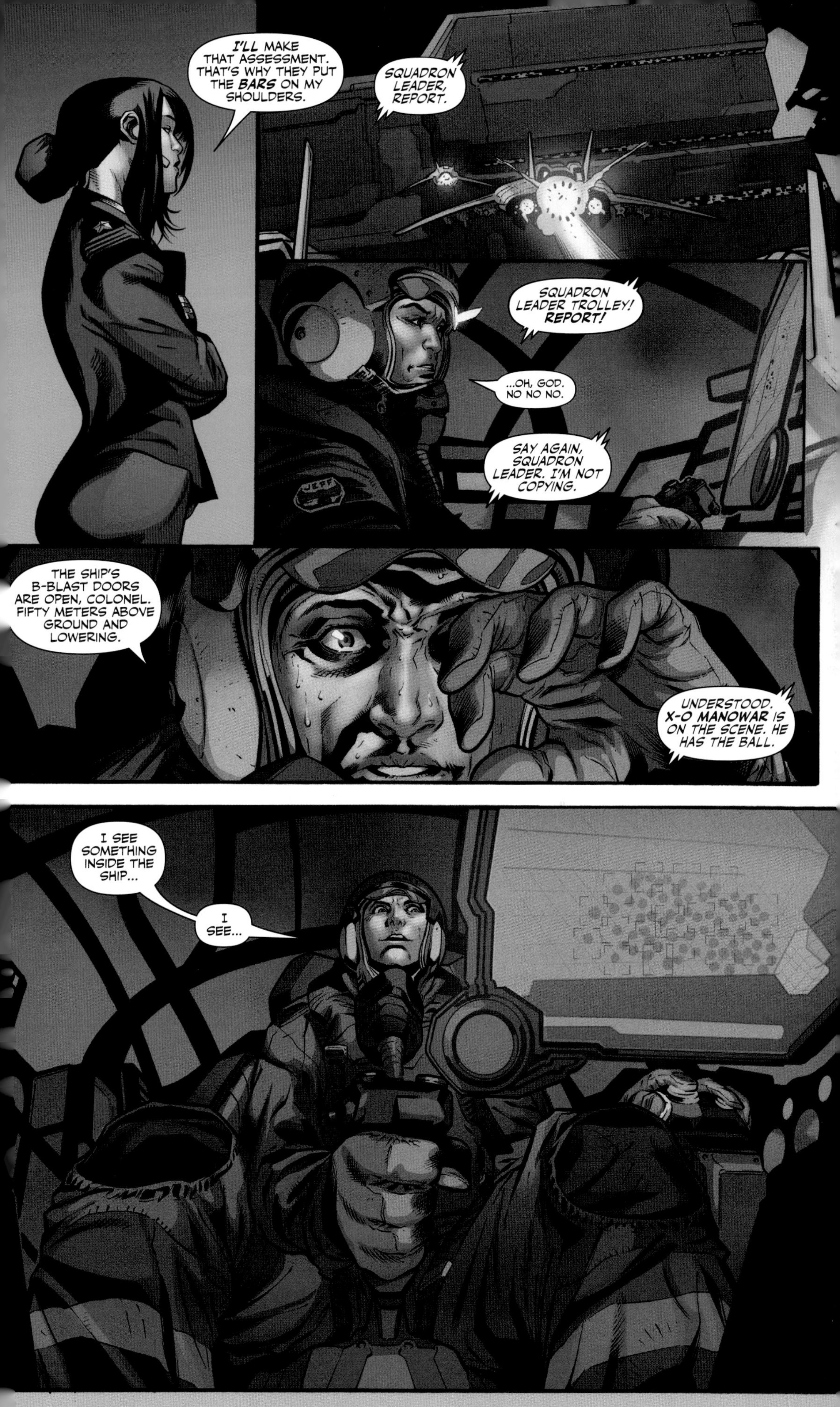
I'LL MAKE THAT ASSESSMENT. THAT'S WHY THEY PUT THE BARS ON MY SHOULDERS.
SQUADRON LEADER, REPORT.
SQUADRON LEADER TROLLEY! REPORT!
...OH, GOD. NO NO NO.
SAY AGAIN, SQUADRON LEADER. I'M NOT COPYING.
THE SHIP'S B-BLAST DOORS ARE OPEN, COLONEL. FIFTY METERS ABOVE GROUND AND LOWERING.
UNDERSTOOD. X-O MANOWAR IS ON THE SCENE. HE HAS THE BALL.
I SEE SOMETHING INSIDE THE SHIP...
I SEE...

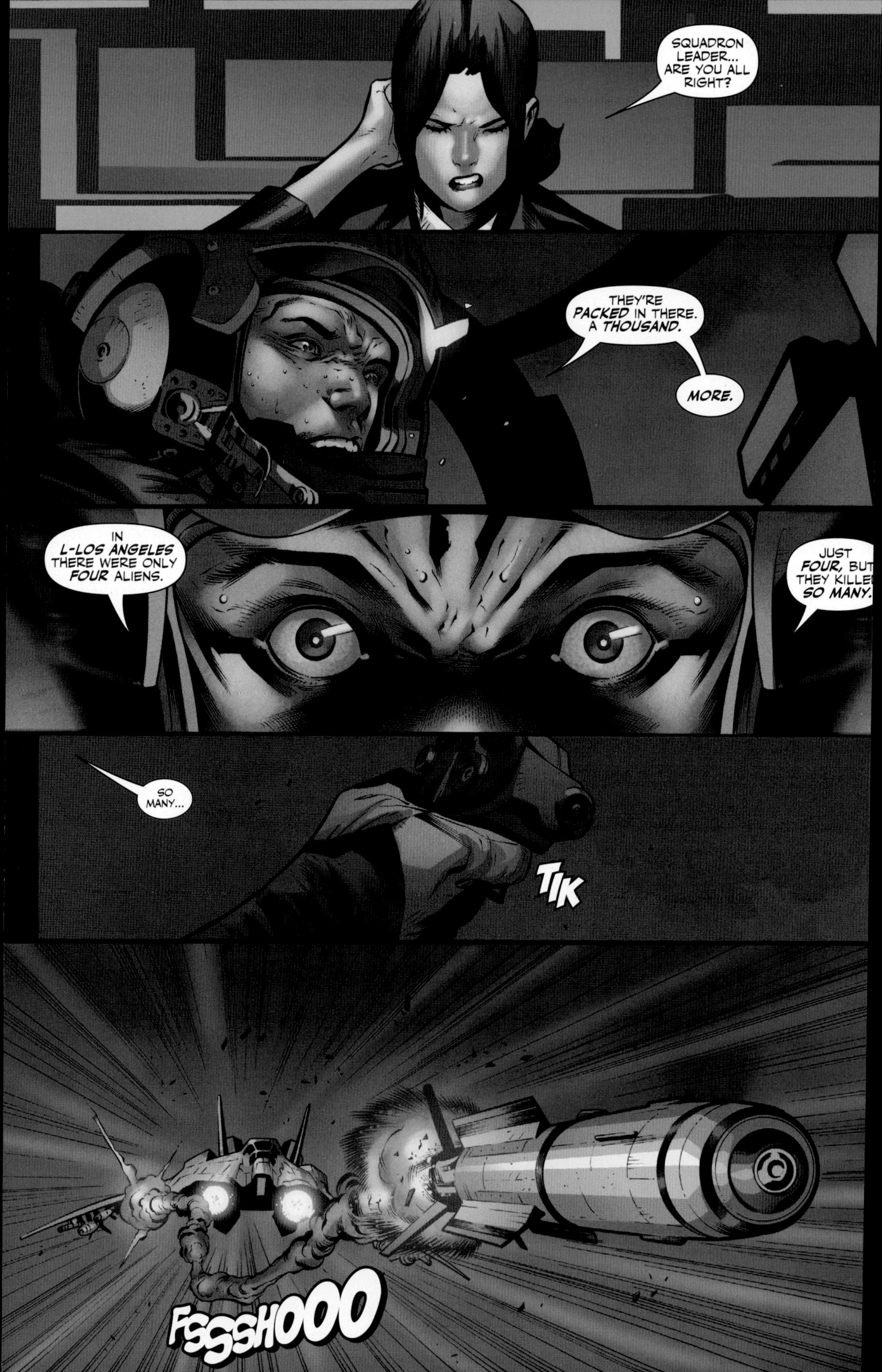

SQUADRON LEADER... ARE YOU ALL RIGHT?
THEY'RE *PACKED* IN THERE. A *THOUSAND.*
MORE.
IN *L-LOS ANGELES* THERE WERE ONLY *FOUR* ALIENS.
JUST *FOUR,* BUT THEY KILLED *SO MANY.*
SO MANY...
TIK
FSSSHOOO

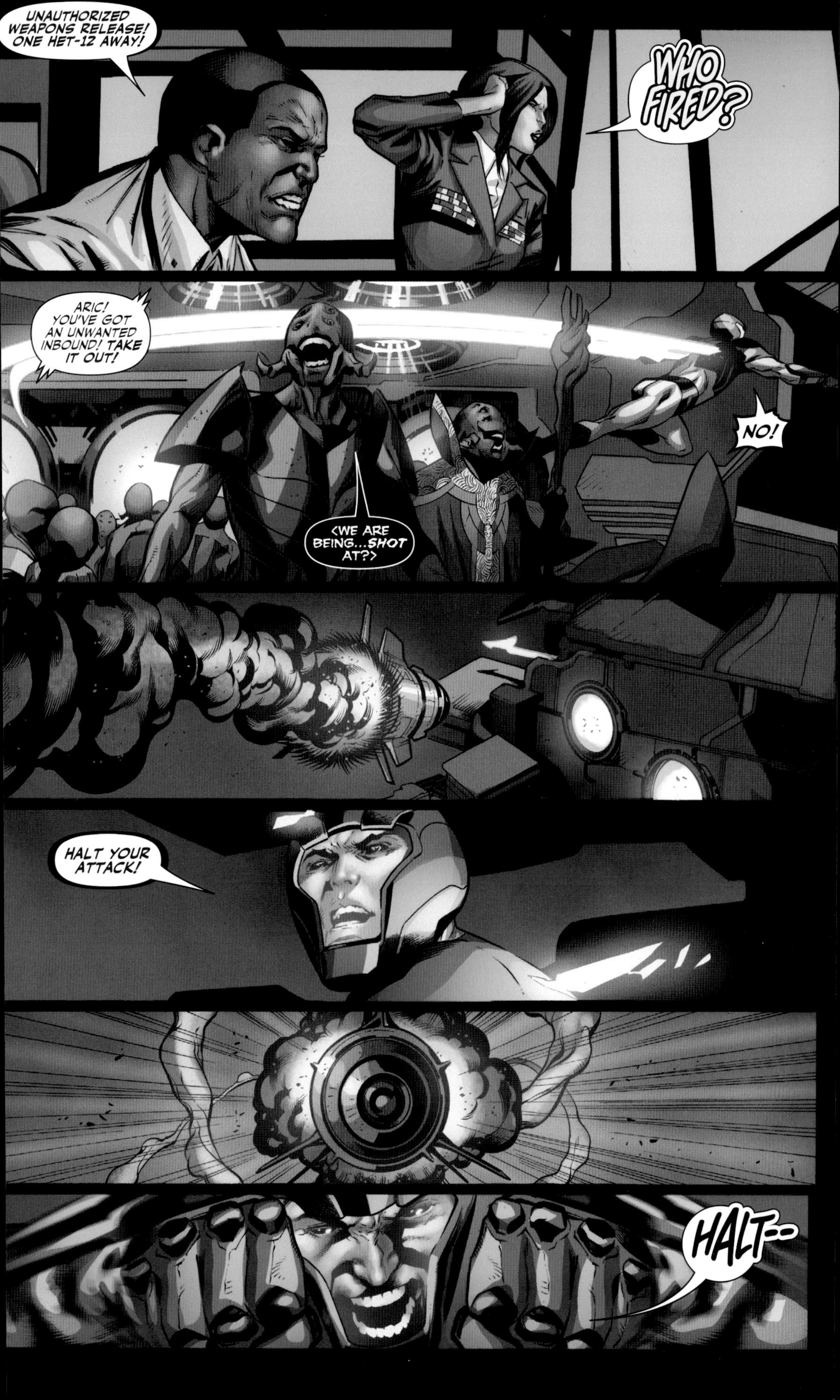
UNAUTHORIZED WEAPONS RELEASE! ONE HET-12 AWAY!
WHO FIRED?
ARIC! YOU'VE GOT AN UNWANTED INBOUND! TAKE IT OUT!
NO!
<WE ARE BEING...SHOT AT?>
HALT YOUR ATTACK!
HALT--

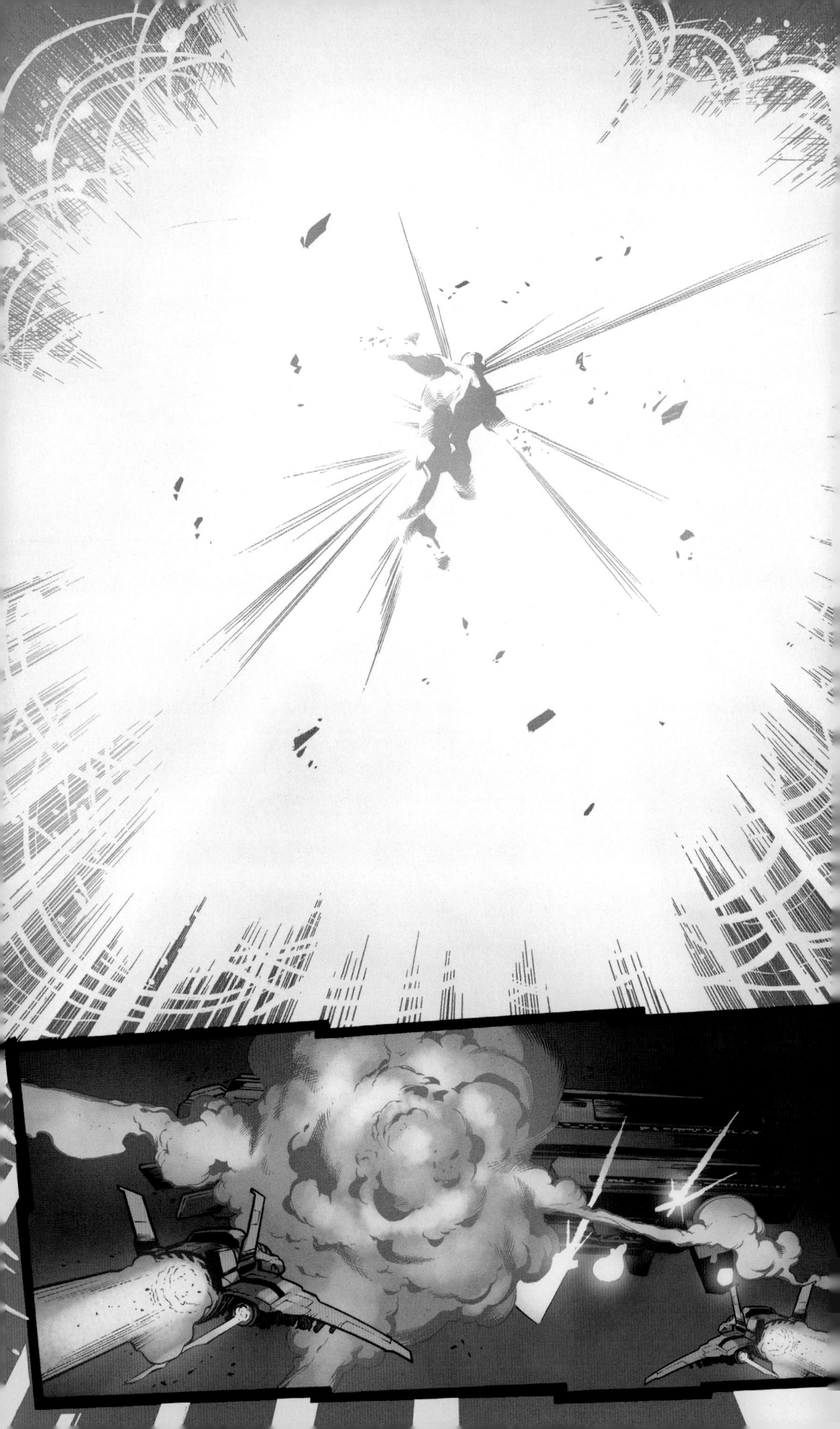

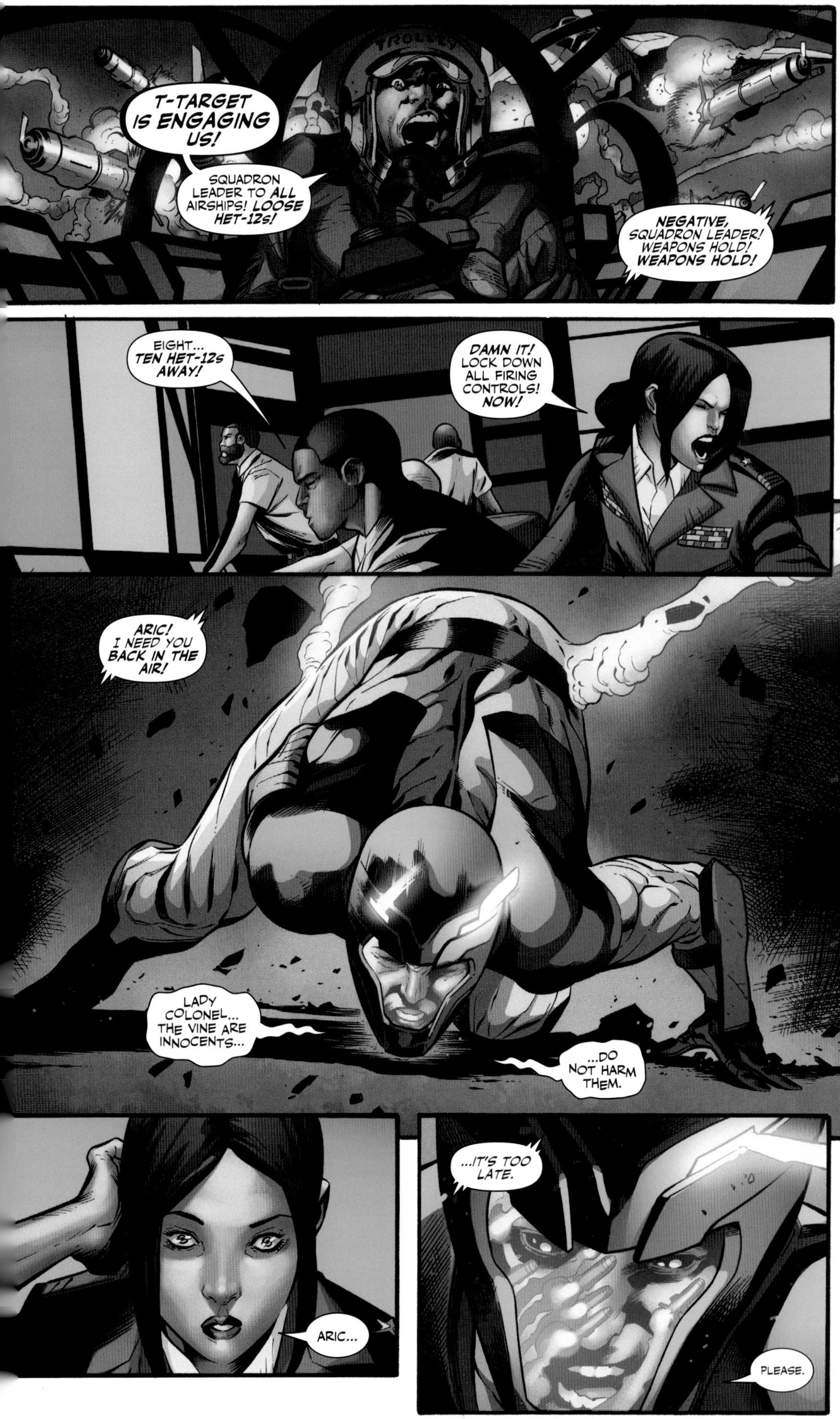
T-TARGET IS ENGAGING US!
SQUADRON LEADER TO ALL AIRSHIPS! LOOSE HET-12s!
NEGATIVE, SQUADRON LEADER! WEAPONS HOLD! WEAPONS HOLD!
EIGHT... TEN HET-12s AWAY!
DAMN IT! LOCK DOWN ALL FIRING CONTROLS! NOW!
ARIC! I NEED YOU BACK IN THE AIR!
LADY COLONEL... THE VINE ARE INNOCENTS...
...DO NOT HARM THEM.
ARIC...
...IT'S TOO LATE.
PLEASE.

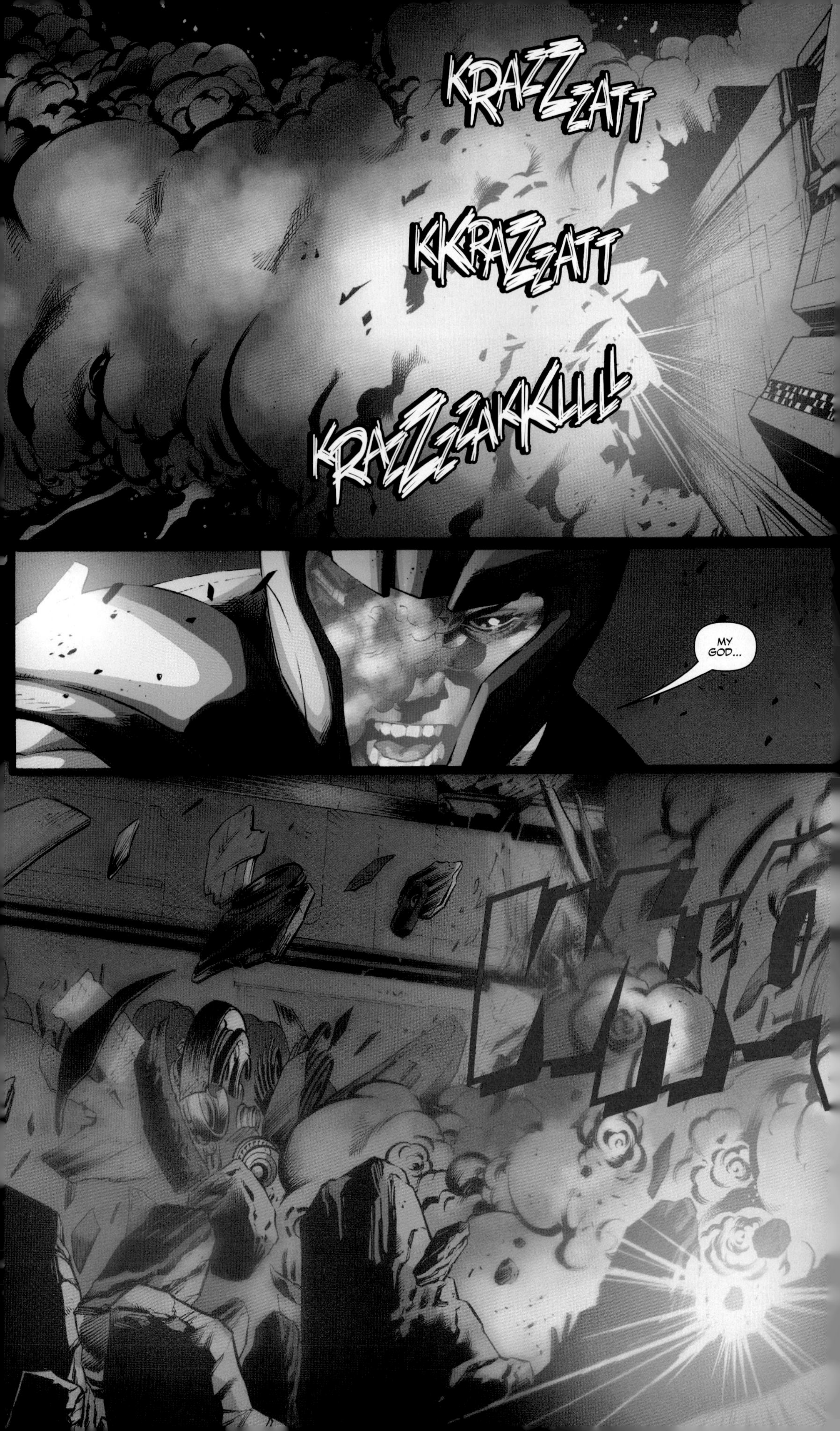
KRAZZZATT
KKRAZZZATT
KRAZZZZAKKLLLL
MY GOD...

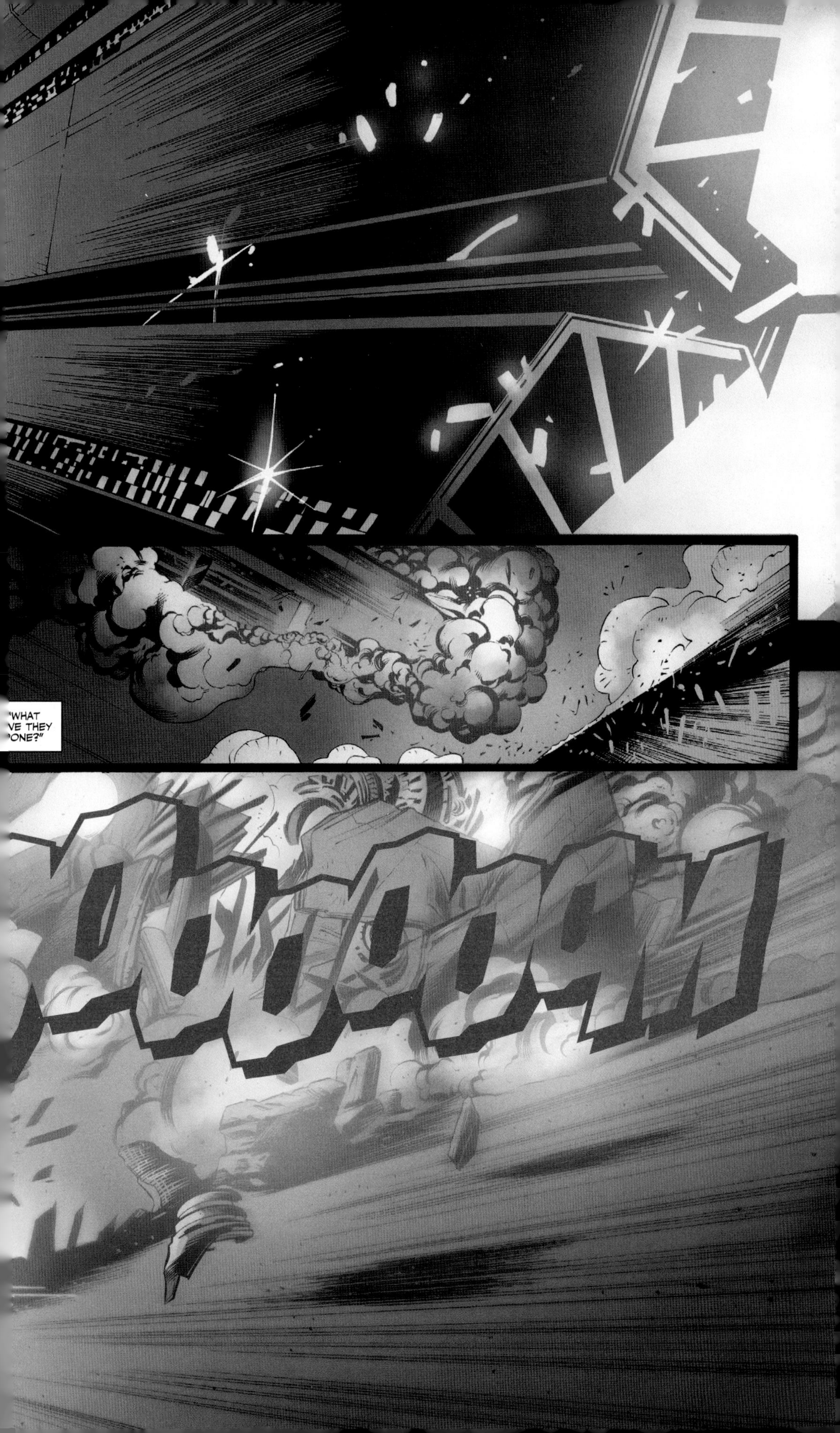
"WHAT
VE THEY
ONE?"

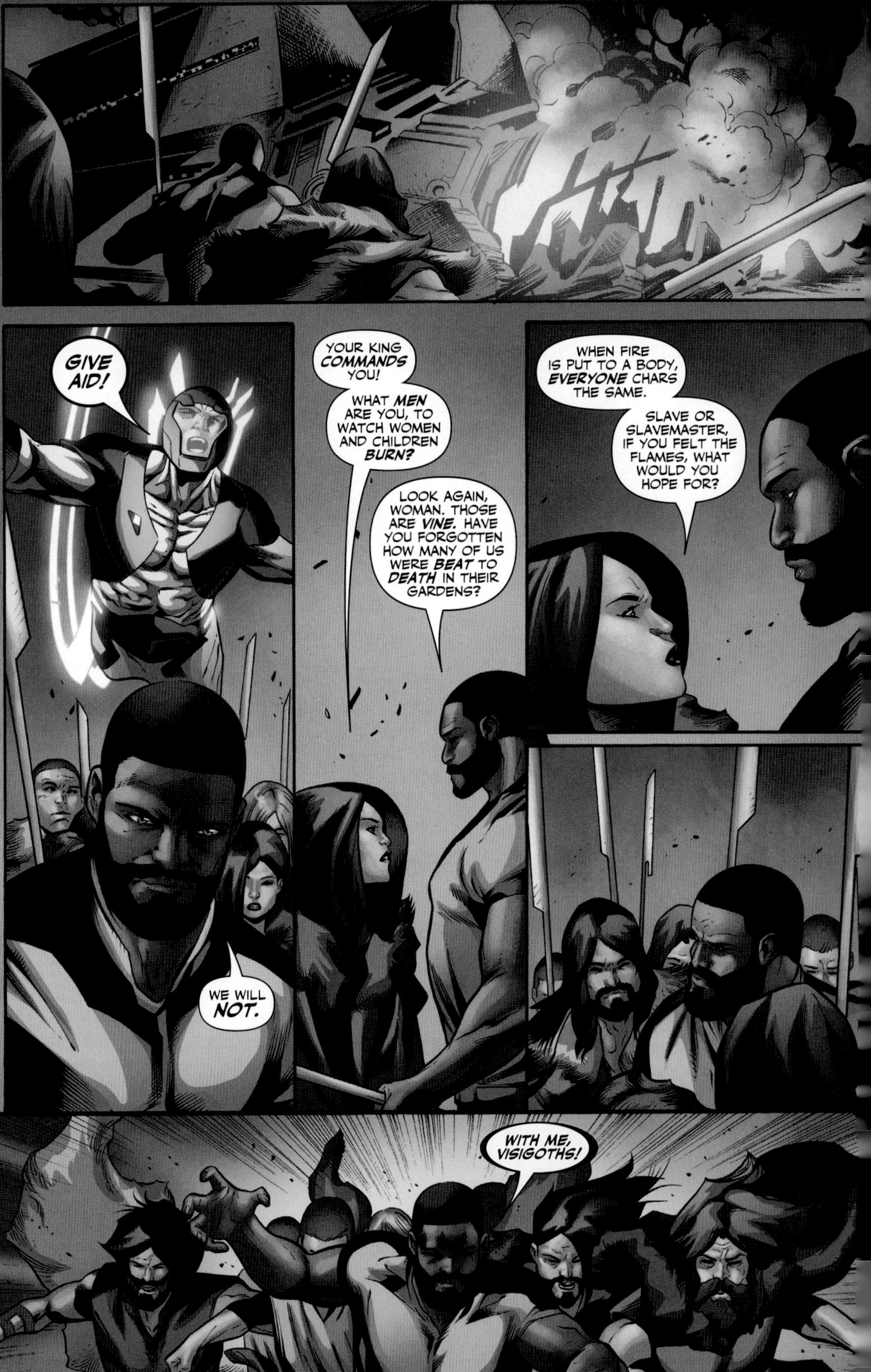
GIVE AID!
YOUR KING COMMANDS YOU!
WHAT MEN ARE YOU, TO WATCH WOMEN AND CHILDREN BURN?
WE WILL NOT.
LOOK AGAIN, WOMAN. THOSE ARE VINE. HAVE YOU FORGOTTEN HOW MANY OF US WERE BEAT TO DEATH IN THEIR GARDENS?
WHEN FIRE IS PUT TO A BODY, EVERYONE CHARS THE SAME.
SLAVE OR SLAVEMASTER, IF YOU FELT THE FLAMES, WHAT WOULD YOU HOPE FOR?
WITH ME, VISIGOTHS!

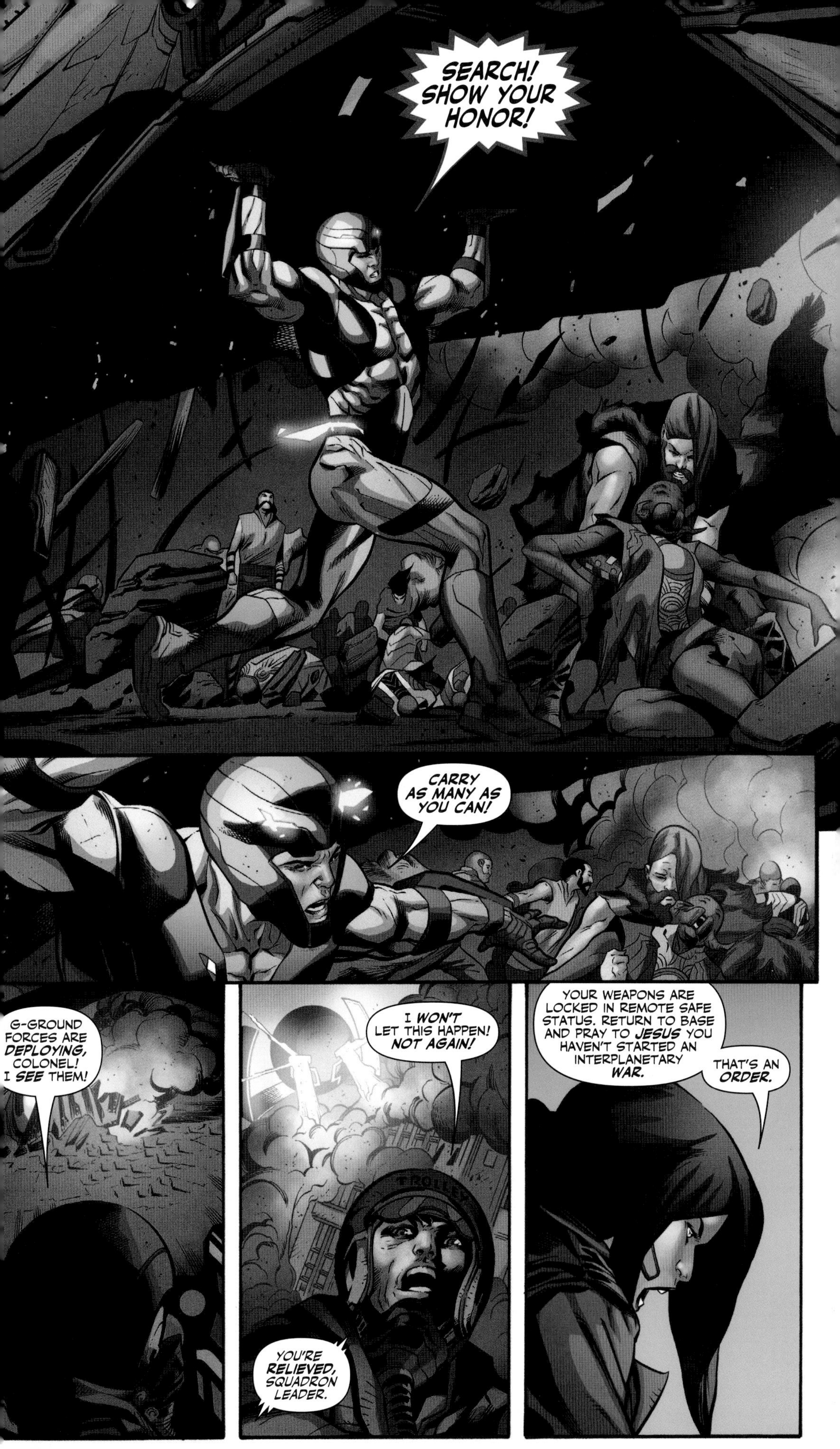
SEARCH! SHOW YOUR HONOR!
CARRY AS MANY AS YOU CAN!
G-GROUND FORCES ARE DEPLOYING, COLONEL! I SEE THEM!
I WON'T LET THIS HAPPEN! NOT AGAIN!
YOU'RE RELIEVED, SQUADRON LEADER.
YOUR WEAPONS ARE LOCKED IN REMOTE SAFE STATUS. RETURN TO BASE AND PRAY TO JESUS YOU HAVEN'T STARTED AN INTERPLANETARY WAR.
THAT'S AN ORDER.

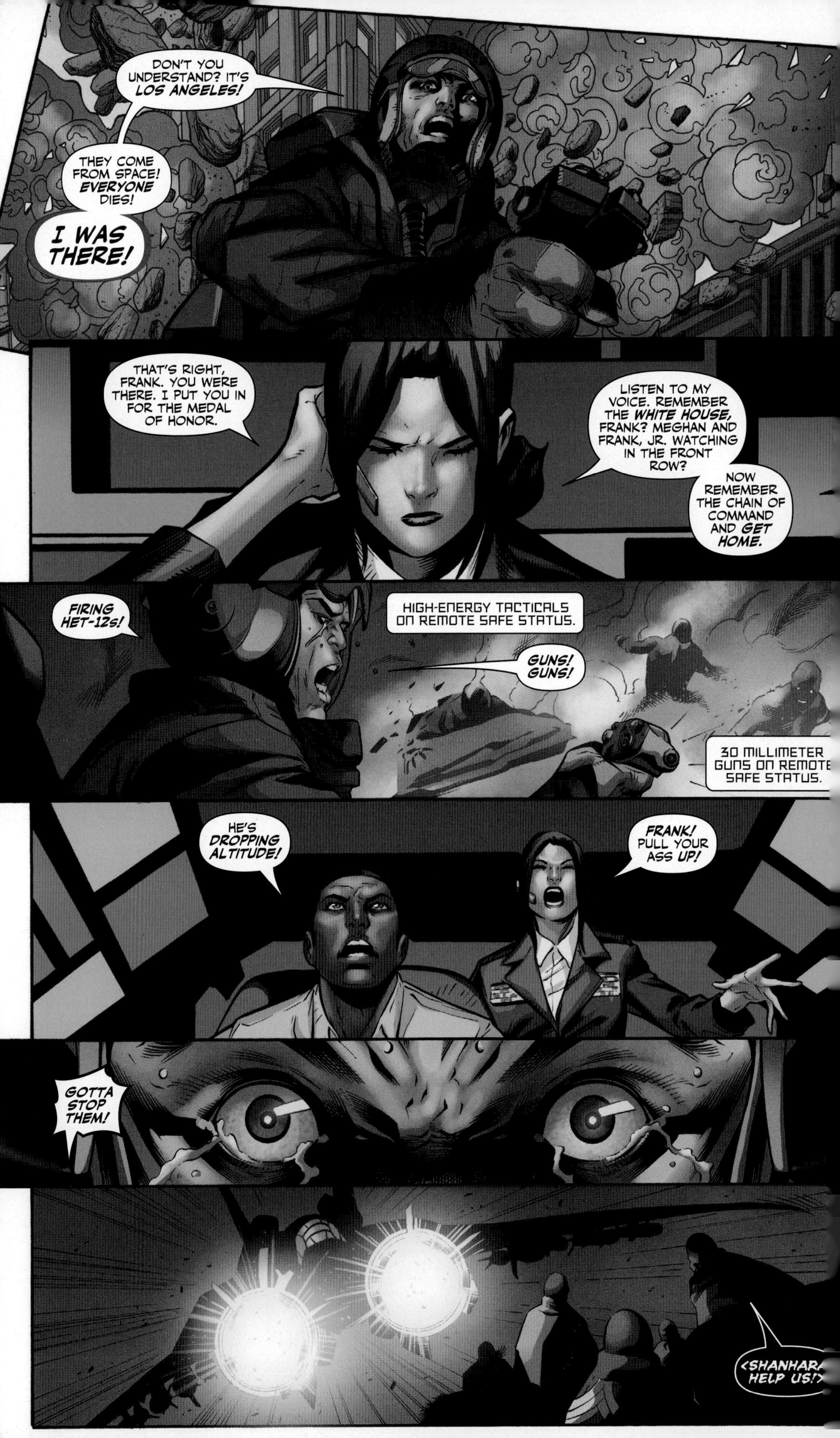
DON'T YOU UNDERSTAND? IT'S LOS ANGELES!
THEY COME FROM SPACE! EVERYONE DIES!
I WAS THERE!
THAT'S RIGHT, FRANK. YOU WERE THERE. I PUT YOU IN FOR THE MEDAL OF HONOR.
LISTEN TO MY VOICE. REMEMBER THE WHITE HOUSE, FRANK? MEGHAN AND FRANK, JR. WATCHING IN THE FRONT ROW?
NOW REMEMBER THE CHAIN OF COMMAND AND GET HOME.
FIRING HET-12s!
HIGH-ENERGY TACTICALS ON REMOTE SAFE STATUS.
GUNS! GUNS!
30 MILLIMETER GUNS ON REMOTE SAFE STATUS.
HE'S DROPPING ALTITUDE!
FRANK! PULL YOUR ASS UP!
GOTTA STOP THEM!
<SHANHARA HELP US!>

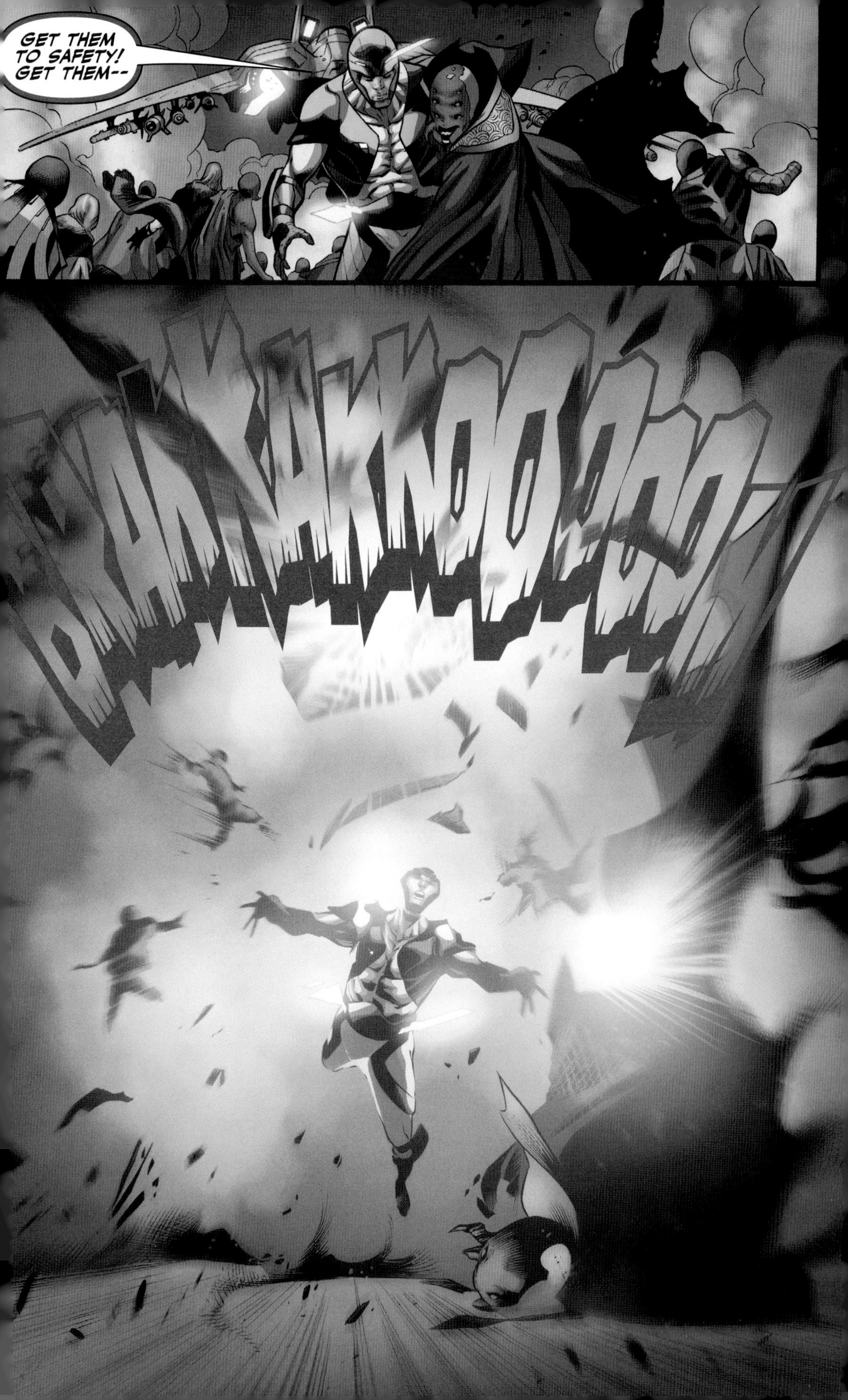
GET THEM TO SAFETY! GET THEM--

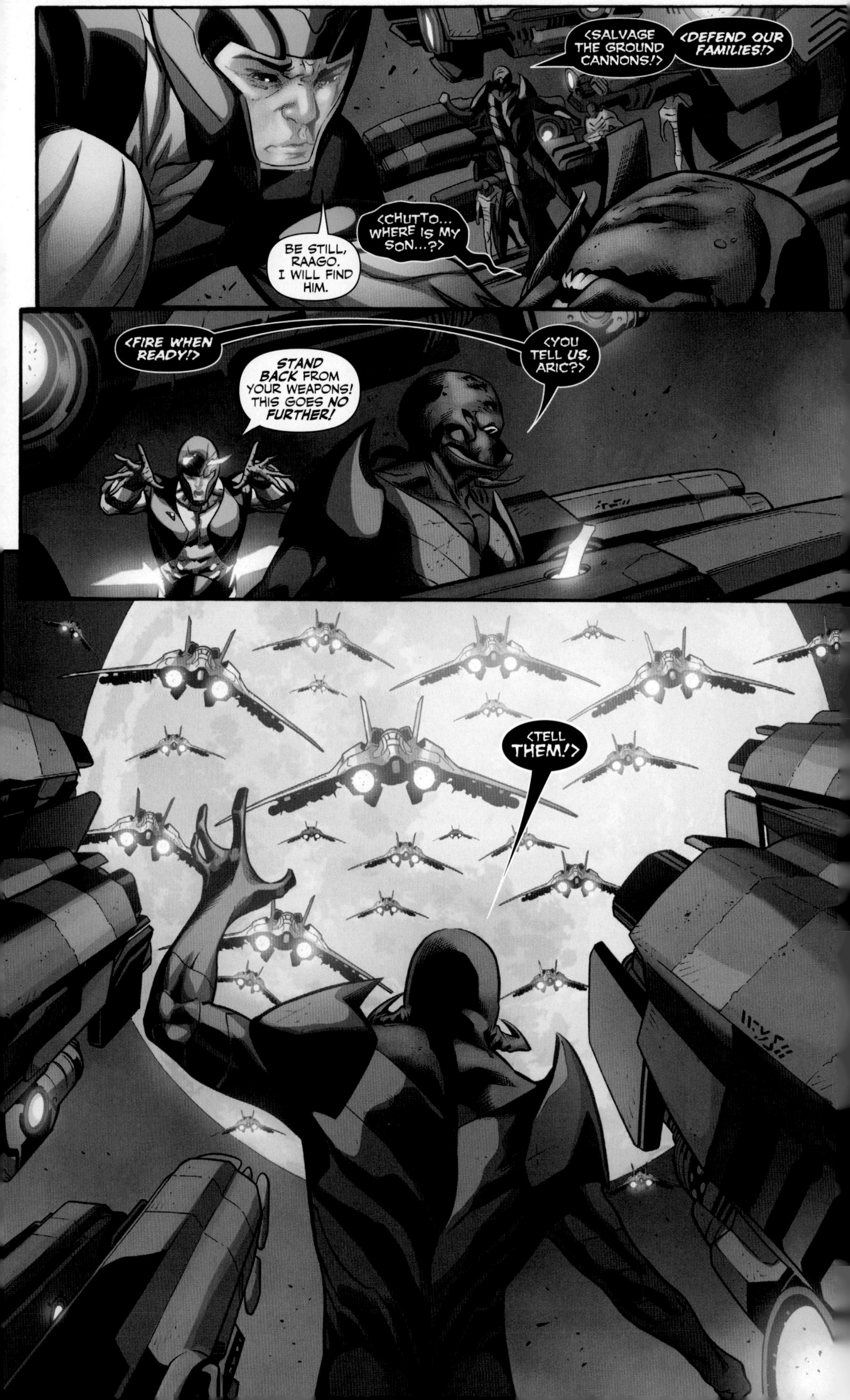
<SALVAGE THE GROUND CANNONS!>
<DEFEND OUR FAMILIES!>
<CHUTTO... WHERE IS MY SON...?>
BE STILL, RAAGO. I WILL FIND HIM.
<FIRE WHEN READY!>
STAND BACK FROM YOUR WEAPONS! THIS GOES NO FURTHER!
<YOU TELL US, ARIC?>
<TELL THEM!>

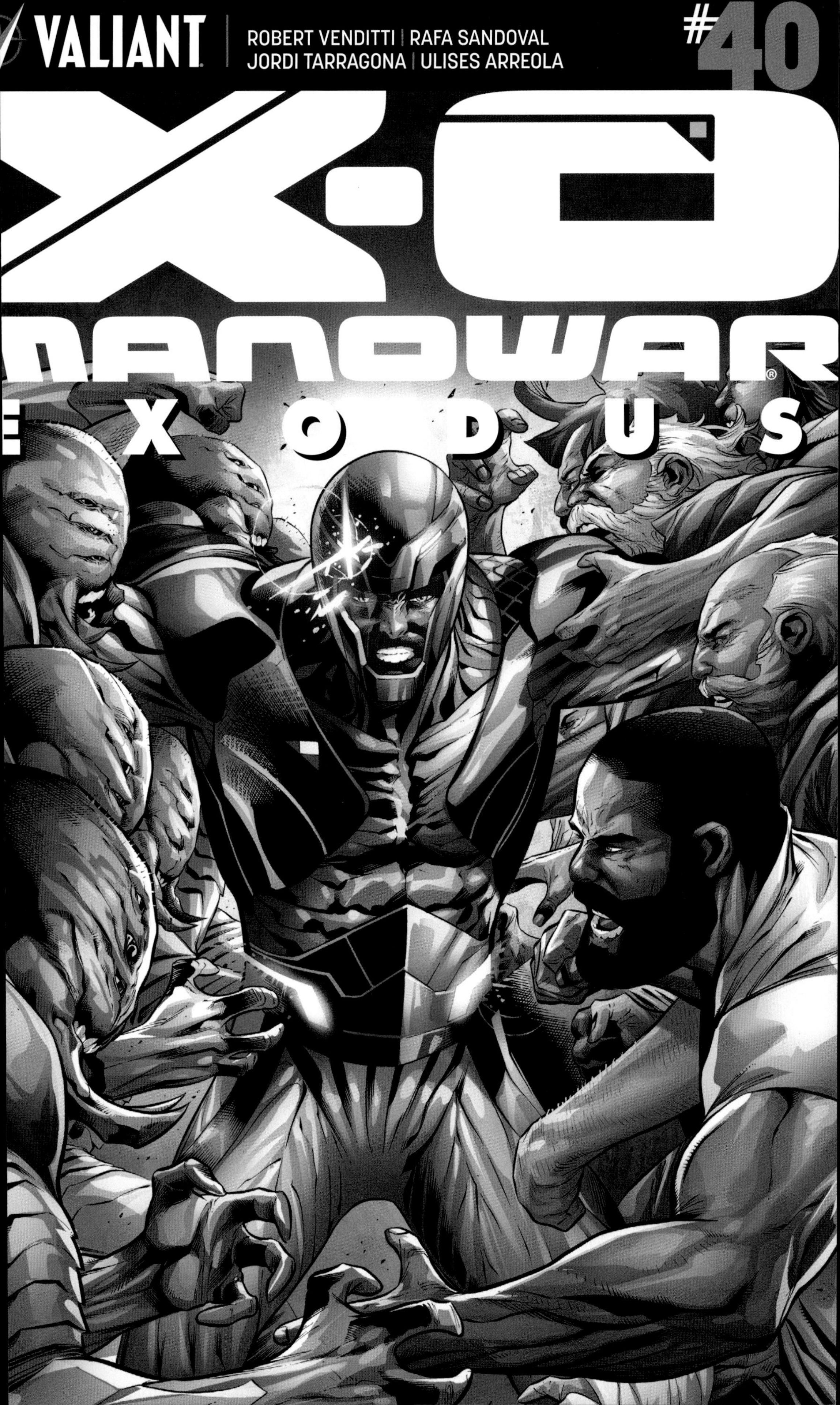
VALIANT
ROBERT VENDITTI | RAFA SANDOVAL
JORDI TARRAGONA | ULISES ARREOLA
#40
X-O MANOWAR
EXODUS

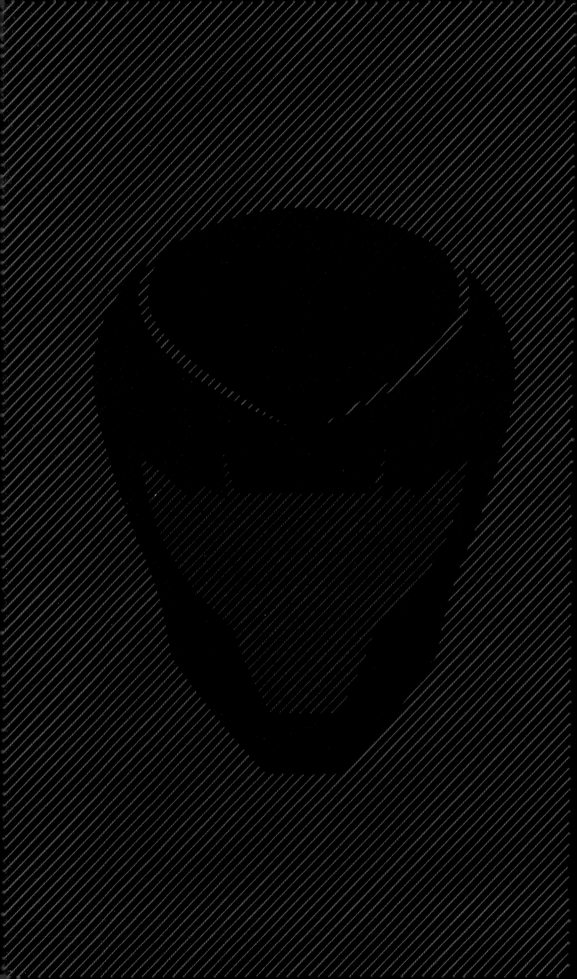

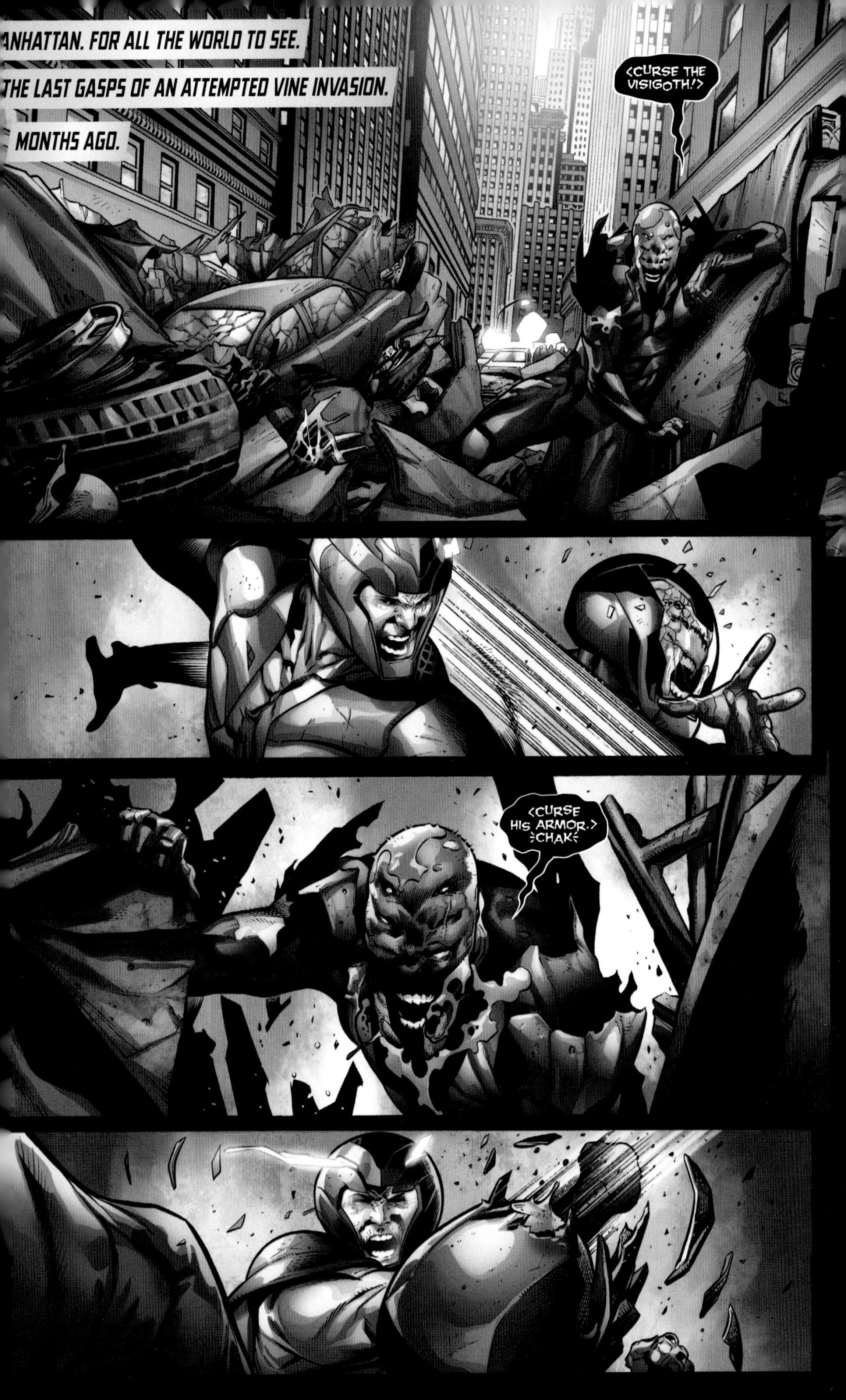
ANHATTAN. FOR ALL THE WORLD TO SEE.
THE LAST GASPS OF AN ATTEMPTED VINE INVASION.
MONTHS AGO.
<CURSE THE VISIGOTH!>
<CURSE HIS ARMOR.> CHAK

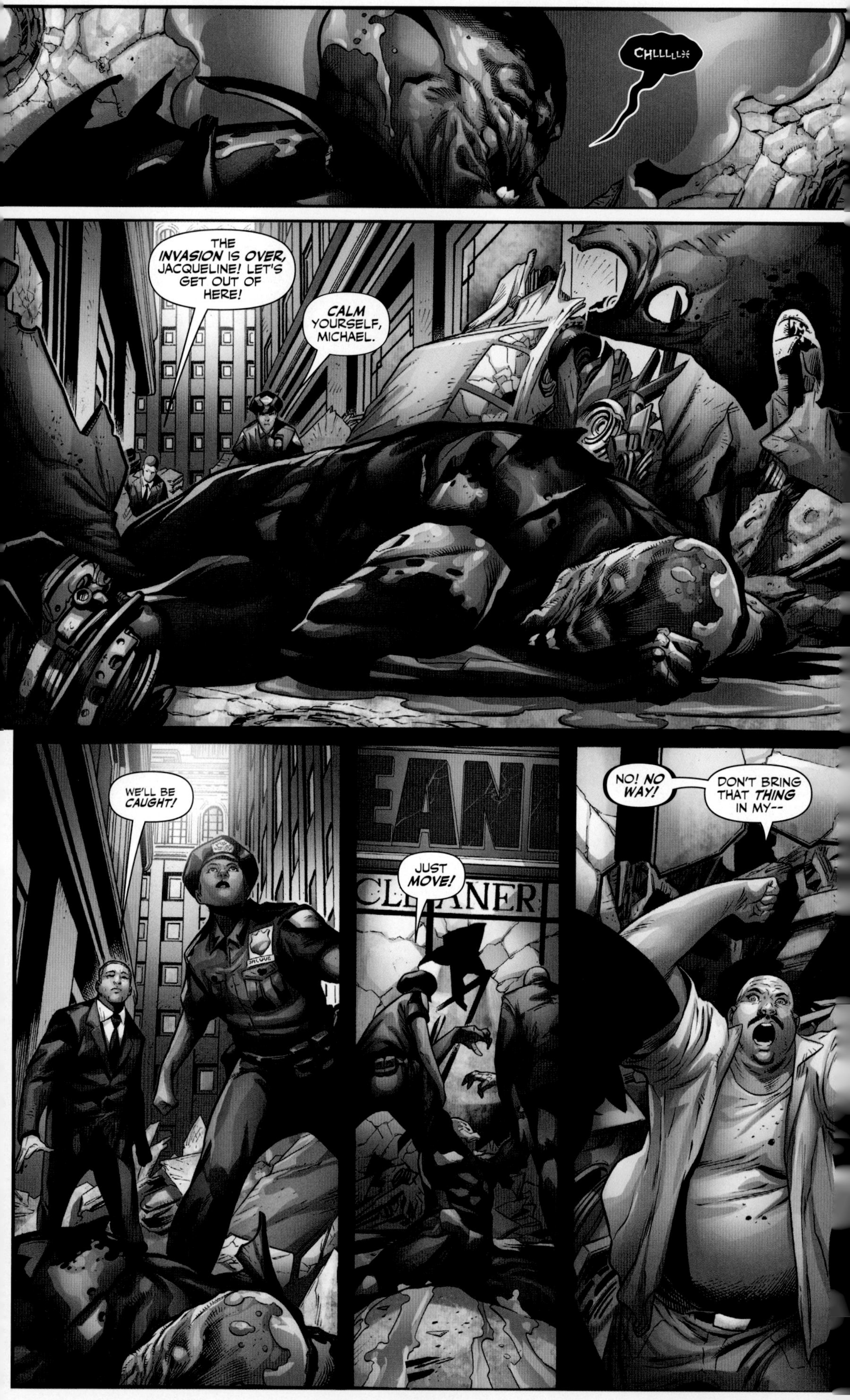
CHLLLLL
THE INVASION IS OVER, JACQUELINE! LET'S GET OUT OF HERE!
CALM YOURSELF, MICHAEL.
WE'LL BE CAUGHT!
JUST MOVE!
CLEANER
NO! NO WAY!
DON'T BRING THAT THING IN MY--

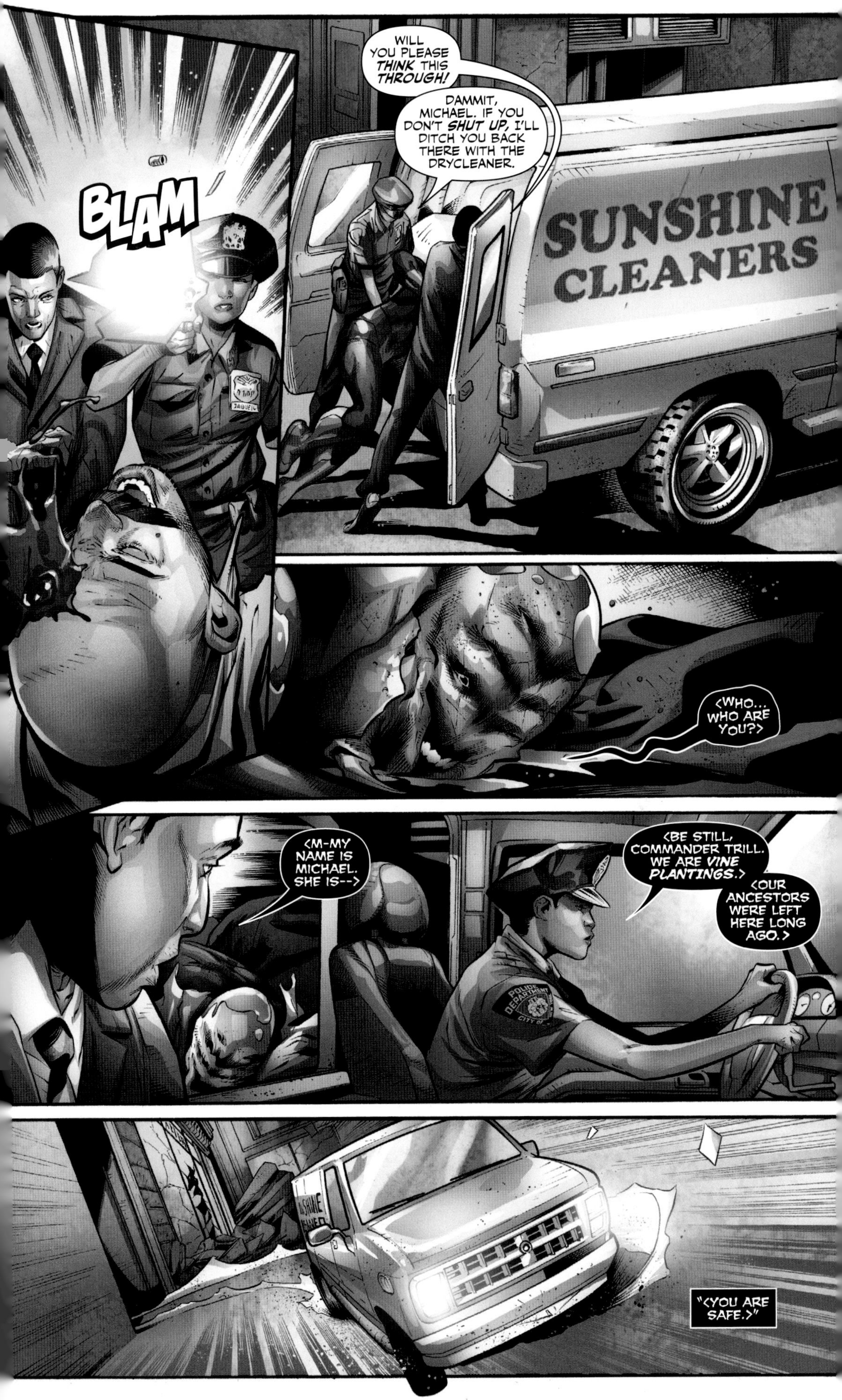
WILL YOU PLEASE *THINK* THIS *THROUGH!*
DAMMIT, MICHAEL. IF YOU DON'T *SHUT UP*, I'LL DITCH YOU BACK THERE WITH THE DRYCLEANER.
BLAM
SUNSHINE CLEANERS
<WHO... WHO ARE YOU?>
<M-MY NAME IS MICHAEL. SHE IS-->
<BE STILL, COMMANDER TRILL. WE ARE *VINE PLANTINGS*.>
<OUR ANCESTORS WERE LEFT HERE LONG AGO.>
"<YOU ARE SAFE.>"

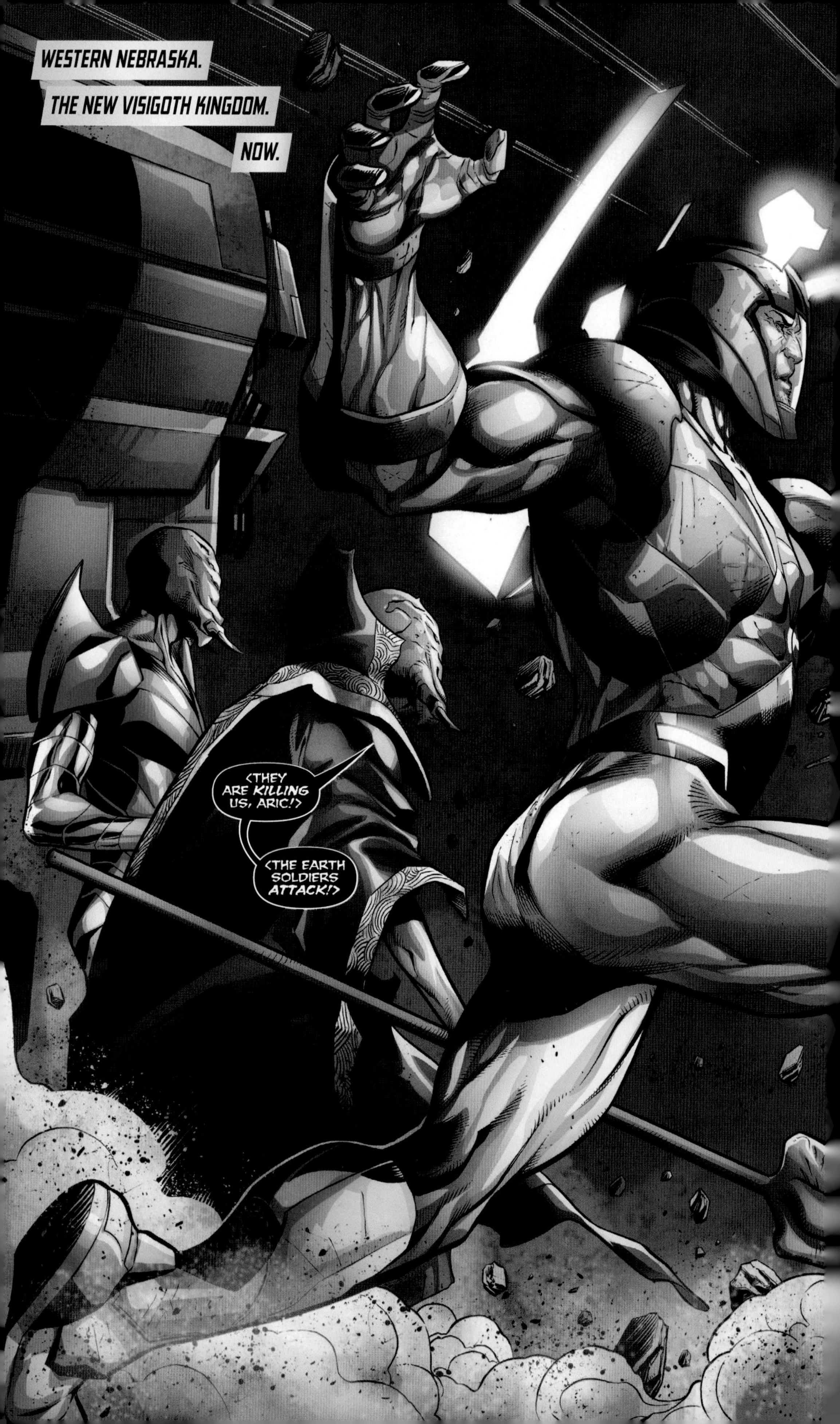
WESTERN NEBRASKA.
THE NEW VISIGOTH KINGDOM.
NOW.
<THEY ARE KILLING US, ARIC!>
<THE EARTH SOLDIERS ATTACK!>

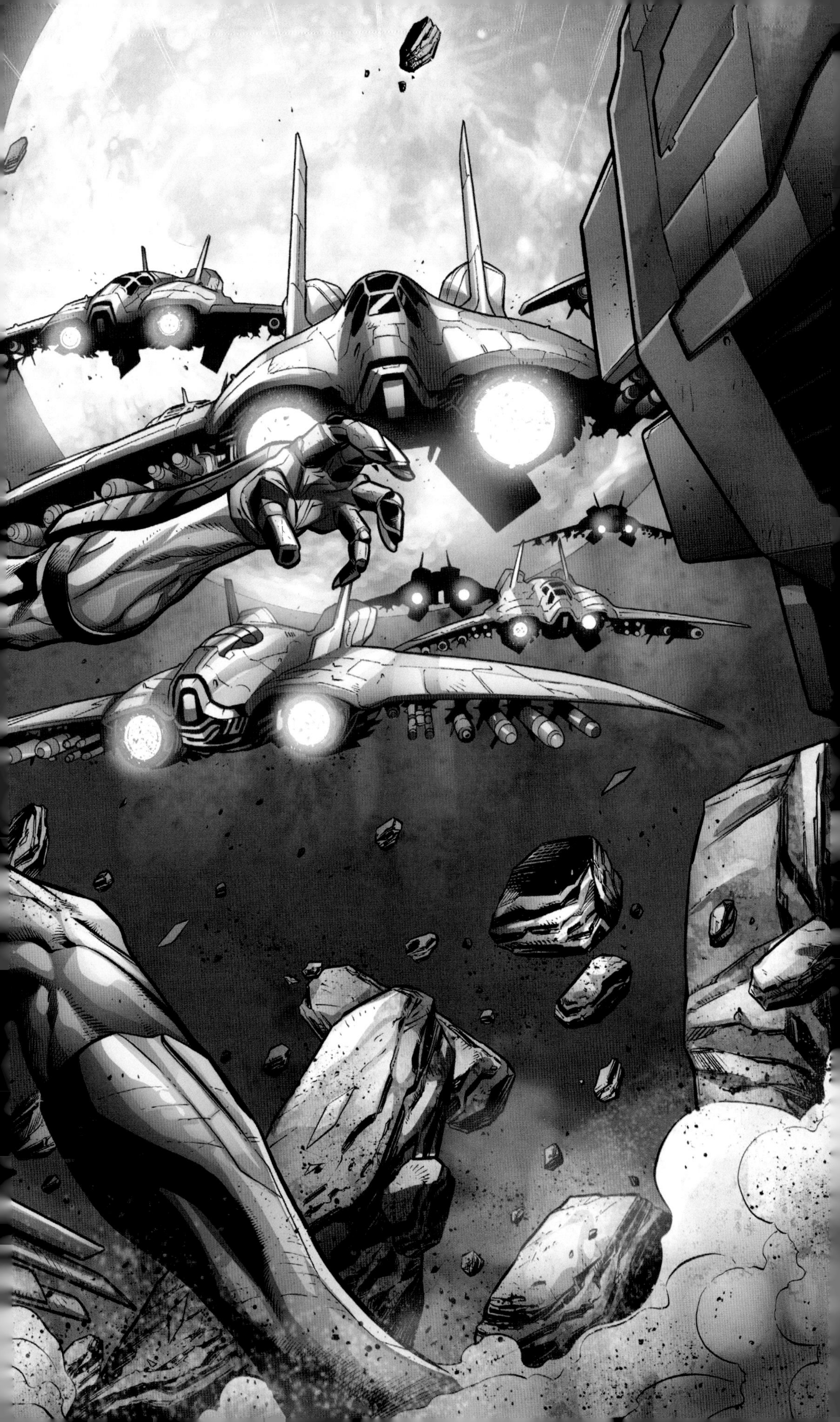

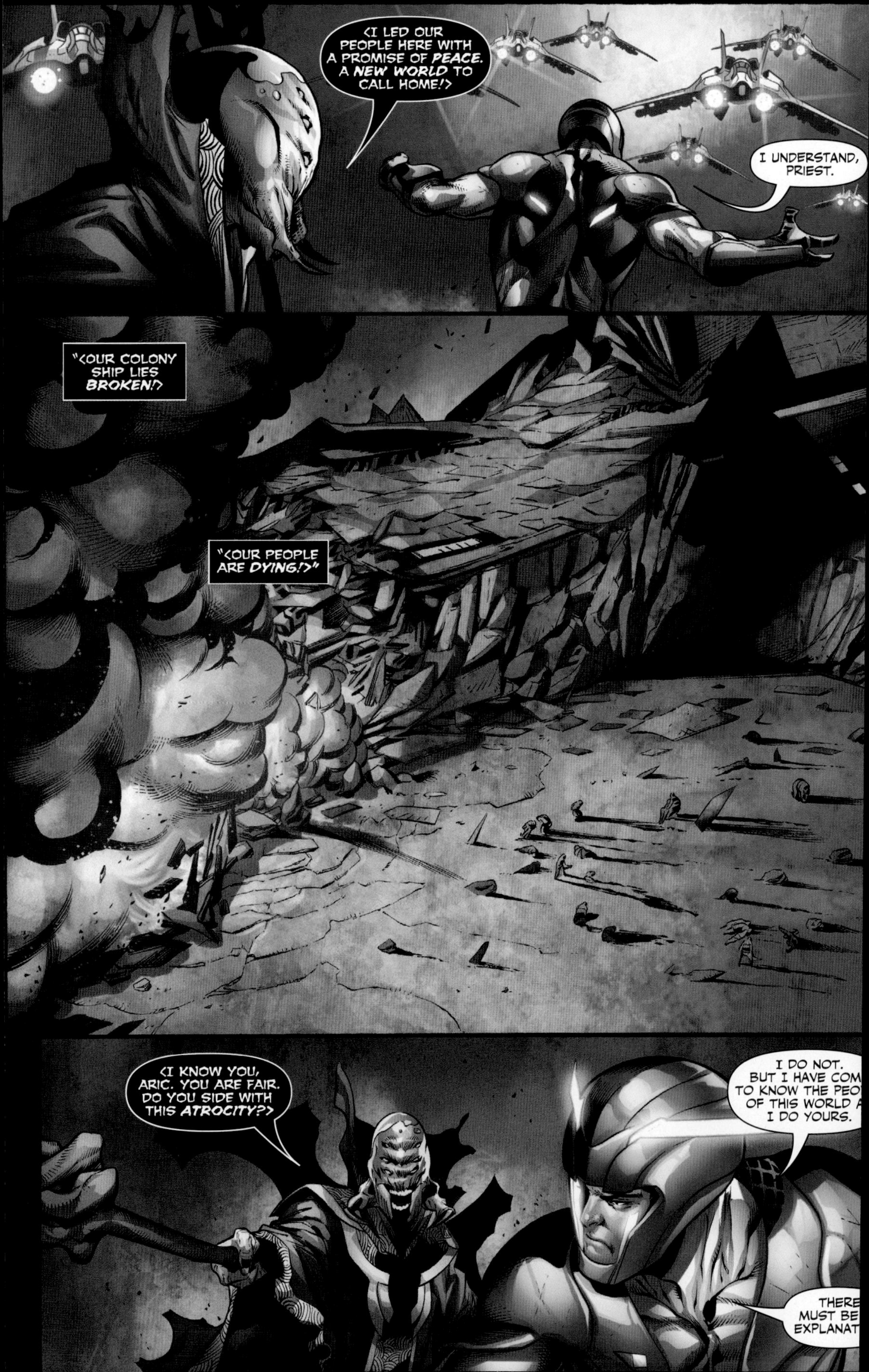

<I LED OUR PEOPLE HERE WITH A PROMISE OF *PEACE*. A *NEW WORLD* TO CALL HOME!>
I UNDERSTAND, PRIEST.
"<OUR COLONY SHIP LIES *BROKEN!*>
"<OUR PEOPLE ARE *DYING!*>"
<I KNOW YOU, ARIC. YOU ARE FAIR. DO YOU SIDE WITH THIS *ATROCITY?*>
I DO NOT. BUT I HAVE COM TO KNOW THE PEO OF THIS WORLD A I DO YOURS.
THERE MUST BE EXPLANAT

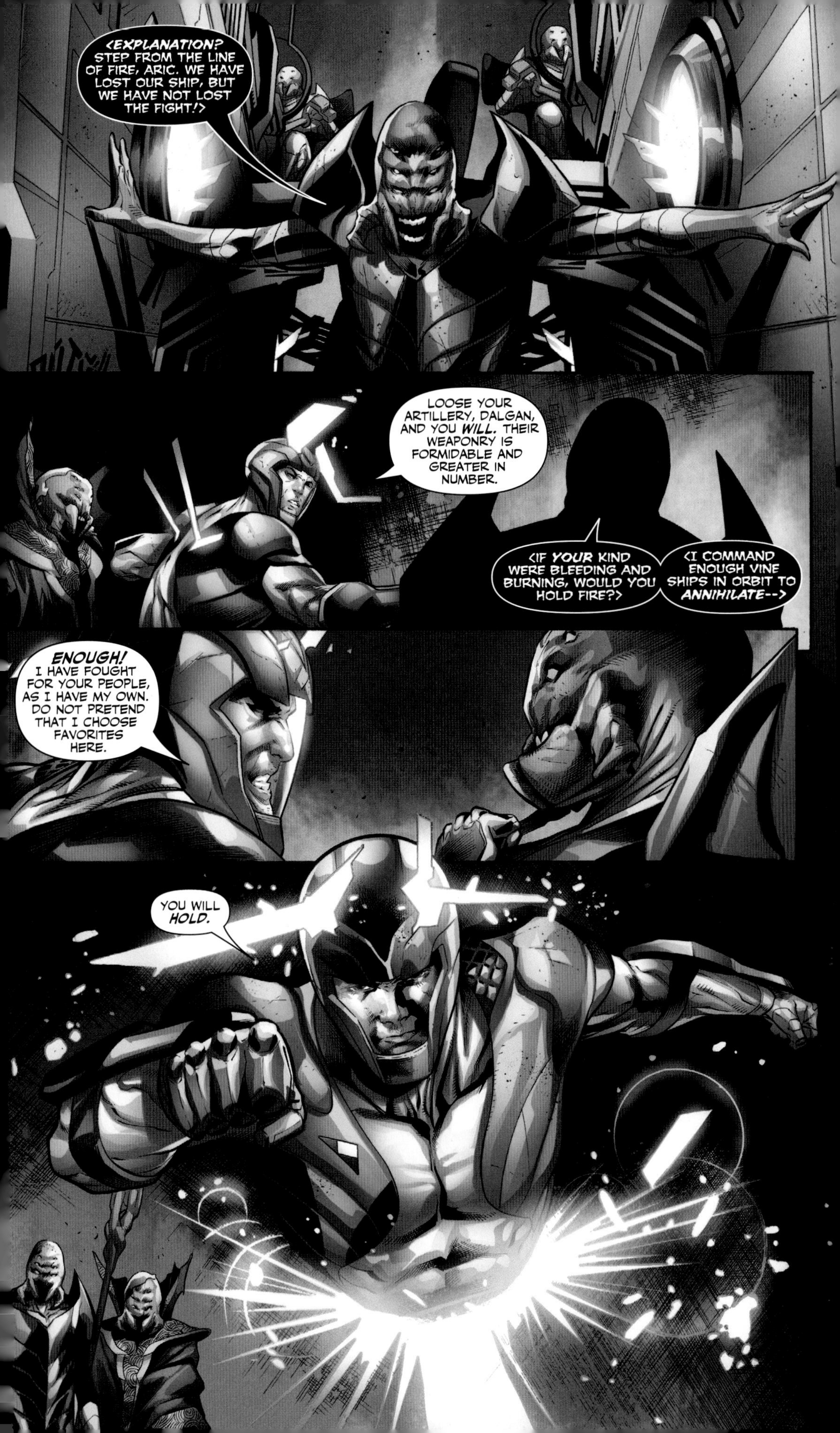
<EXPLANATION? STEP FROM THE LINE OF FIRE, ARIC. WE HAVE LOST OUR SHIP, BUT WE HAVE NOT LOST THE FIGHT!>
LOOSE YOUR ARTILLERY, DALGAN, AND YOU WILL. THEIR WEAPONRY IS FORMIDABLE AND GREATER IN NUMBER.
<IF YOUR KIND WERE BLEEDING AND BURNING, WOULD YOU HOLD FIRE?>
<I COMMAND ENOUGH VINE SHIPS IN ORBIT TO ANNIHILATE-->
ENOUGH! I HAVE FOUGHT FOR YOUR PEOPLE, AS I HAVE MY OWN. DO NOT PRETEND THAT I CHOOSE FAVORITES HERE.
YOU WILL HOLD.

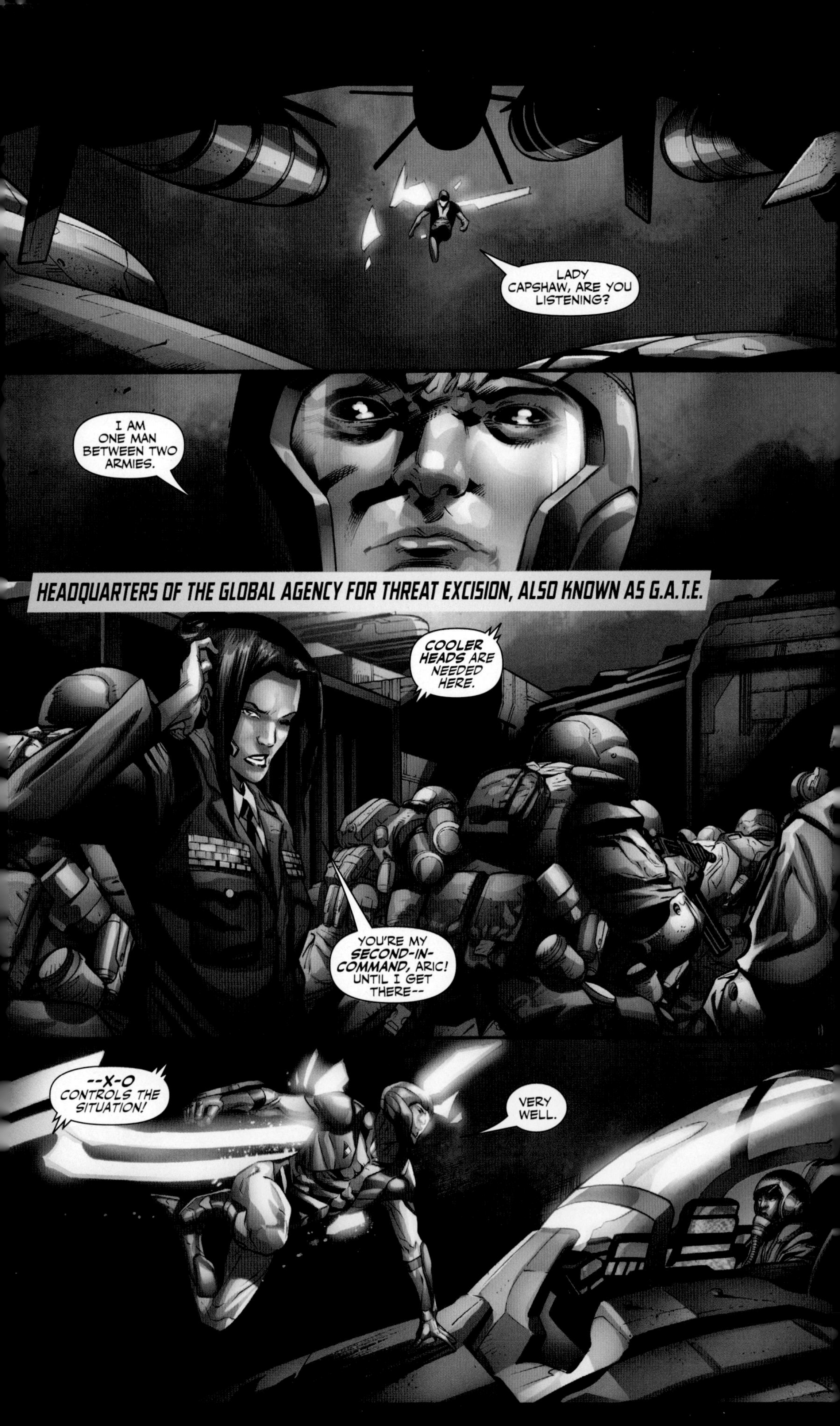
LADY CAPSHAW, ARE YOU LISTENING?
I AM ONE MAN BETWEEN TWO ARMIES.
HEADQUARTERS OF THE GLOBAL AGENCY FOR THREAT EXCISION, ALSO KNOWN AS G.A.T.E.
COOLER HEADS ARE NEEDED HERE.
YOU'RE MY SECOND-IN-COMMAND, ARIC! UNTIL I GET THERE--
--X-O CONTROLS THE SITUATION!
VERY WELL.

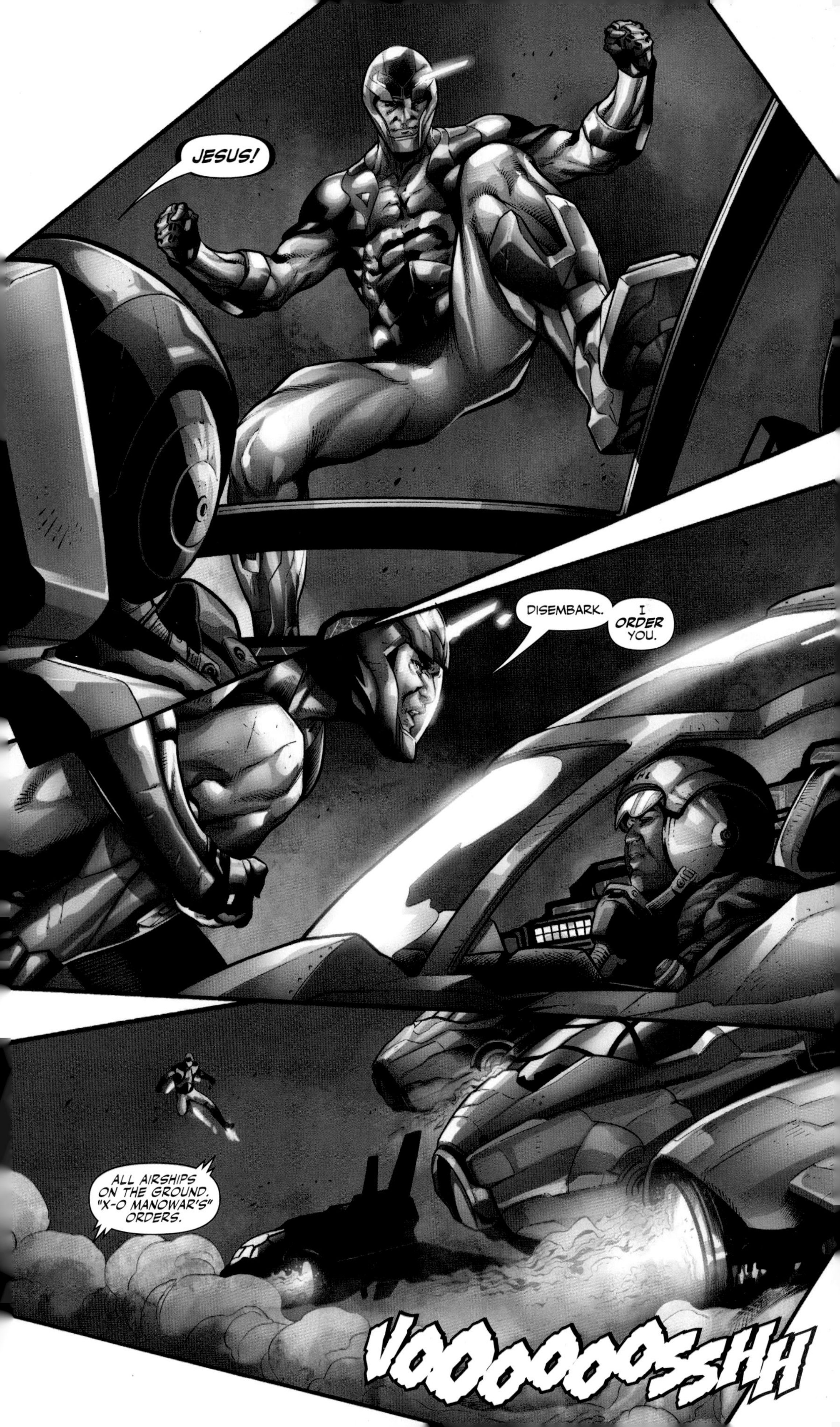
JESUS!
DISEMBARK.
I ORDER YOU.
ALL AIRSHIPS ON THE GROUND. "X-O MANOWAR'S" ORDERS.
VOOOOOOOSSHH

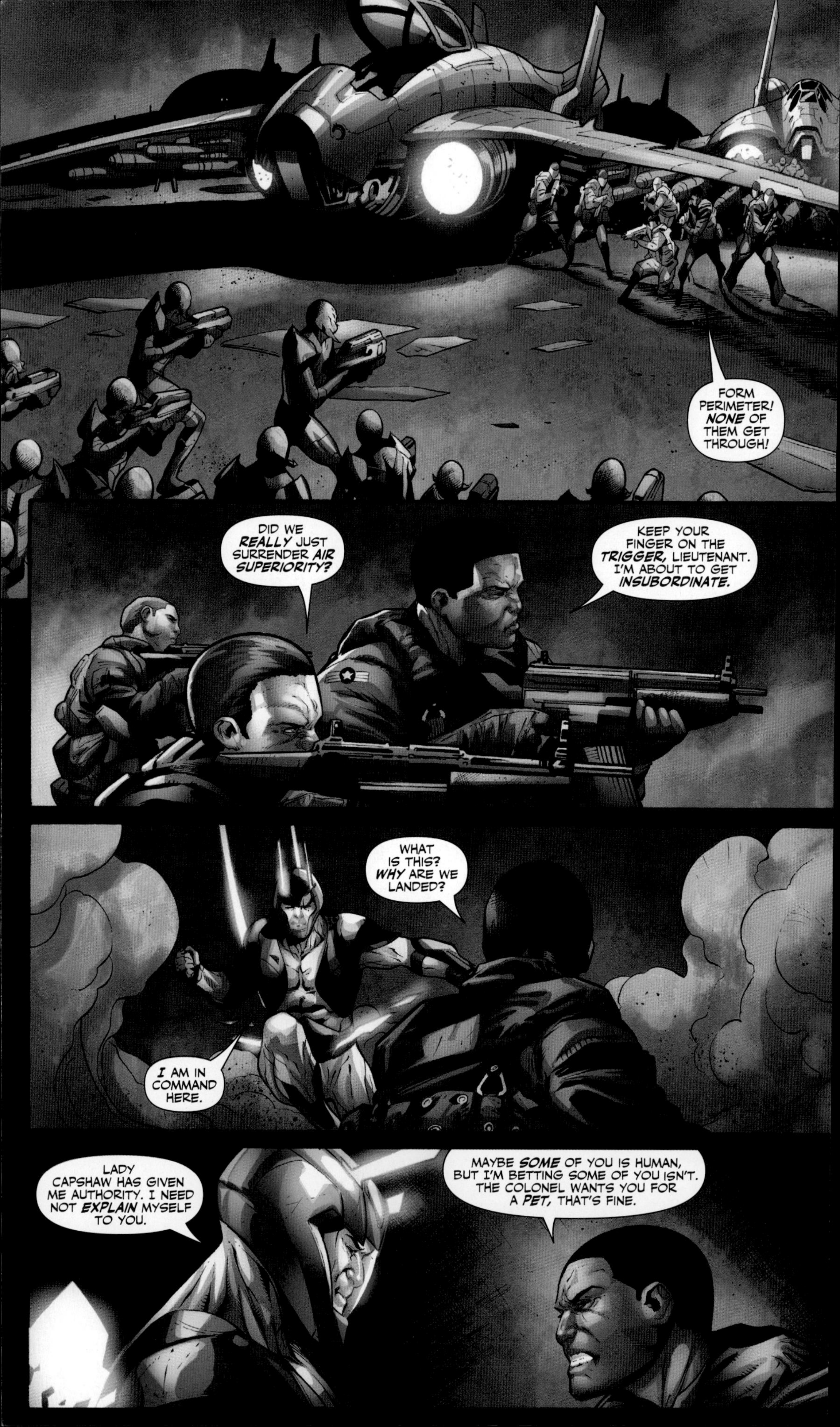
FORM PERIMETER! NONE OF THEM GET THROUGH!
DID WE REALLY JUST SURRENDER AIR SUPERIORITY?
KEEP YOUR FINGER ON THE TRIGGER, LIEUTENANT. I'M ABOUT TO GET INSUBORDINATE.
WHAT IS THIS? WHY ARE WE LANDED?
I AM IN COMMAND HERE.
LADY CAPSHAW HAS GIVEN ME AUTHORITY. I NEED NOT EXPLAIN MYSELF TO YOU.
MAYBE SOME OF YOU IS HUMAN, BUT I'M BETTING SOME OF YOU ISN'T. THE COLONEL WANTS YOU FOR A PET, THAT'S FINE.

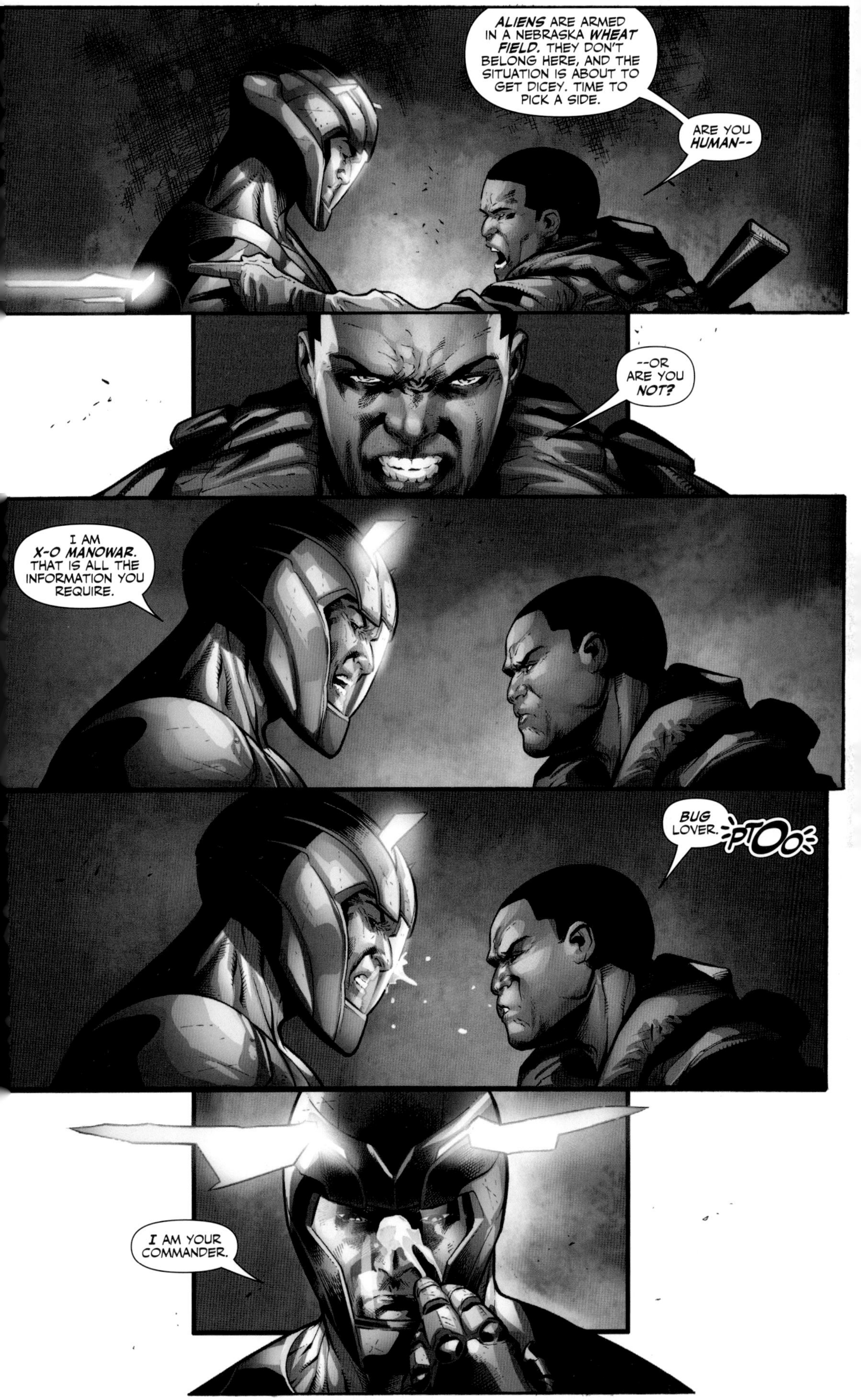
ALIENS ARE ARMED IN A NEBRASKA WHEAT FIELD. THEY DON'T BELONG HERE, AND THE SITUATION IS ABOUT TO GET DICEY. TIME TO PICK A SIDE.
ARE YOU HUMAN--
--OR ARE YOU NOT?
I AM X-O MANOWAR. THAT IS ALL THE INFORMATION YOU REQUIRE.
BUG LOVER.
PTOO
I AM YOUR COMMANDER.

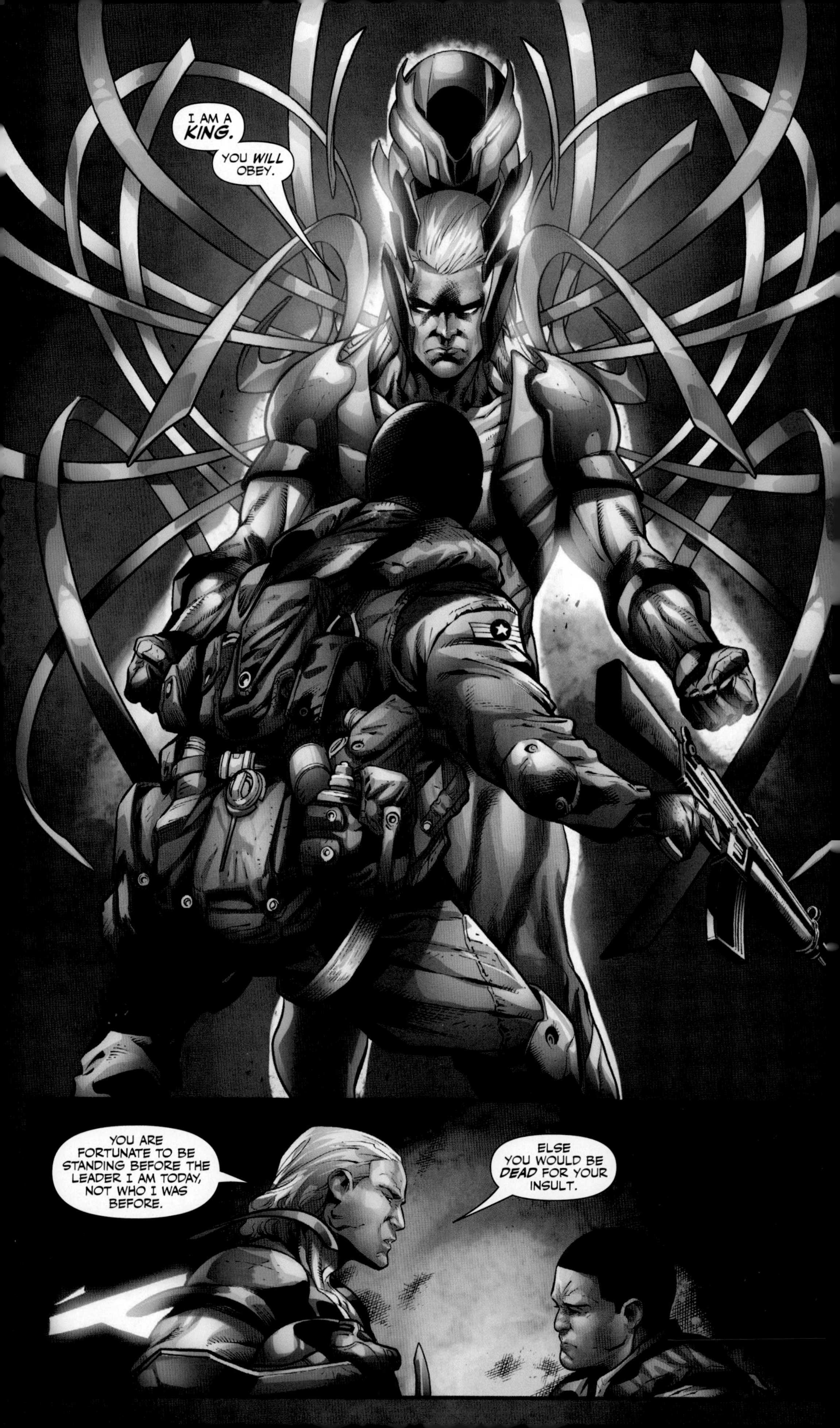
I AM A KING.
YOU WILL OBEY.
YOU ARE FORTUNATE TO BE STANDING BEFORE THE LEADER I AM TODAY, NOT WHO I WAS BEFORE.
ELSE YOU WOULD BE DEAD FOR YOUR INSULT.

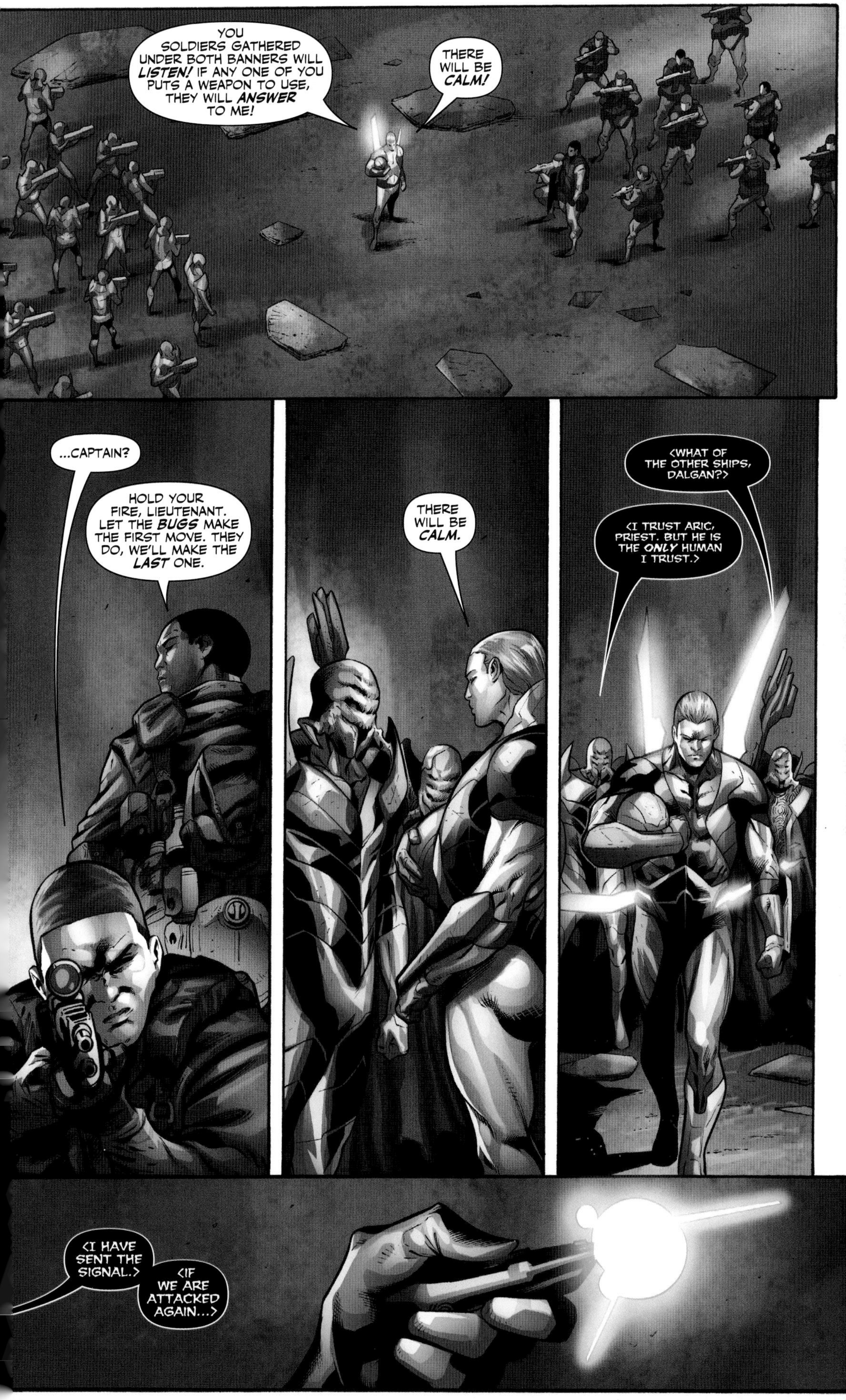
YOU SOLDIERS GATHERED UNDER BOTH BANNERS WILL LISTEN! IF ANY ONE OF YOU PUTS A WEAPON TO USE, THEY WILL ANSWER TO ME!
THERE WILL BE CALM!
...CAPTAIN?
HOLD YOUR FIRE, LIEUTENANT. LET THE BUGS MAKE THE FIRST MOVE. THEY DO, WE'LL MAKE THE LAST ONE.
THERE WILL BE CALM.
<WHAT OF THE OTHER SHIPS, DALGAN?>
<I TRUST ARIC, PRIEST. BUT HE IS THE ONLY HUMAN I TRUST.>
<I HAVE SENT THE SIGNAL.>
<IF WE ARE ATTACKED AGAIN...>

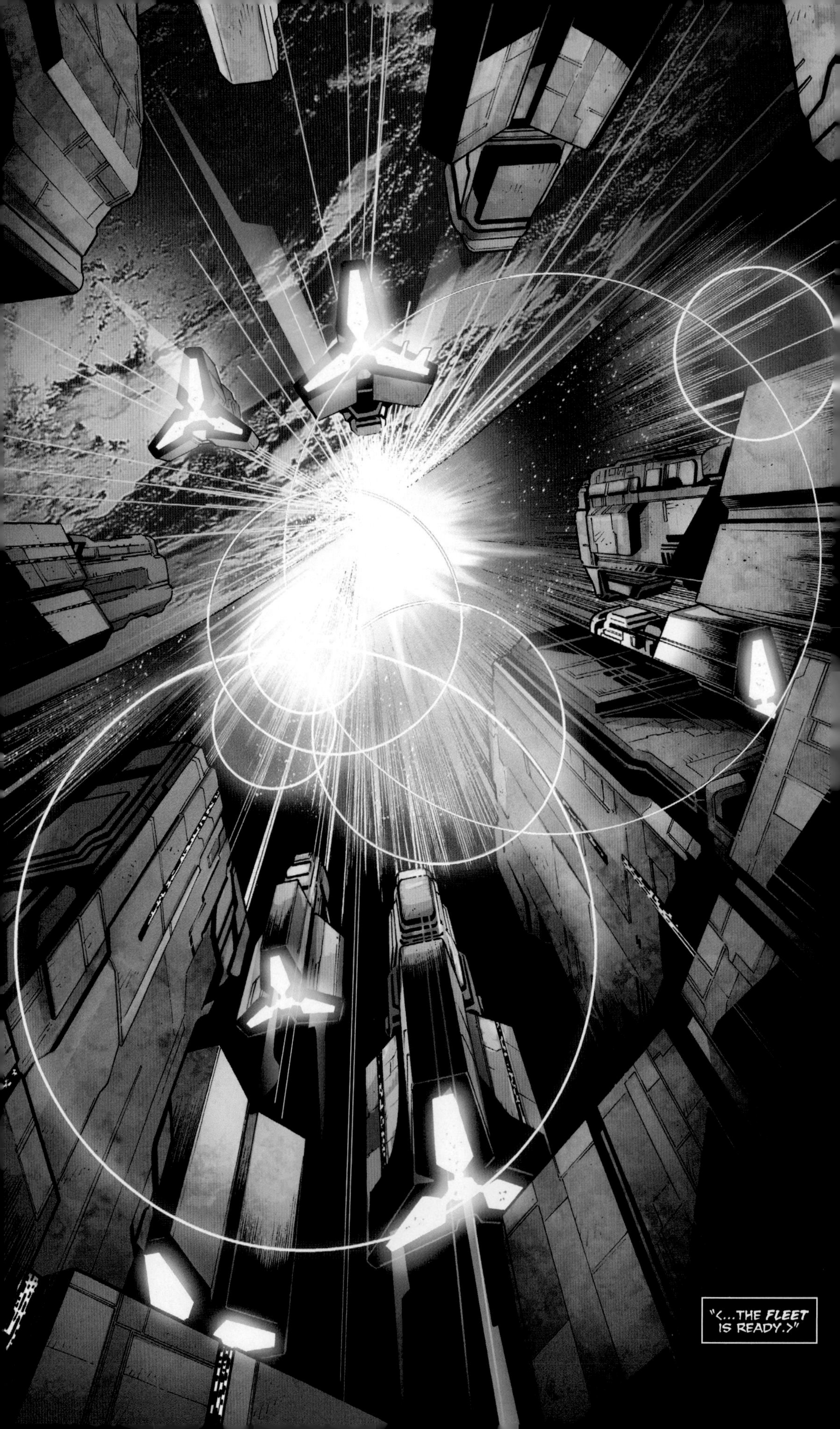
"<...THE *FLEET* IS READY.>"

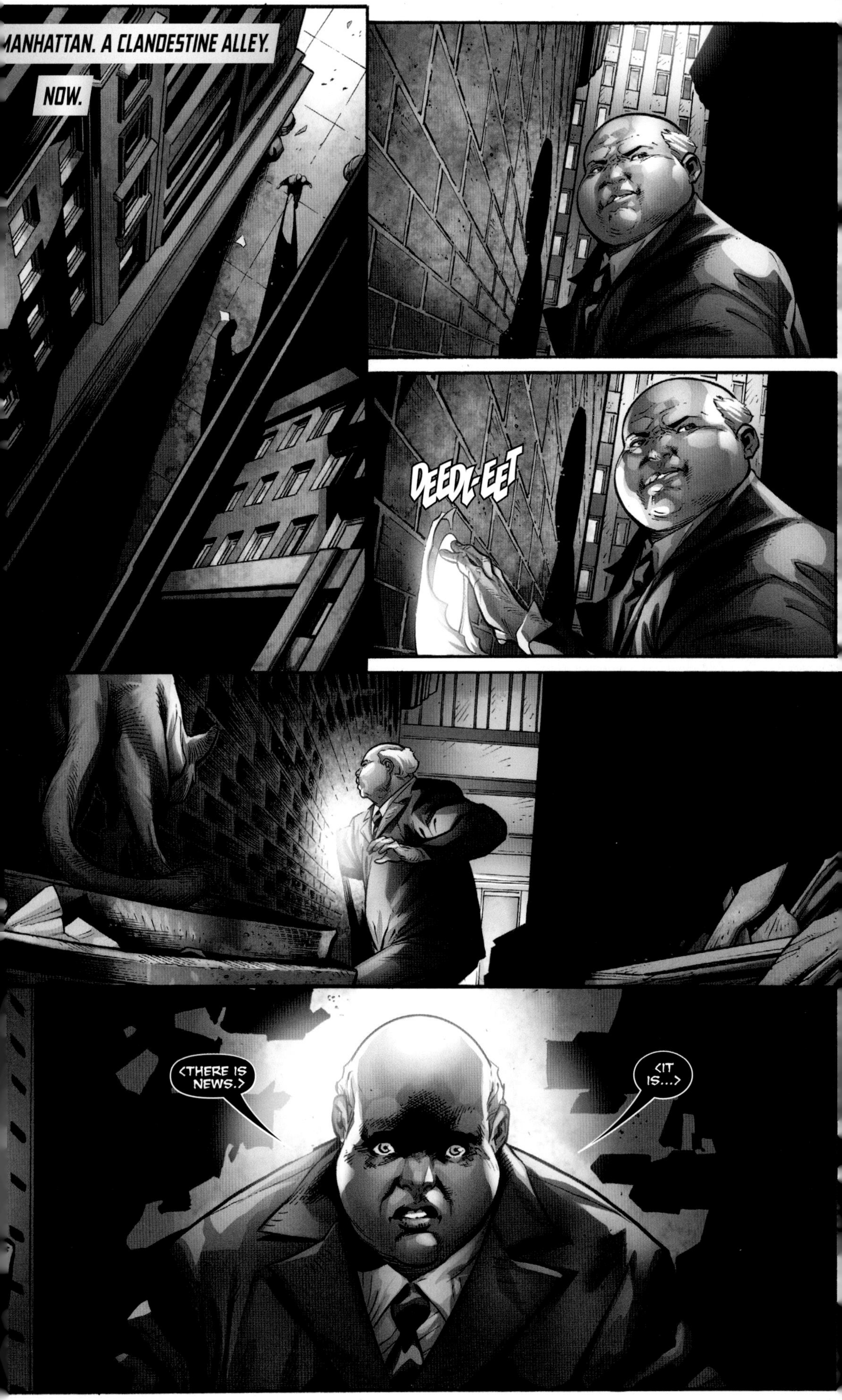
MANHATTAN. A CLANDESTINE ALLEY.
NOW.
DEEDL-EET
<THERE IS NEWS.>
<IT IS...>

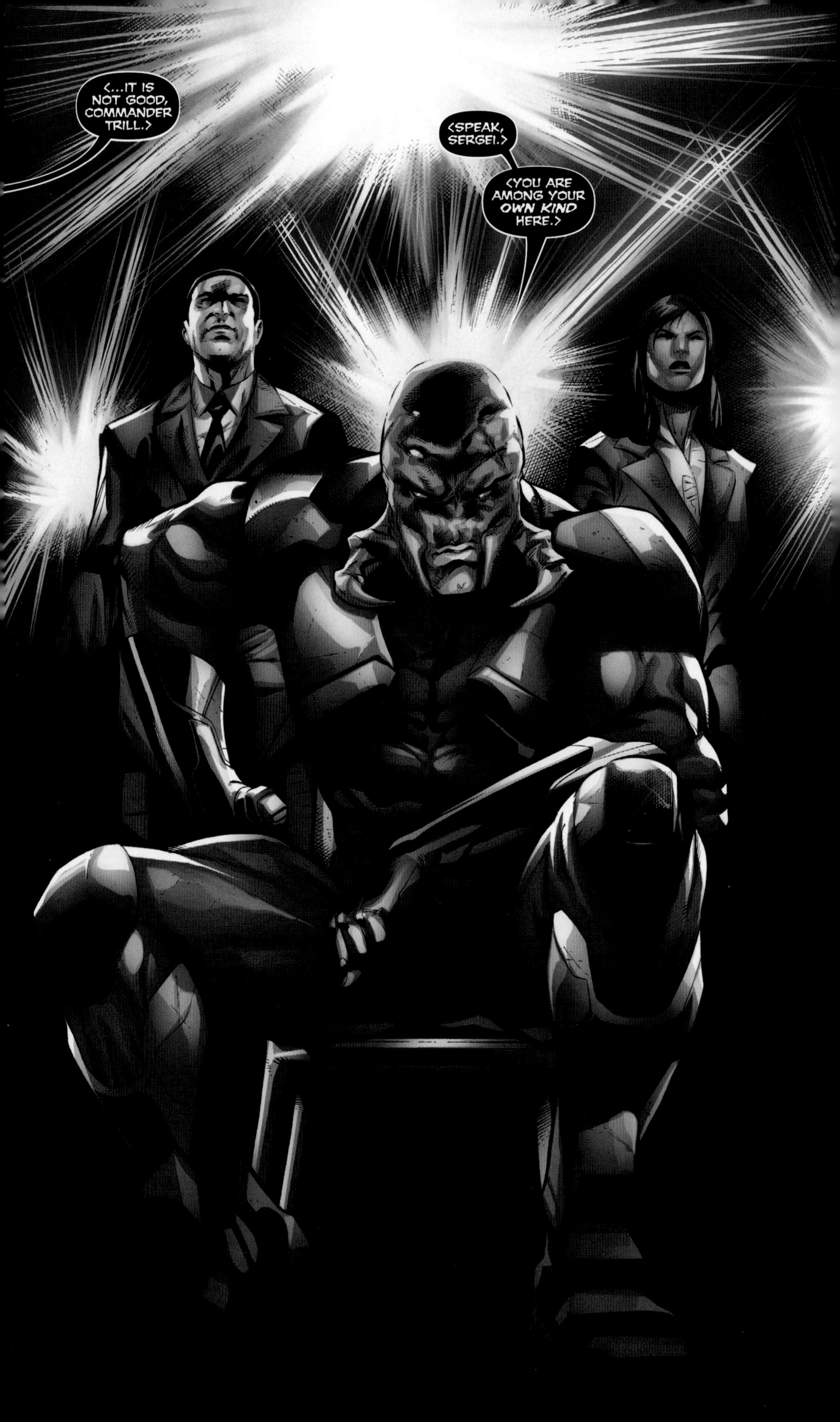
<...IT IS NOT GOOD, COMMANDER TRILL.>
<SPEAK, SERGEI.>
<YOU ARE AMONG YOUR OWN KIND HERE.>

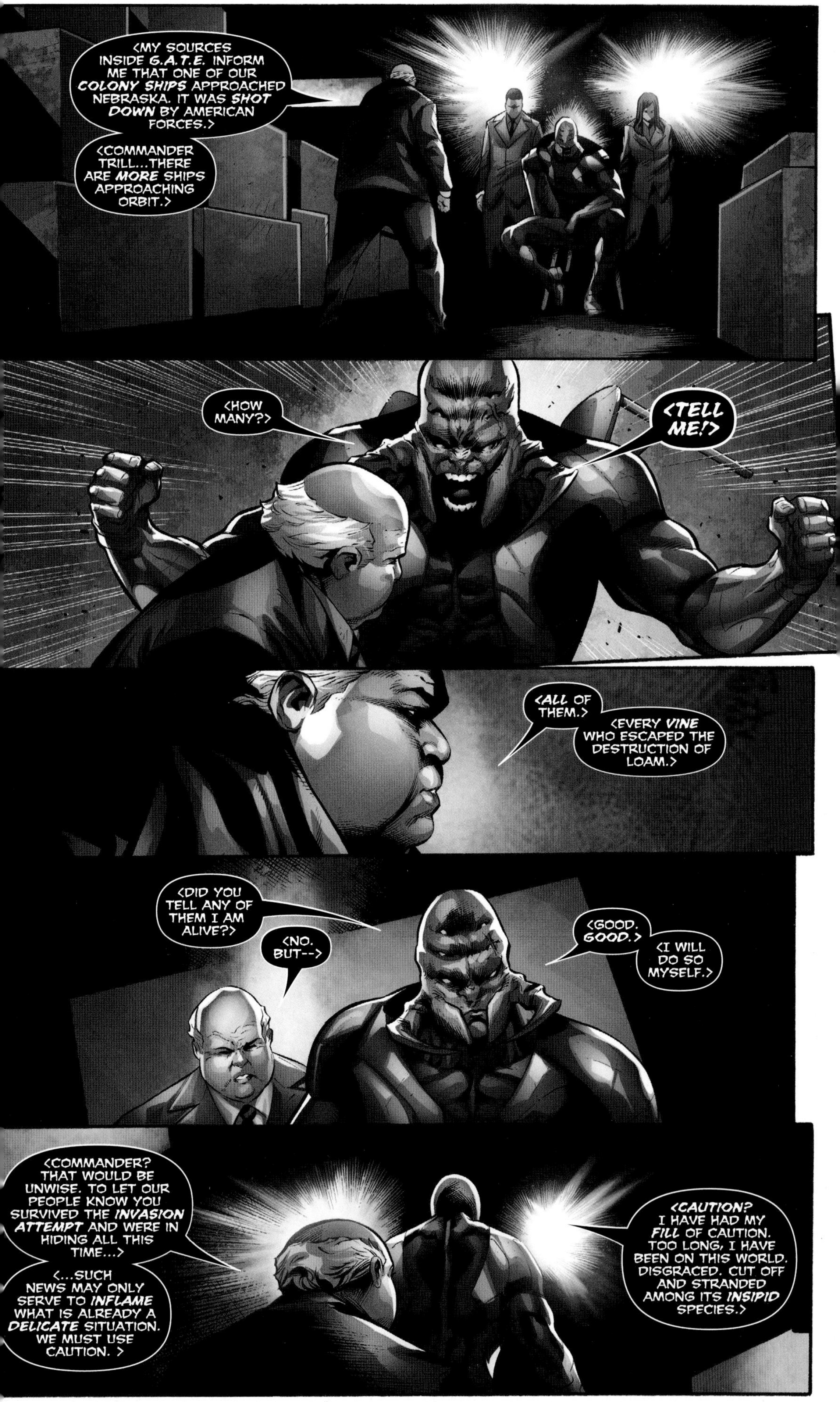
<MY SOURCES INSIDE G.A.T.E. INFORM ME THAT ONE OF OUR COLONY SHIPS APPROACHED NEBRASKA. IT WAS SHOT DOWN BY AMERICAN FORCES.>
<COMMANDER TRILL...THERE ARE MORE SHIPS APPROACHING ORBIT.>
<HOW MANY?>
<TELL ME!>
<ALL OF THEM.>
<EVERY VINE WHO ESCAPED THE DESTRUCTION OF LOAM.>
<DID YOU TELL ANY OF THEM I AM ALIVE?>
<NO. BUT-->
<GOOD. GOOD.>
<I WILL DO SO MYSELF.>
<COMMANDER? THAT WOULD BE UNWISE. TO LET OUR PEOPLE KNOW YOU SURVIVED THE INVASION ATTEMPT AND WERE IN HIDING ALL THIS TIME...>
<...SUCH NEWS MAY ONLY SERVE TO INFLAME WHAT IS ALREADY A DELICATE SITUATION. WE MUST USE CAUTION. >
<CAUTION? I HAVE HAD MY FILL OF CAUTION. TOO LONG, I HAVE BEEN ON THIS WORLD. DISGRACED. CUT OFF AND STRANDED AMONG ITS INSIPID SPECIES.>

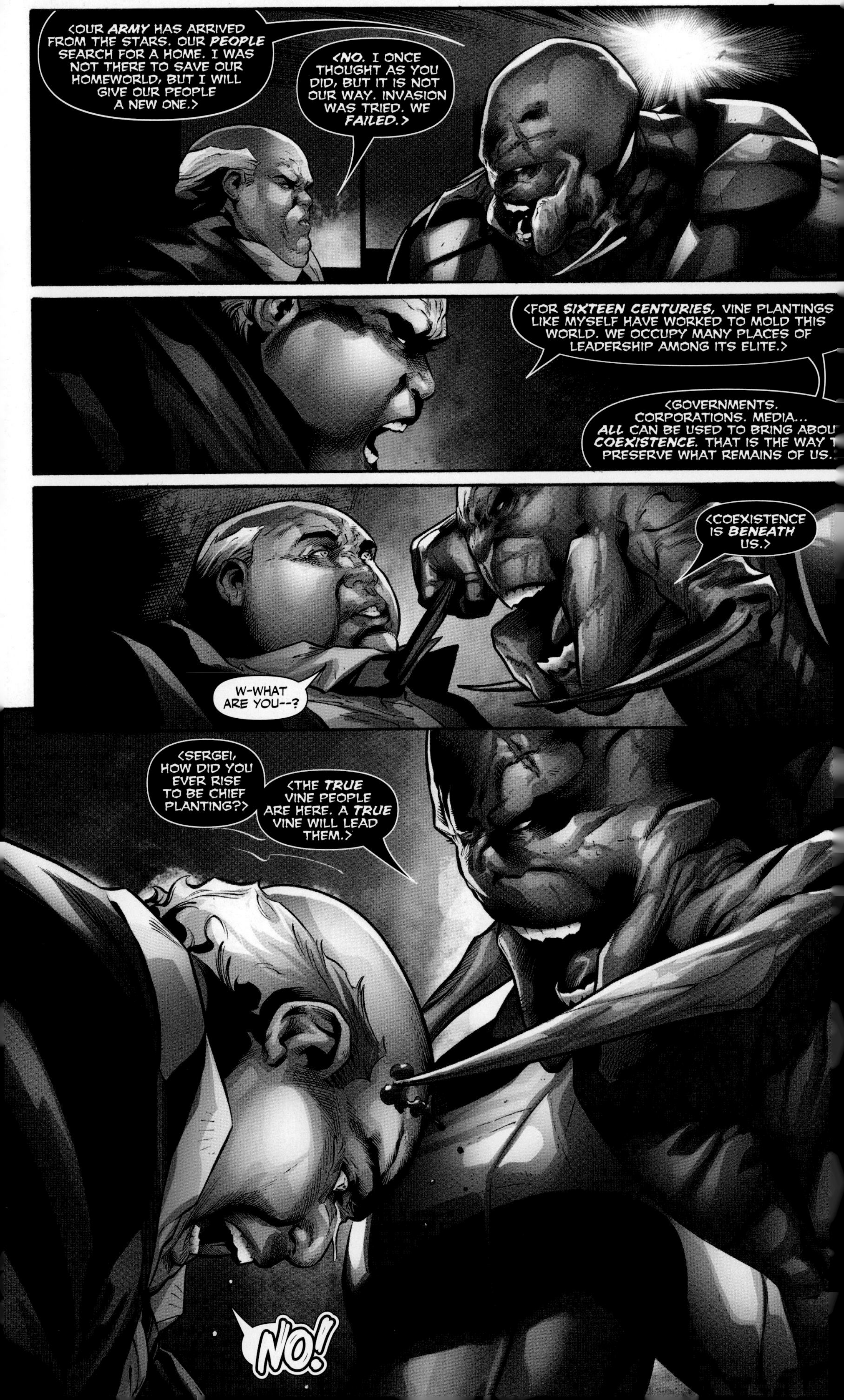

<OUR ARMY HAS ARRIVED FROM THE STARS. OUR PEOPLE SEARCH FOR A HOME. I WAS NOT THERE TO SAVE OUR HOMEWORLD, BUT I WILL GIVE OUR PEOPLE A NEW ONE.>
<NO. I ONCE THOUGHT AS YOU DID, BUT IT IS NOT OUR WAY. INVASION WAS TRIED. WE FAILED.>
<FOR SIXTEEN CENTURIES, VINE PLANTINGS LIKE MYSELF HAVE WORKED TO MOLD THIS WORLD. WE OCCUPY MANY PLACES OF LEADERSHIP AMONG ITS ELITE.>
<GOVERNMENTS. CORPORATIONS. MEDIA... ALL CAN BE USED TO BRING ABOU COEXISTENCE. THAT IS THE WAY T PRESERVE WHAT REMAINS OF US.
<COEXISTENCE IS BENEATH US.>
W-WHAT ARE YOU--?
<SERGEI, HOW DID YOU EVER RISE TO BE CHIEF PLANTING?>
<THE TRUE VINE PEOPLE ARE HERE. A TRUE VINE WILL LEAD THEM.>
NO!

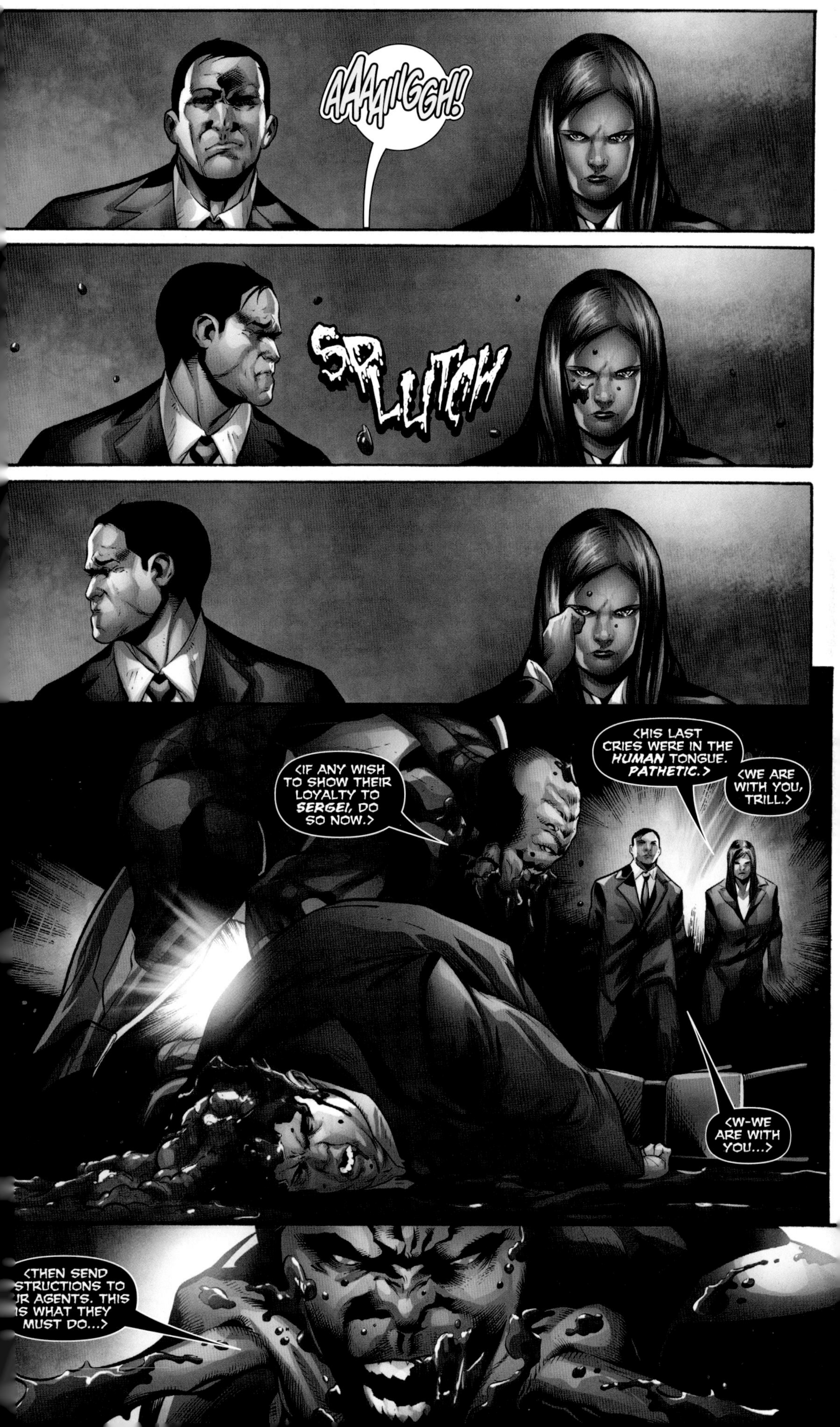
AAAAIIIGGH!
SPLUTCH
<IF ANY WISH TO SHOW THEIR LOYALTY TO SERGEI, DO SO NOW.>
<HIS LAST CRIES WERE IN THE HUMAN TONGUE. PATHETIC.>
<WE ARE WITH YOU, TRILL.>
<W-WE ARE WITH YOU...>
<THEN SEND STRUCTIONS TO UR AGENTS. THIS IS WHAT THEY MUST DO...>

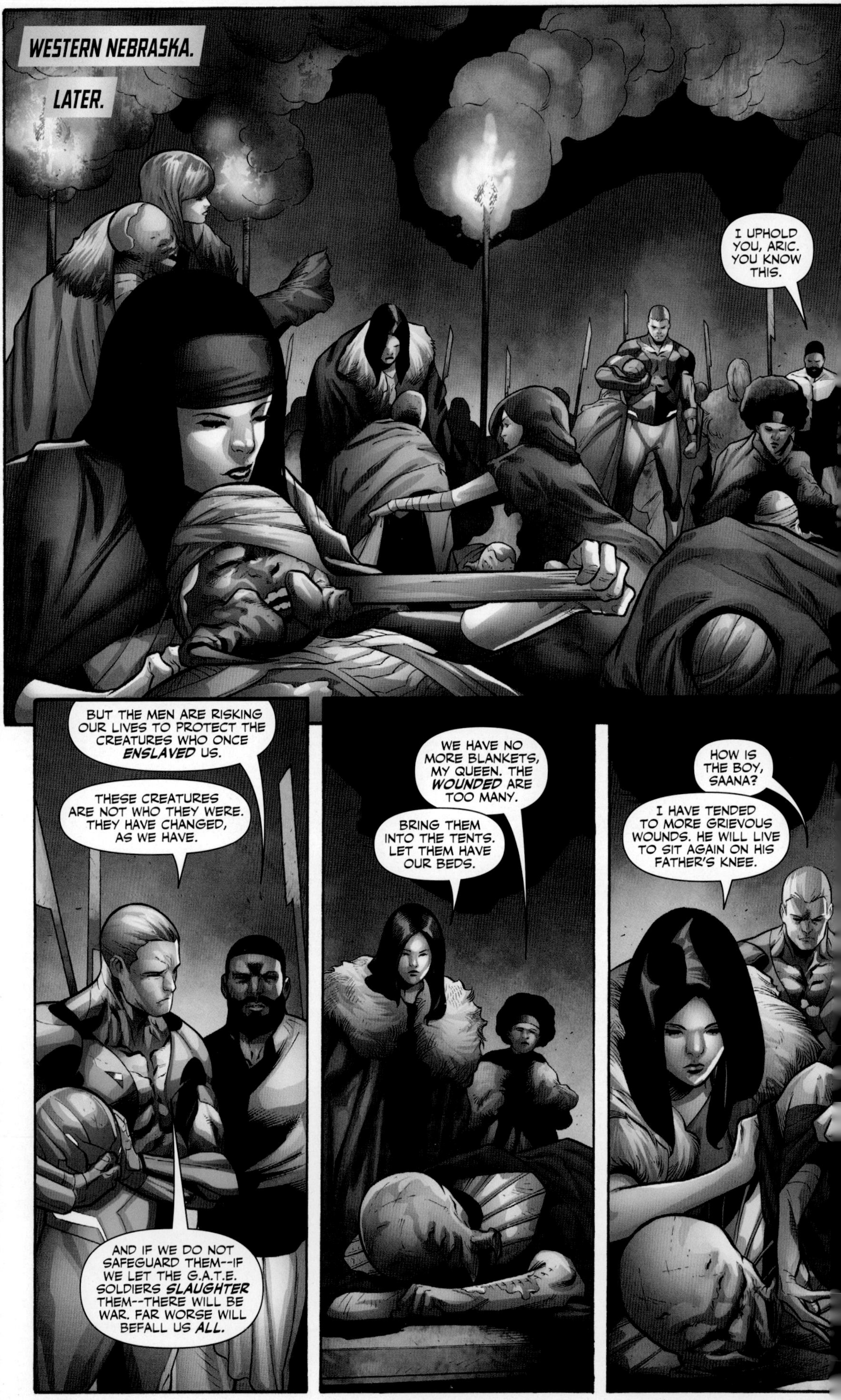
WESTERN NEBRASKA.
LATER.
I UPHOLD YOU, ARIC. YOU KNOW THIS.
BUT THE MEN ARE RISKING OUR LIVES TO PROTECT THE CREATURES WHO ONCE ENSLAVED US.
THESE CREATURES ARE NOT WHO THEY WERE. THEY HAVE CHANGED, AS WE HAVE.
AND IF WE DO NOT SAFEGUARD THEM--IF WE LET THE G.A.T.E. SOLDIERS SLAUGHTER THEM--THERE WILL BE WAR. FAR WORSE WILL BEFALL US ALL.
WE HAVE NO MORE BLANKETS, MY QUEEN. THE WOUNDED ARE TOO MANY.
BRING THEM INTO THE TENTS. LET THEM HAVE OUR BEDS.
HOW IS THE BOY, SAANA?
I HAVE TENDED TO MORE GRIEVOUS WOUNDS. HE WILL LIVE TO SIT AGAIN ON HIS FATHER'S KNEE.

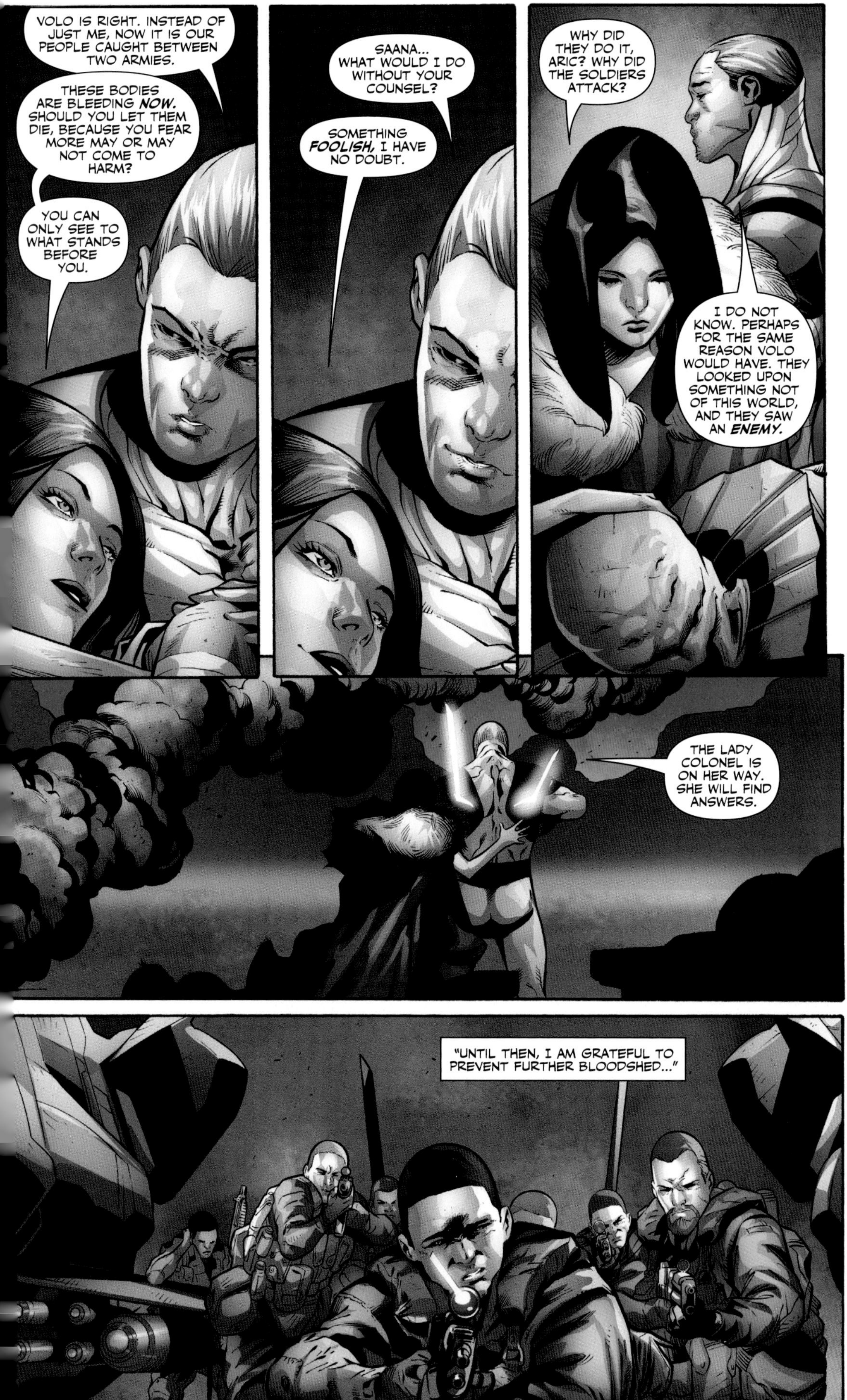

VOLO IS RIGHT. INSTEAD OF JUST ME, NOW IT IS OUR PEOPLE CAUGHT BETWEEN TWO ARMIES.
THESE BODIES ARE BLEEDING *NOW.* SHOULD YOU LET THEM DIE, BECAUSE YOU FEAR MORE MAY OR MAY NOT COME TO HARM?
YOU CAN ONLY SEE TO WHAT STANDS BEFORE YOU.
SAANA... WHAT WOULD I DO WITHOUT YOUR COUNSEL?
SOMETHING *FOOLISH,* I HAVE NO DOUBT.
WHY DID THEY DO IT, ARIC? WHY DID THE SOLDIERS ATTACK?
I DO NOT KNOW. PERHAPS FOR THE SAME REASON VOLO WOULD HAVE. THEY LOOKED UPON SOMETHING NOT OF THIS WORLD, AND THEY SAW AN *ENEMY.*
THE LADY COLONEL IS ON HER WAY. SHE WILL FIND ANSWERS.
"UNTIL THEN, I AM GRATEFUL TO PREVENT FURTHER BLOODSHED..."

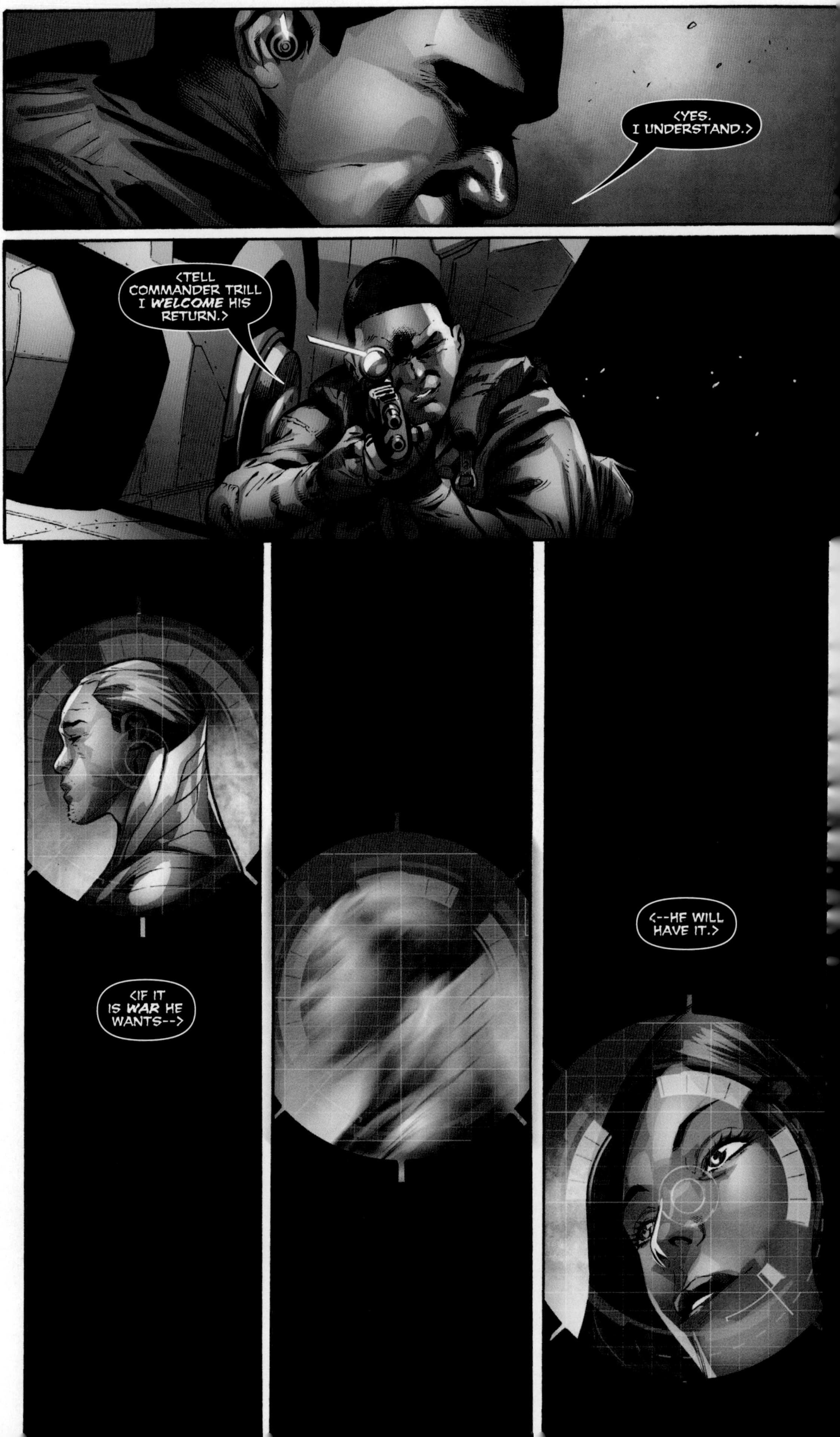

<YES. I UNDERSTAND.>
<TELL COMMANDER TRILL I WELCOME HIS RETURN.>
<IF IT IS WAR HE WANTS-->
<--HE WILL HAVE IT.>

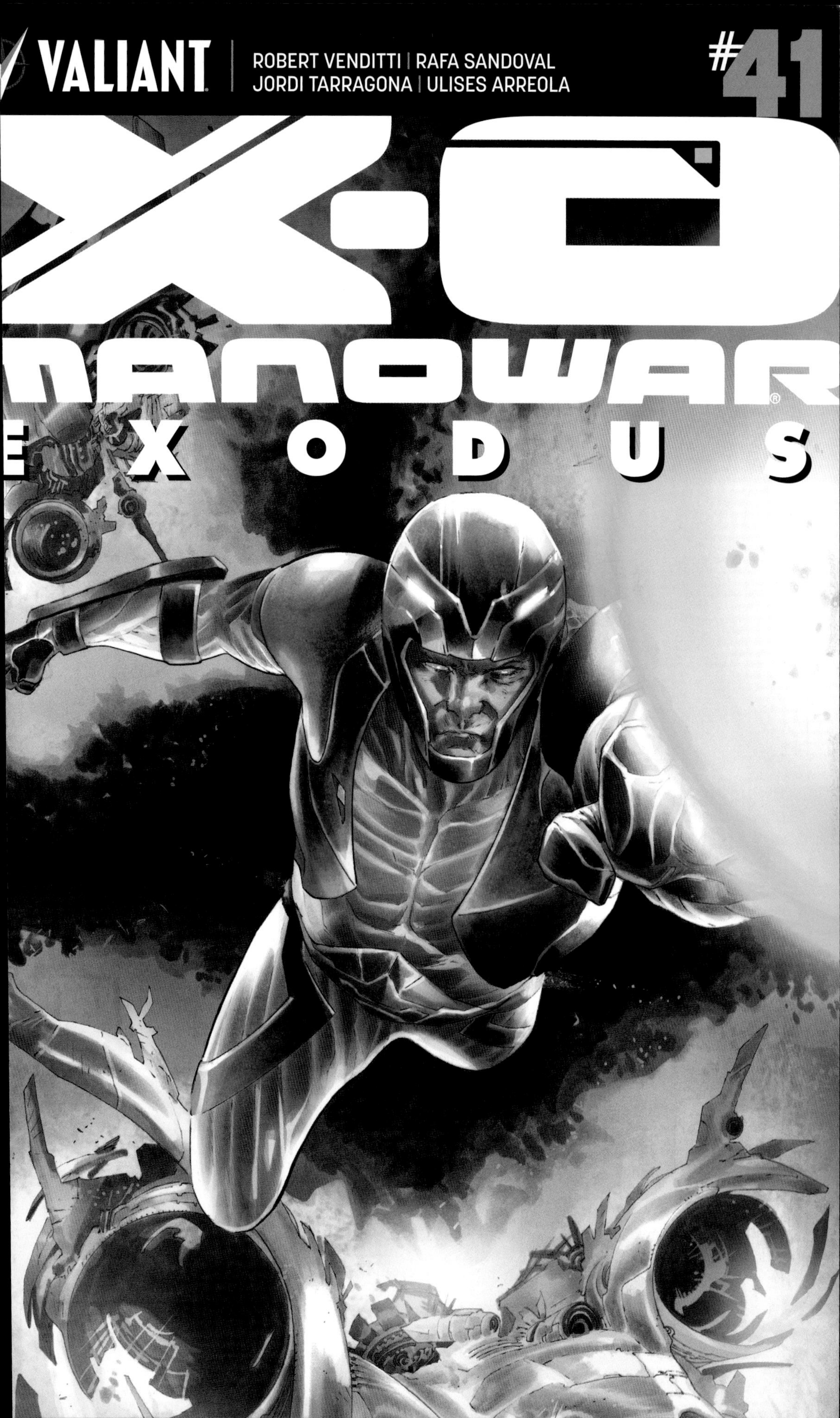
VALIANT
ROBERT VENDITTI | RAFA SANDOVAL
JORDI TARRAGONA | ULISES ARREOLA
#41
X-O MANOWAR
EXODUS

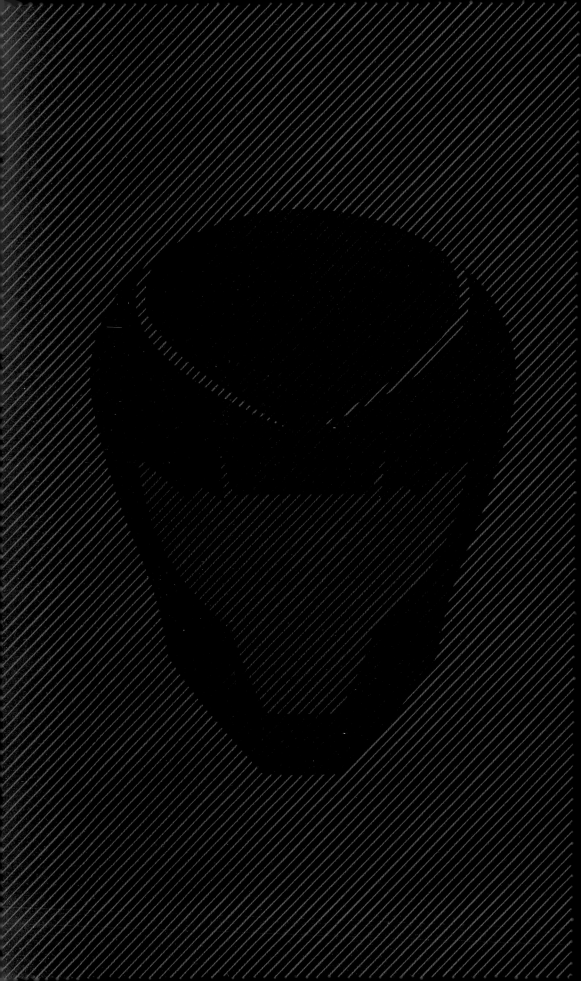

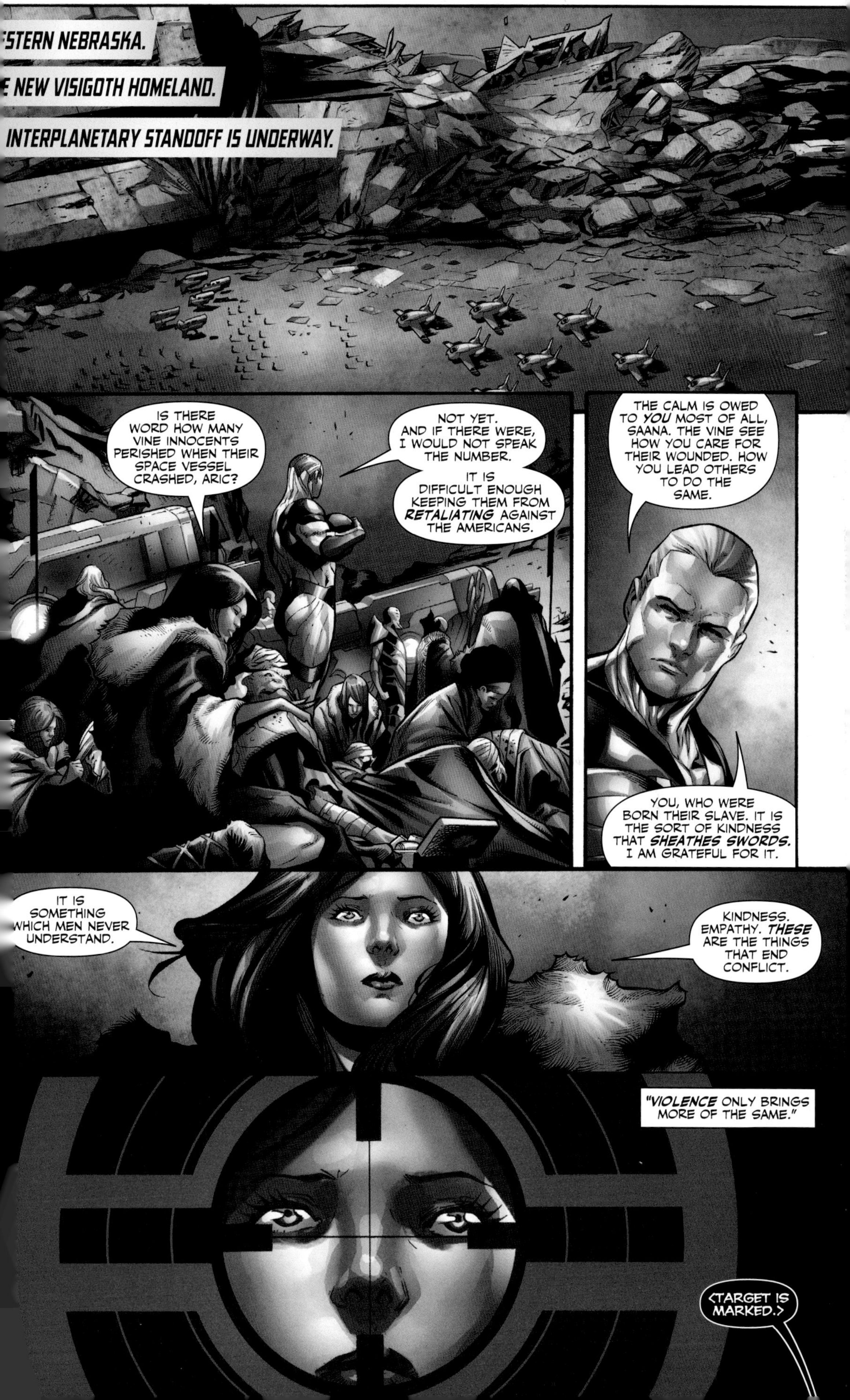

...STERN NEBRASKA.
...E NEW VISIGOTH HOMELAND.
...INTERPLANETARY STANDOFF IS UNDERWAY.
IS THERE WORD HOW MANY VINE INNOCENTS PERISHED WHEN THEIR SPACE VESSEL CRASHED, ARIC?
NOT YET. AND IF THERE WERE, I WOULD NOT SPEAK THE NUMBER.
IT IS DIFFICULT ENOUGH KEEPING THEM FROM RETALIATING AGAINST THE AMERICANS.
THE CALM IS OWED TO YOU MOST OF ALL, SAANA. THE VINE SEE HOW YOU CARE FOR THEIR WOUNDED. HOW YOU LEAD OTHERS TO DO THE SAME.
YOU, WHO WERE BORN THEIR SLAVE. IT IS THE SORT OF KINDNESS THAT SHEATHES SWORDS. I AM GRATEFUL FOR IT.
IT IS SOMETHING WHICH MEN NEVER UNDERSTAND.
KINDNESS. EMPATHY. THESE ARE THE THINGS THAT END CONFLICT.
"VIOLENCE ONLY BRINGS MORE OF THE SAME."
<TARGET IS MARKED.>

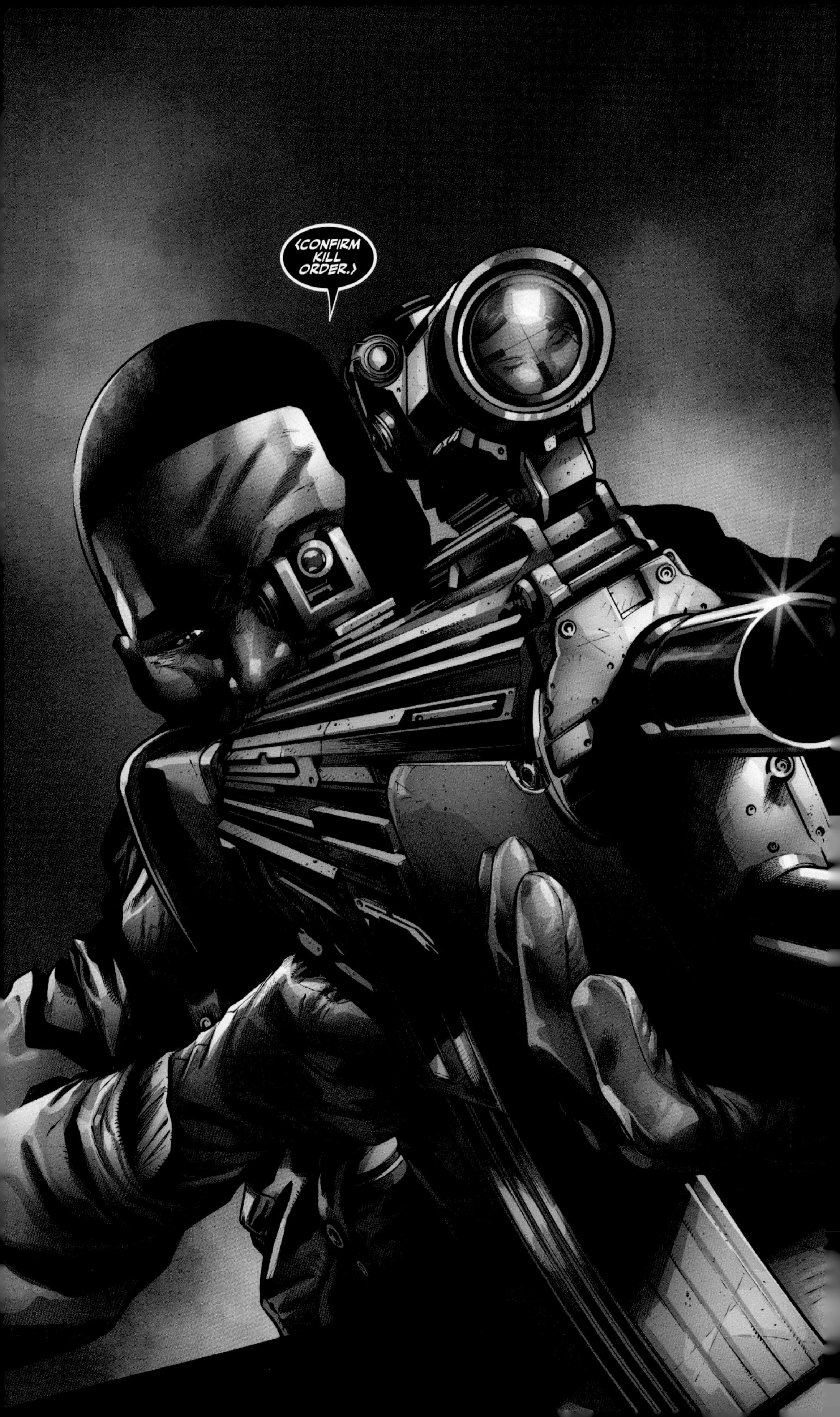
‹CONFIRM KILL ORDER.›

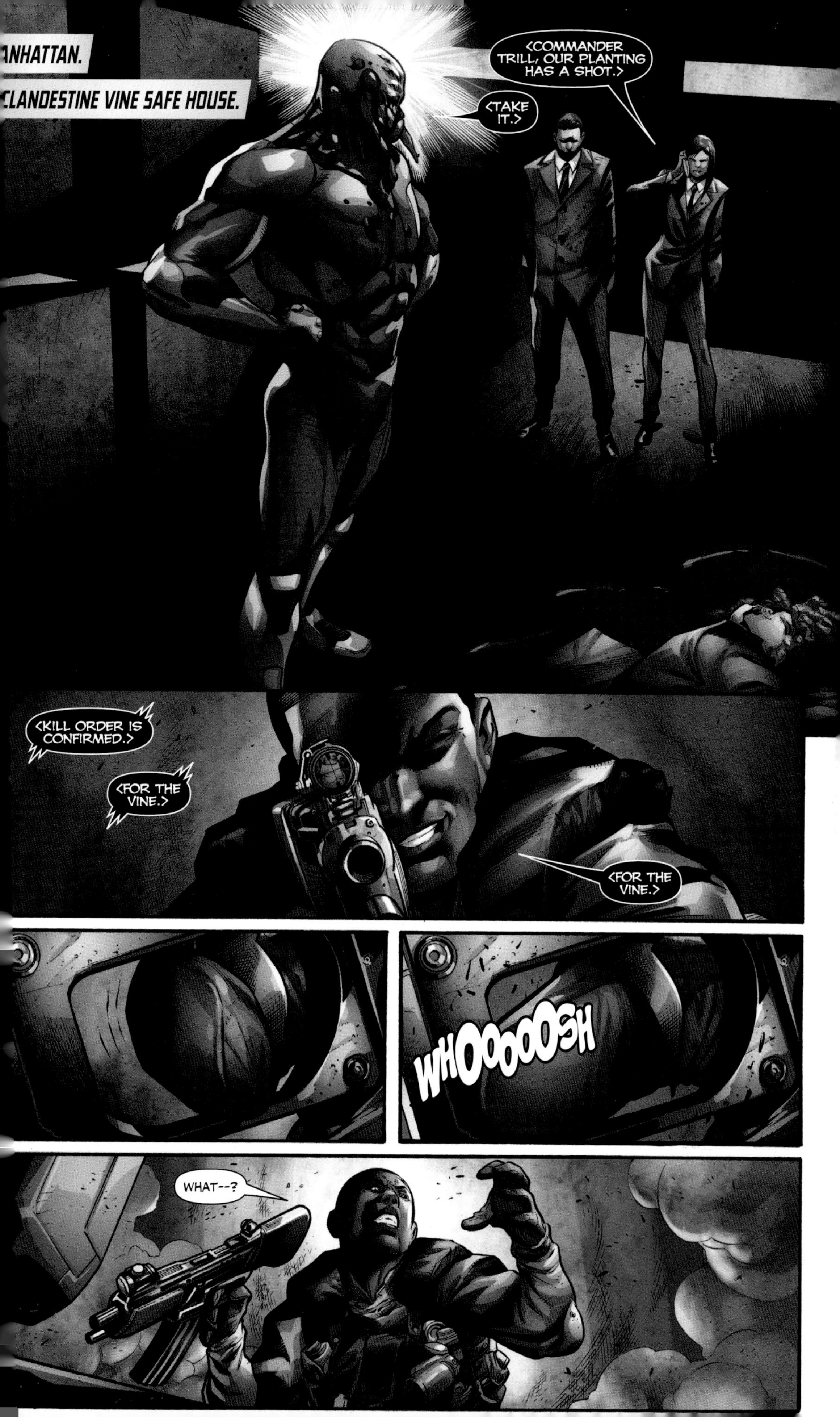
ANHATTAN.
CLANDESTINE VINE SAFE HOUSE.
<COMMANDER TRILL, OUR PLANTING HAS A SHOT.>
<TAKE IT.>
<KILL ORDER IS CONFIRMED.>
<FOR THE VINE.>
<FOR THE VINE.>
WHOOOOOOSH
WHAT--?

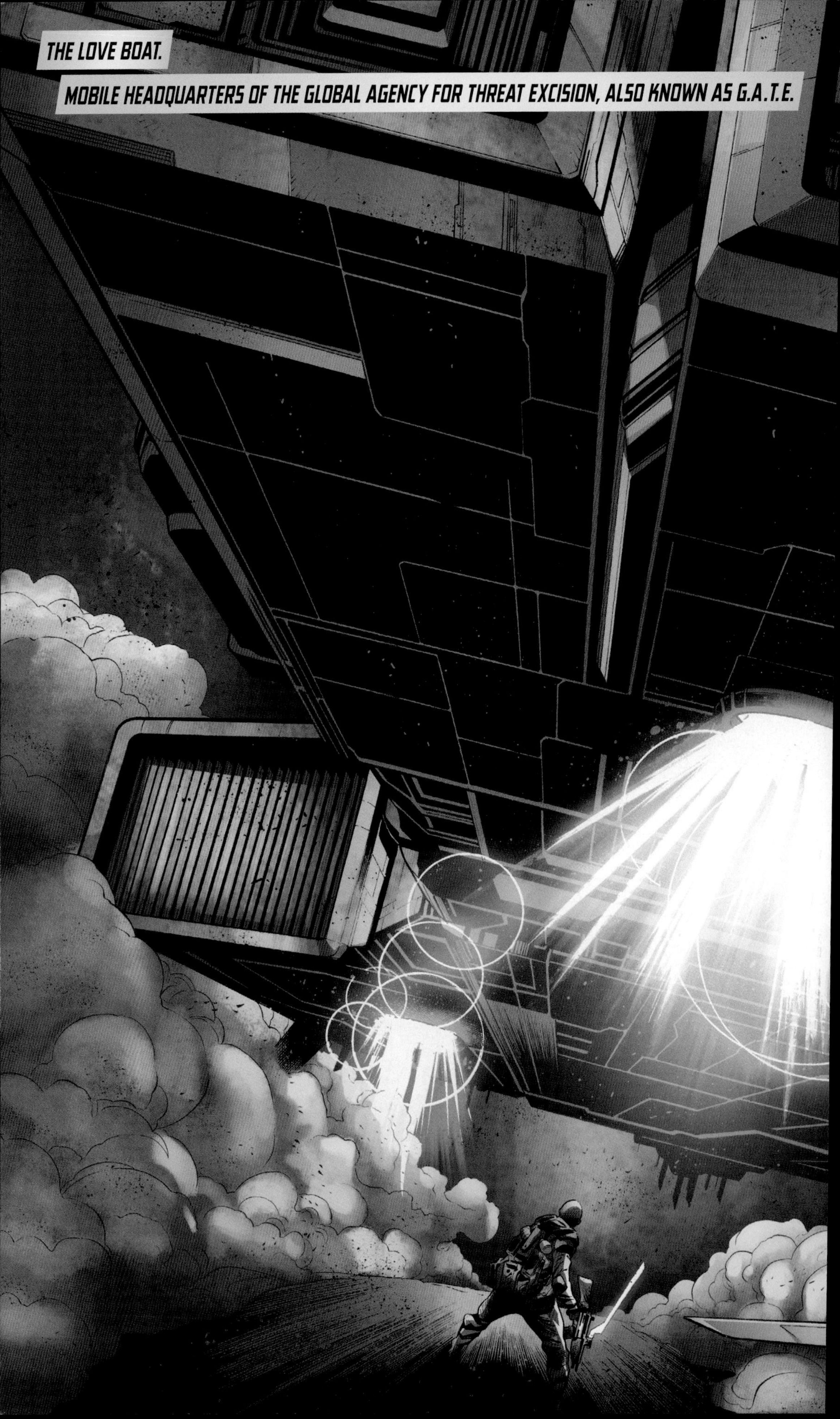
THE LOVE BOAT.
MOBILE HEADQUARTERS OF THE GLOBAL AGENCY FOR THREAT EXCISION, ALSO KNOWN AS G.A.T.E.

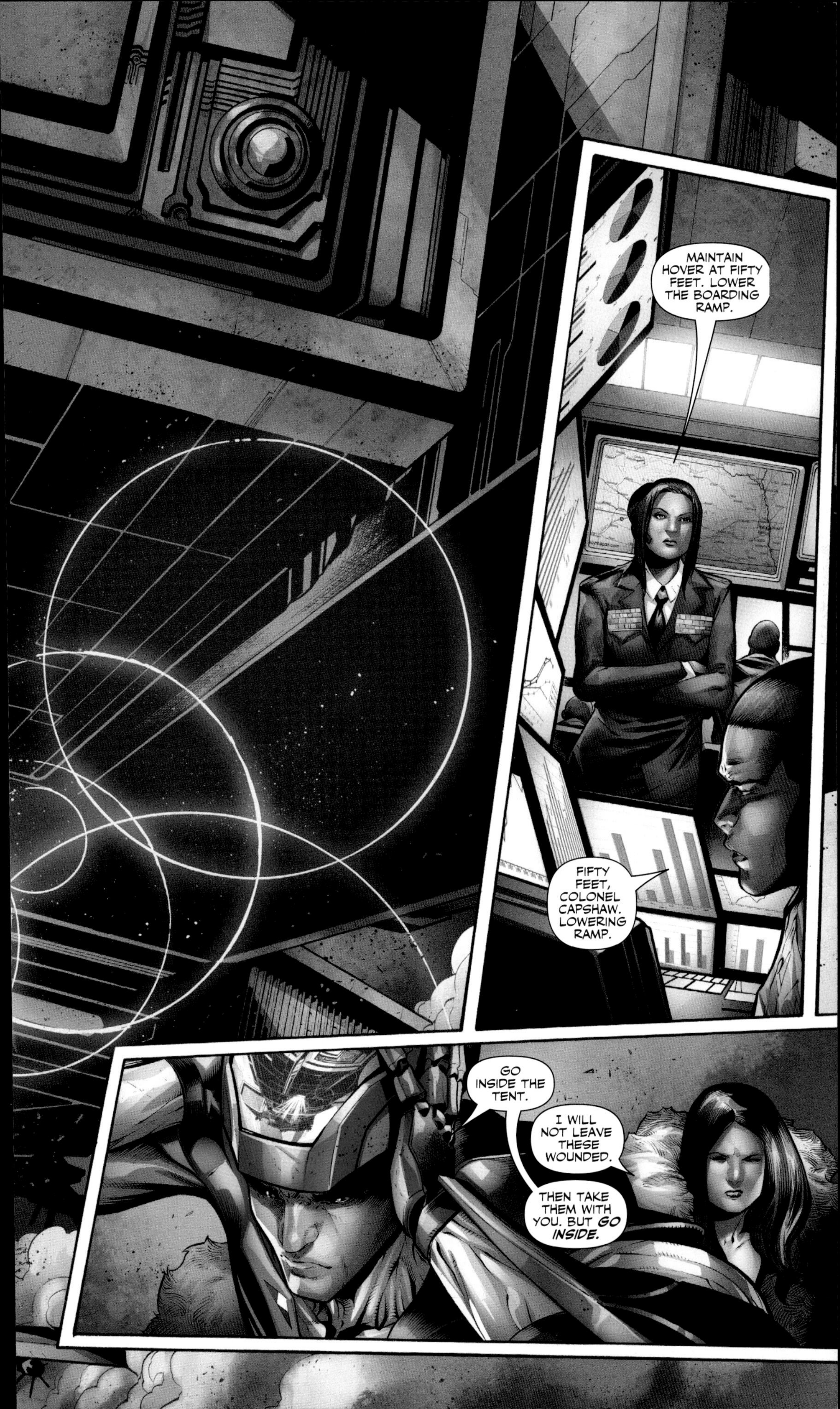
MAINTAIN HOVER AT FIFTY FEET. LOWER THE BOARDING RAMP.
FIFTY FEET, COLONEL CAPSHAW. LOWERING RAMP.
GO INSIDE THE TENT.
I WILL NOT LEAVE THESE WOUNDED.
THEN TAKE THEM WITH YOU. BUT *GO INSIDE.*

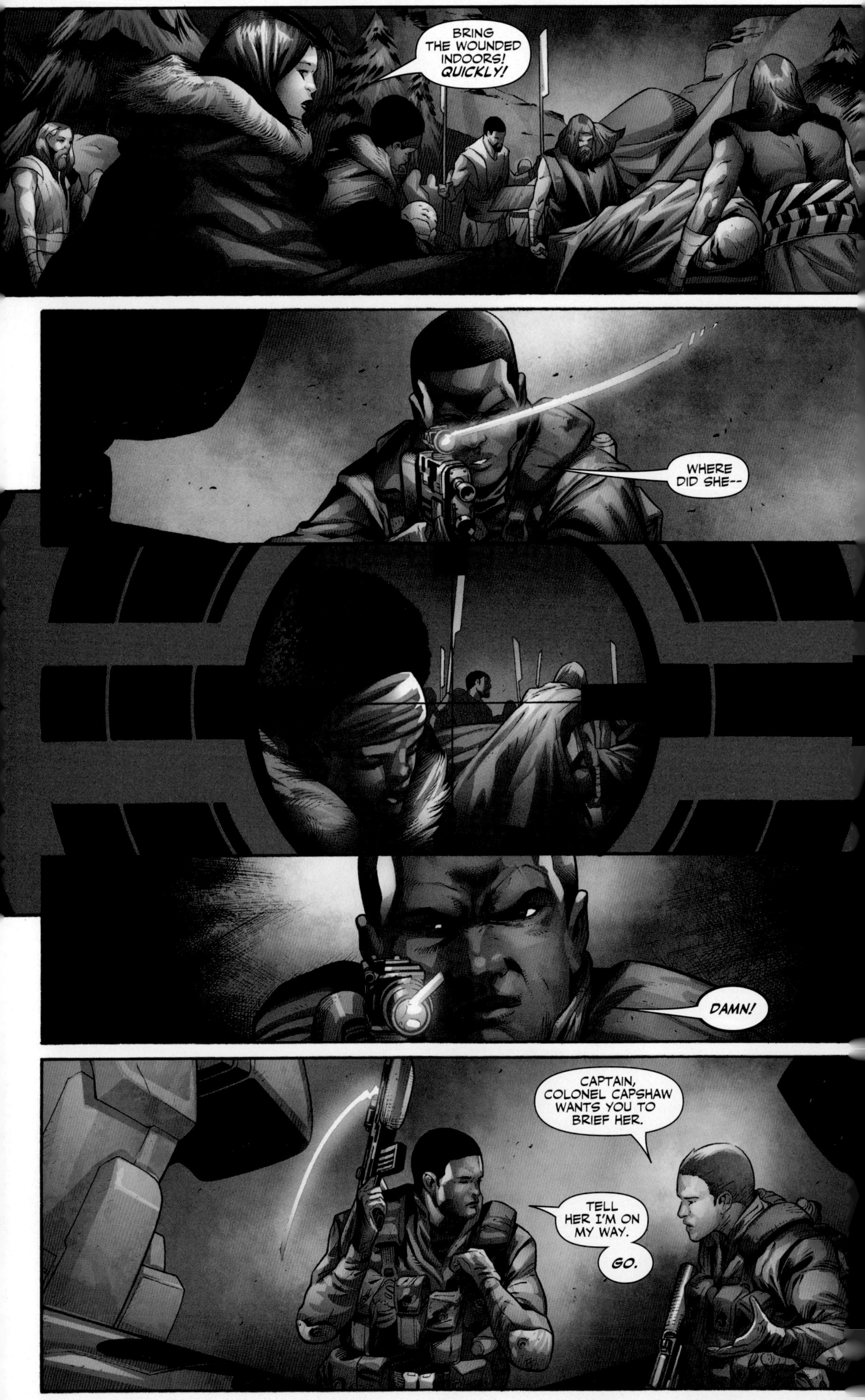
BRING THE WOUNDED INDOORS! QUICKLY!
WHERE DID SHE--
DAMN!
CAPTAIN, COLONEL CAPSHAW WANTS YOU TO BRIEF HER.
TELL HER I'M ON MY WAY.
GO.

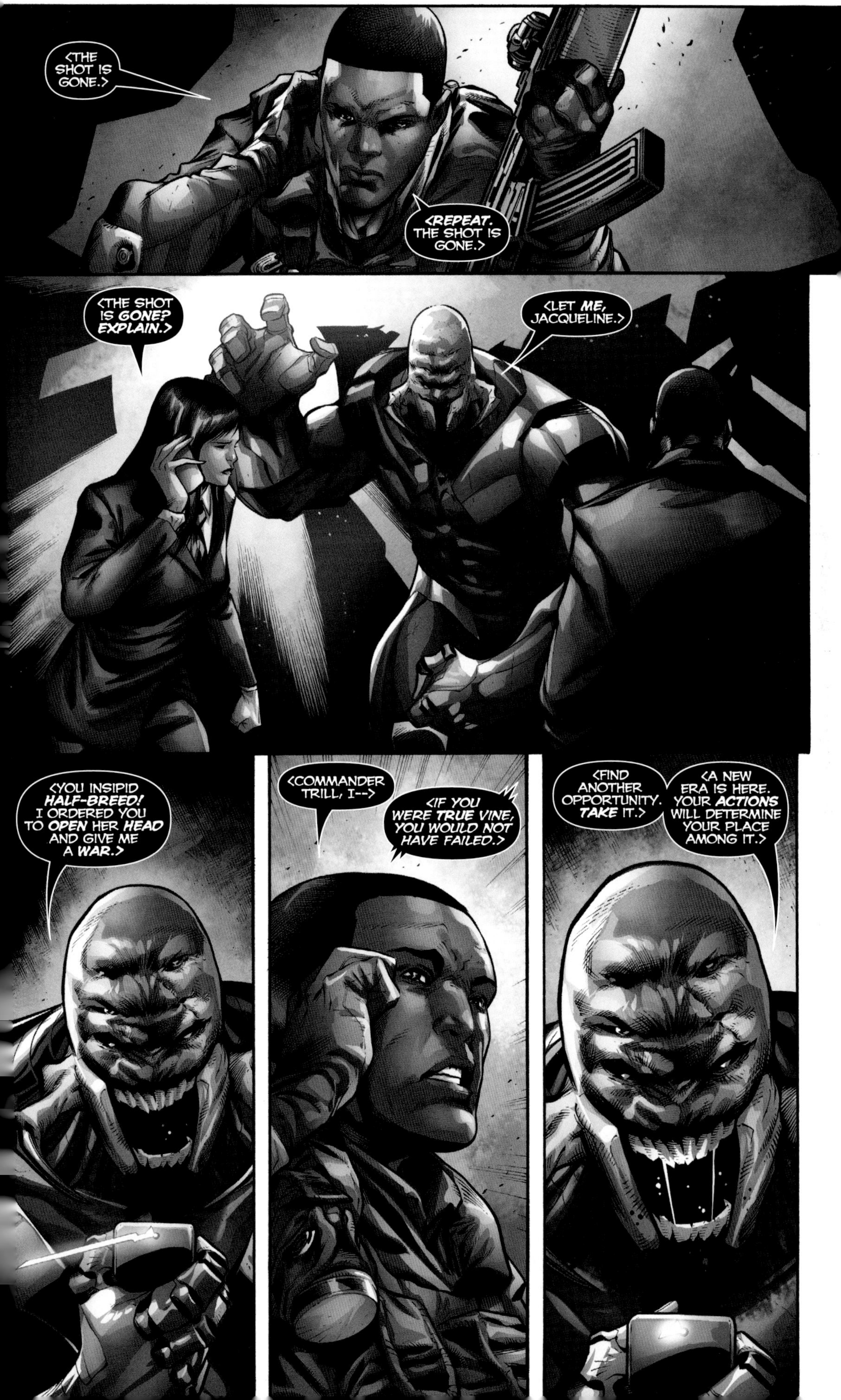
<THE SHOT IS GONE.>
<REPEAT. THE SHOT IS GONE.>
<THE SHOT IS GONE? EXPLAIN.>
<LET ME, JACQUELINE.>
<YOU INSIPID HALF-BREED! I ORDERED YOU TO OPEN HER HEAD AND GIVE ME A WAR.>
<COMMANDER TRILL, I-->
<IF YOU WERE TRUE VINE, YOU WOULD NOT HAVE FAILED.>
<FIND ANOTHER OPPORTUNITY. TAKE IT.>
<A NEW ERA IS HERE. YOUR ACTIONS WILL DETERMINE YOUR PLACE AMONG IT.>

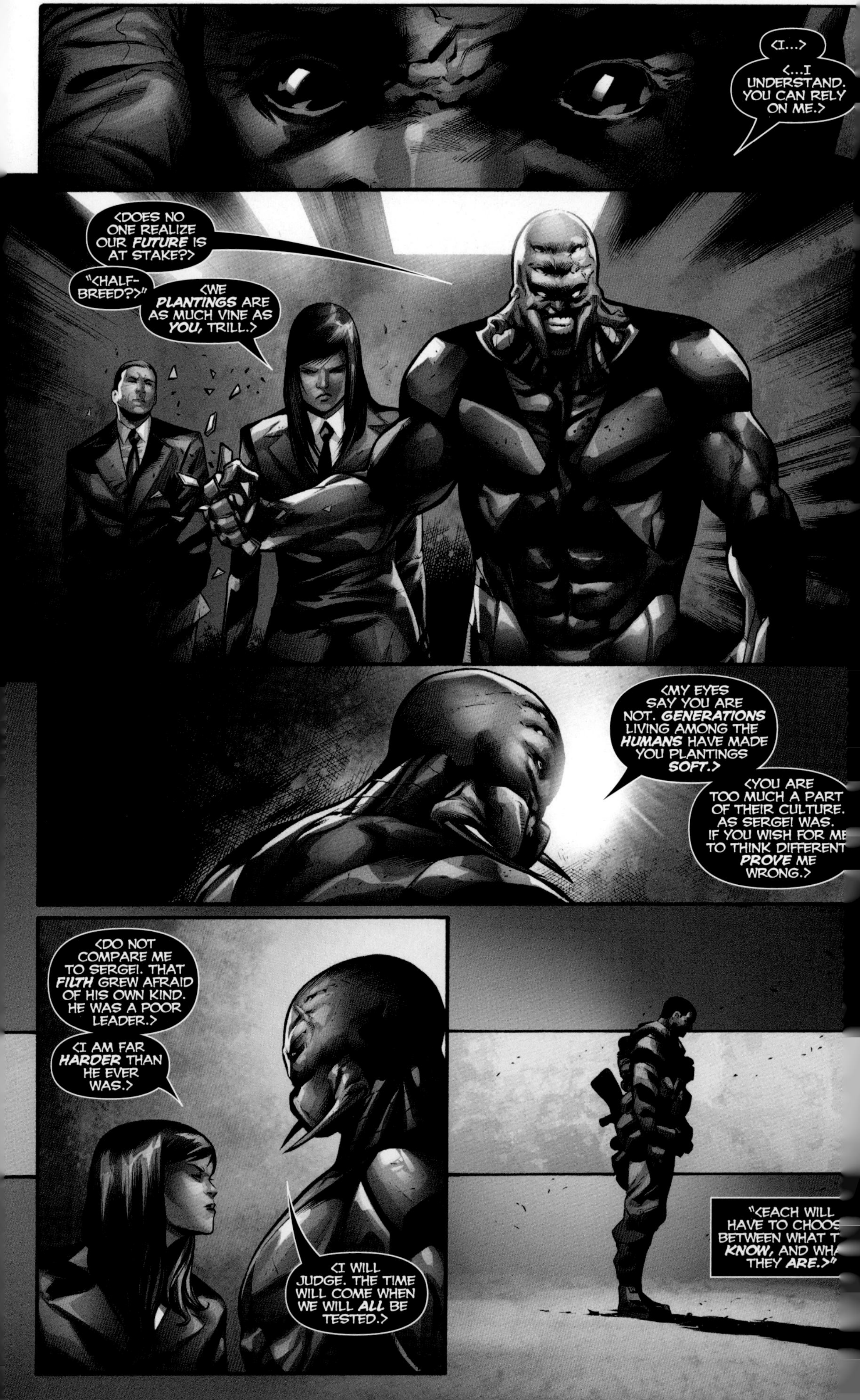
<I...>
<...I UNDERSTAND. YOU CAN RELY ON ME.>
<DOES NO ONE REALIZE OUR FUTURE IS AT STAKE?>
"<HALF-BREED?>"
<WE PLANTINGS ARE AS MUCH VINE AS YOU, TRILL.>
<MY EYES SAY YOU ARE NOT. GENERATIONS LIVING AMONG THE HUMANS HAVE MADE YOU PLANTINGS SOFT.>
<YOU ARE TOO MUCH A PART OF THEIR CULTURE. AS SERGEI WAS. IF YOU WISH FOR ME TO THINK DIFFERENT PROVE ME WRONG.>
<DO NOT COMPARE ME TO SERGEI. THAT FILTH GREW AFRAID OF HIS OWN KIND. HE WAS A POOR LEADER.>
<I AM FAR HARDER THAN HE EVER WAS.>
<I WILL JUDGE. THE TIME WILL COME WHEN WE WILL ALL BE TESTED.>
"<EACH WILL HAVE TO CHOOS BETWEEN WHAT T KNOW, AND WHA THEY ARE.>"

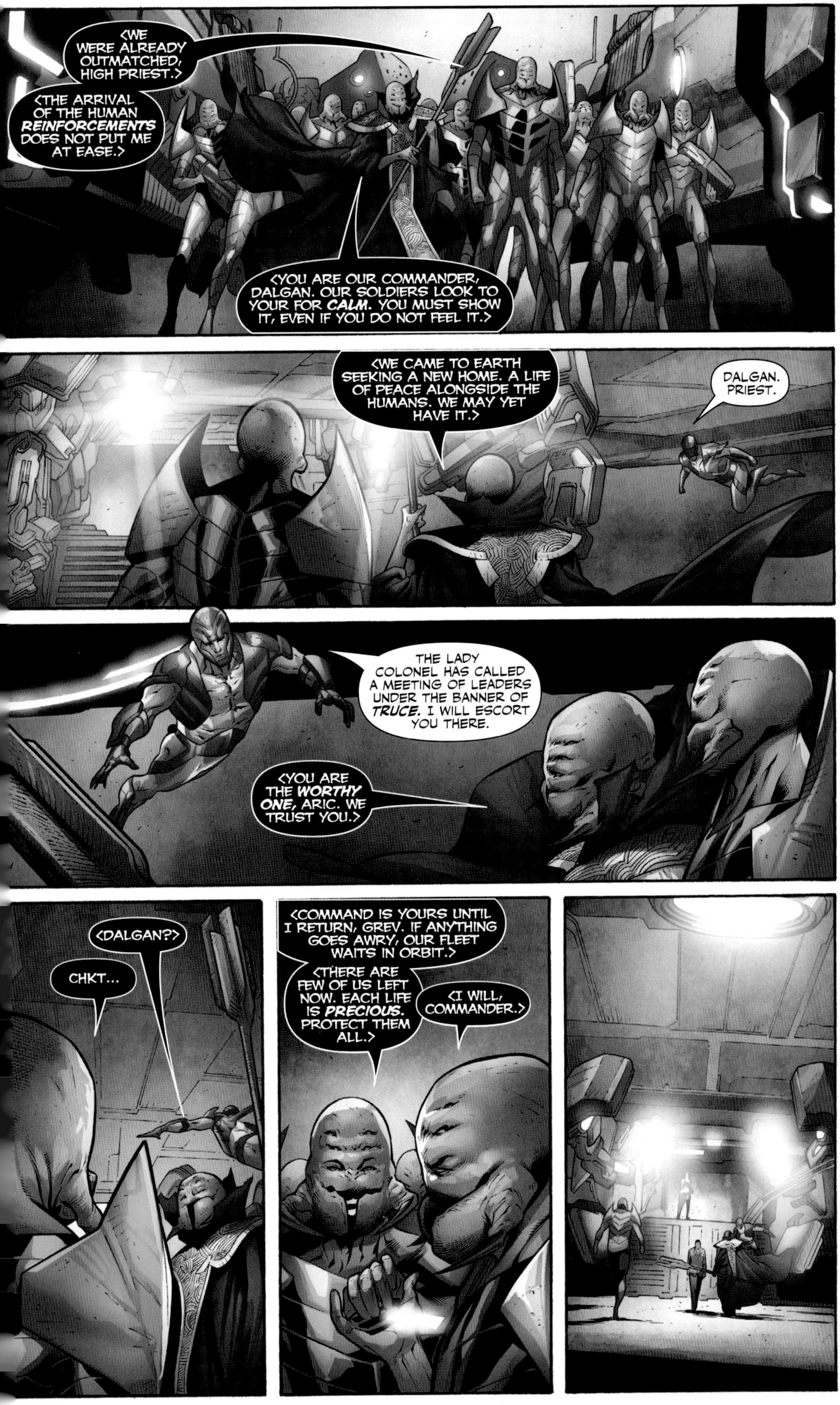
<WE WERE ALREADY OUTMATCHED, HIGH PRIEST.>
<THE ARRIVAL OF THE HUMAN REINFORCEMENTS DOES NOT PUT ME AT EASE.>
<YOU ARE OUR COMMANDER, DALGAN. OUR SOLDIERS LOOK TO YOUR FOR CALM. YOU MUST SHOW IT, EVEN IF YOU DO NOT FEEL IT.>
<WE CAME TO EARTH SEEKING A NEW HOME. A LIFE OF PEACE ALONGSIDE THE HUMANS. WE MAY YET HAVE IT.>
DALGAN. PRIEST.
THE LADY COLONEL HAS CALLED A MEETING OF LEADERS UNDER THE BANNER OF TRUCE. I WILL ESCORT YOU THERE.
<YOU ARE THE WORTHY ONE, ARIC. WE TRUST YOU.>
<DALGAN?>
CHKT...
<COMMAND IS YOURS UNTIL I RETURN, GREV. IF ANYTHING GOES AWRY, OUR FLEET WAITS IN ORBIT.>
<THERE ARE FEW OF US LEFT NOW. EACH LIFE IS PRECIOUS. PROTECT THEM ALL.>
<I WILL, COMMANDER.>

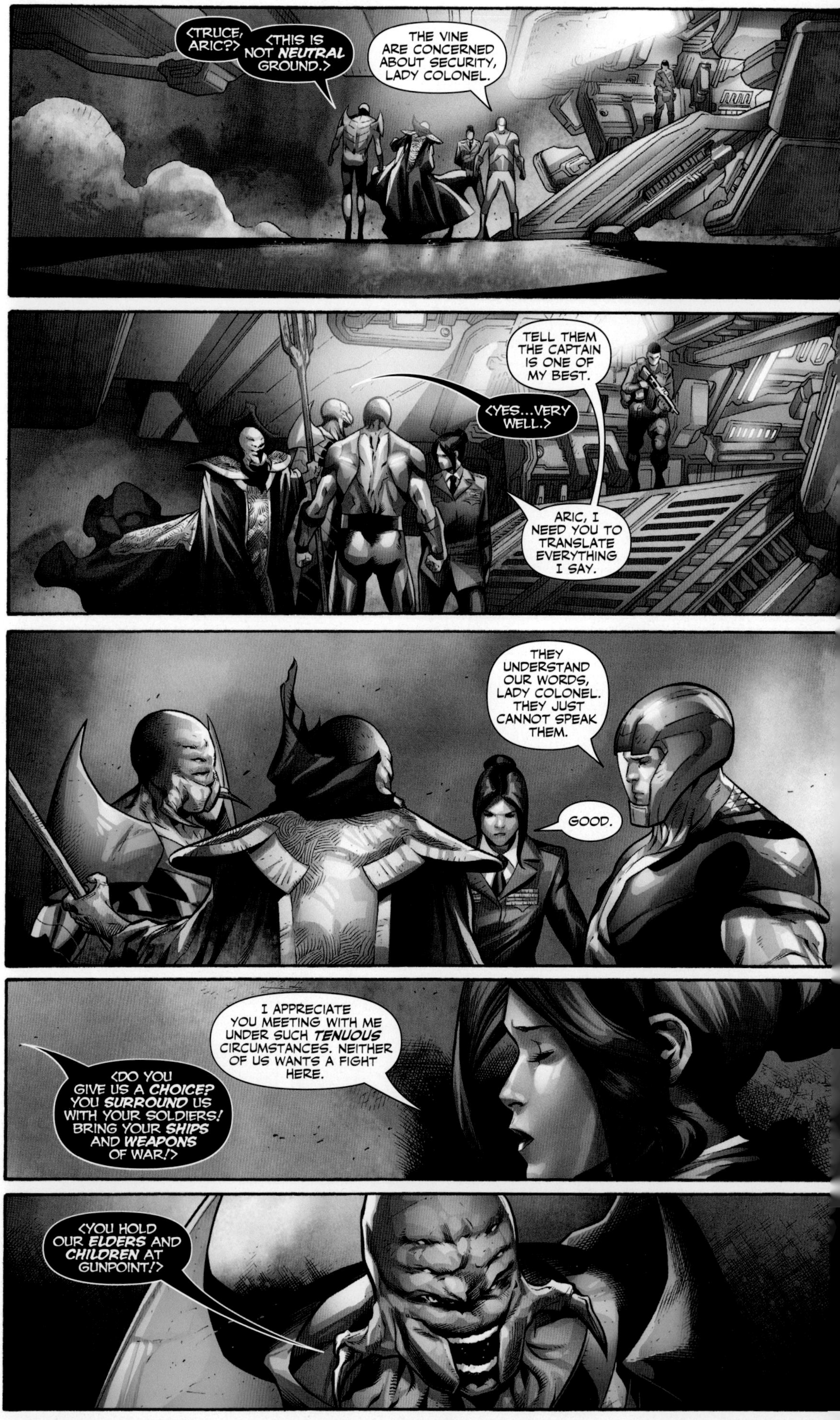
<TRUCE, ARIC?>
<THIS IS NOT NEUTRAL GROUND.>
THE VINE ARE CONCERNED ABOUT SECURITY, LADY COLONEL.
TELL THEM THE CAPTAIN IS ONE OF MY BEST.
<YES...VERY WELL.>
ARIC, I NEED YOU TO TRANSLATE EVERYTHING I SAY.
THEY UNDERSTAND OUR WORDS, LADY COLONEL. THEY JUST CANNOT SPEAK THEM.
GOOD.
I APPRECIATE YOU MEETING WITH ME UNDER SUCH TENUOUS CIRCUMSTANCES. NEITHER OF US WANTS A FIGHT HERE.
<DO YOU GIVE US A CHOICE? YOU SURROUND US WITH YOUR SOLDIERS! BRING YOUR SHIPS AND WEAPONS OF WAR!>
<YOU HOLD OUR ELDERS AND CHILDREN AT GUNPOINT!>

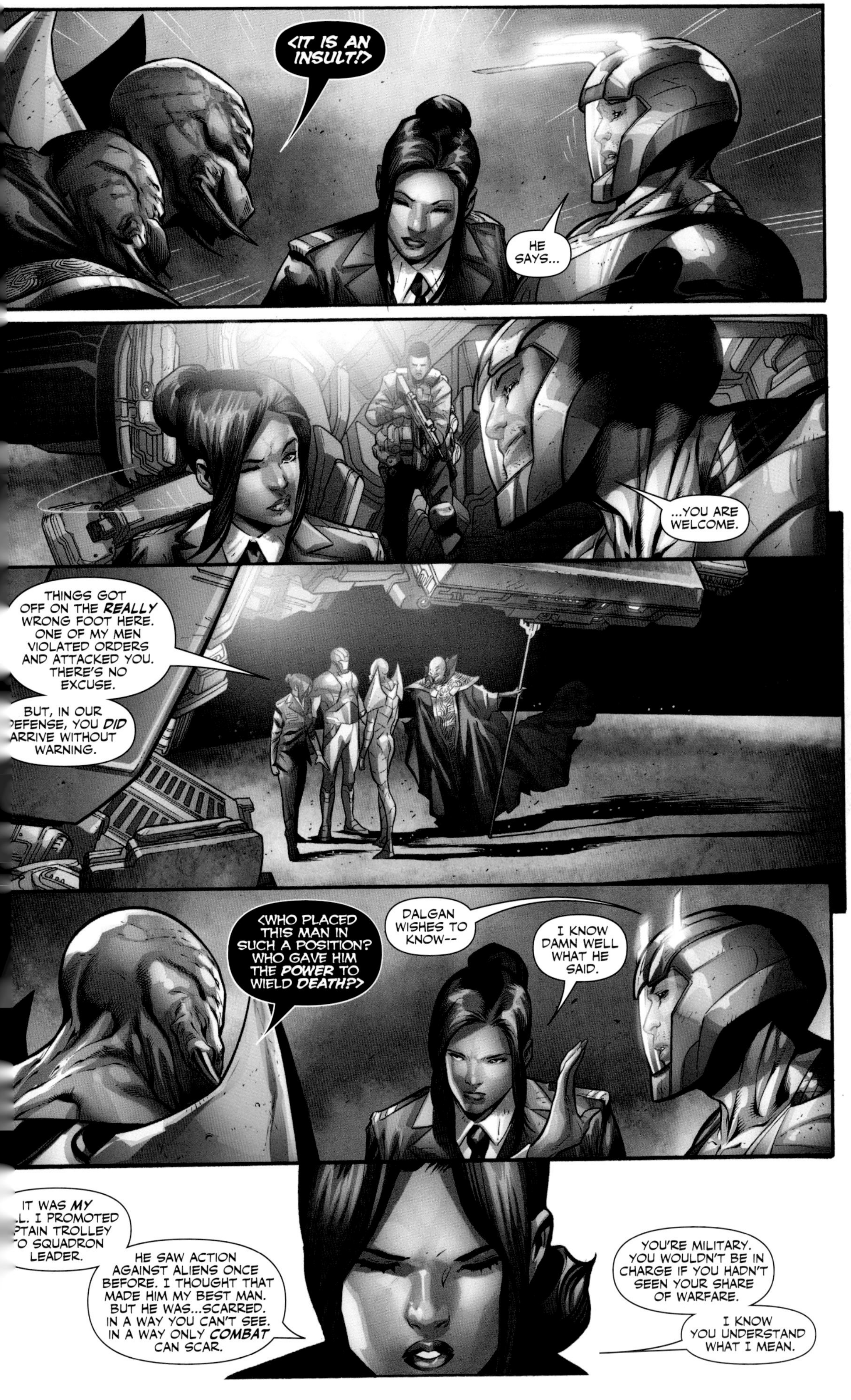
<IT IS AN INSULT!>
HE SAYS...
...YOU ARE WELCOME.
THINGS GOT OFF ON THE *REALLY* WRONG FOOT HERE. ONE OF MY MEN VIOLATED ORDERS AND ATTACKED YOU. THERE'S NO EXCUSE.
BUT, IN OUR DEFENSE, YOU *DID* ARRIVE WITHOUT WARNING.
<WHO PLACED THIS MAN IN SUCH A POSITION? WHO GAVE HIM THE *POWER* TO WIELD *DEATH?*>
DALGAN WISHES TO KNOW--
I KNOW DAMN WELL WHAT HE SAID.
IT WAS *MY* ...L. I PROMOTED ...PTAIN TROLLEY ...O SQUADRON LEADER.
HE SAW ACTION AGAINST ALIENS ONCE BEFORE. I THOUGHT THAT MADE HIM MY BEST MAN. BUT HE WAS...SCARRED. IN A WAY YOU CAN'T SEE. IN A WAY ONLY *COMBAT* CAN SCAR.
YOU'RE MILITARY. YOU WOULDN'T BE IN CHARGE IF YOU HADN'T SEEN YOUR SHARE OF WARFARE.
I KNOW YOU UNDERSTAND WHAT I MEAN.

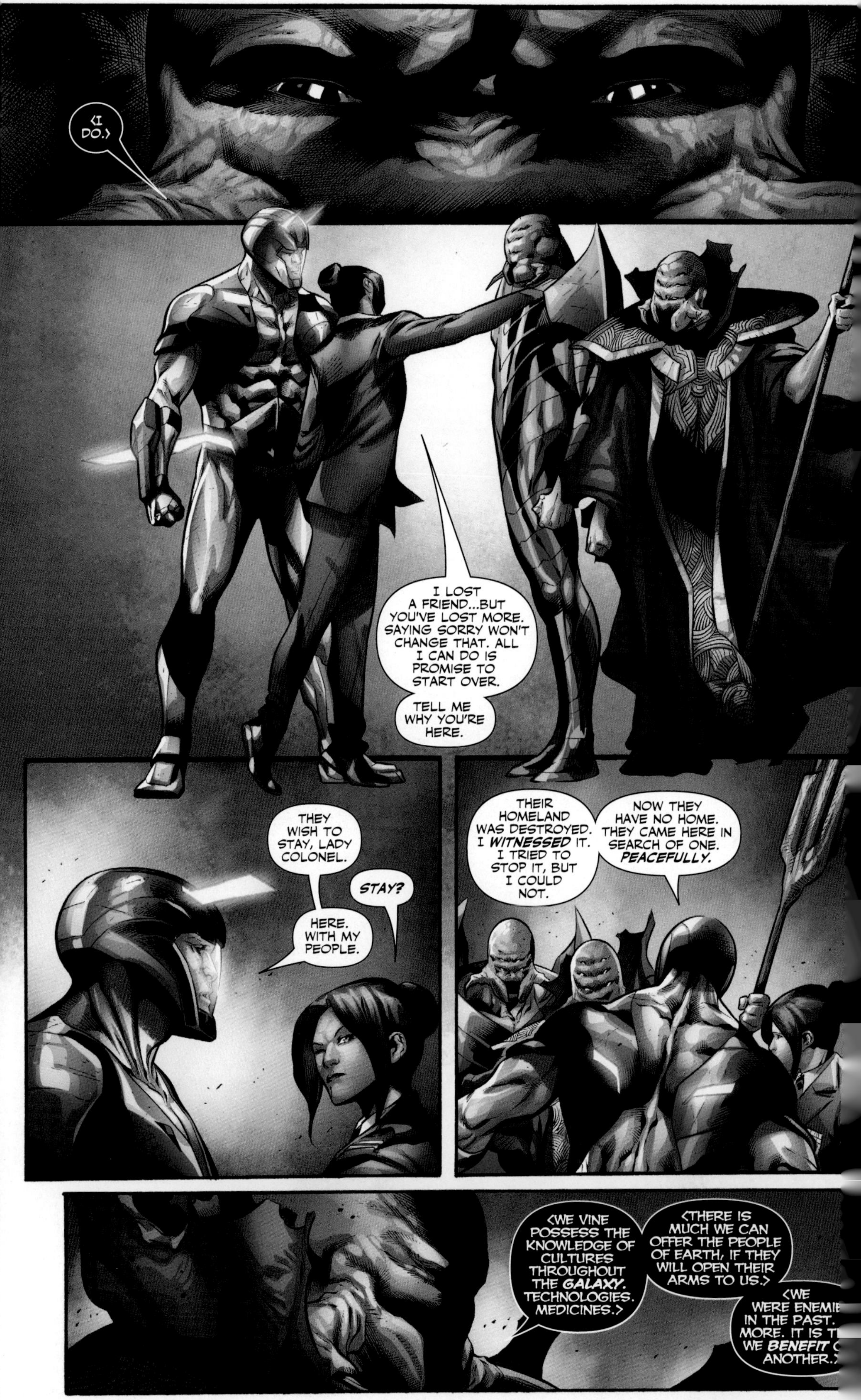
‹I DO.›
I LOST A FRIEND...BUT YOU'VE LOST MORE. SAYING SORRY WON'T CHANGE THAT. ALL I CAN DO IS PROMISE TO START OVER.
TELL ME WHY YOU'RE HERE.
THEY WISH TO STAY, LADY COLONEL.
STAY?
HERE. WITH MY PEOPLE.
THEIR HOMELAND WAS DESTROYED. I WITNESSED IT. I TRIED TO STOP IT, BUT I COULD NOT.
NOW THEY HAVE NO HOME. THEY CAME HERE IN SEARCH OF ONE. PEACEFULLY.
‹WE VINE POSSESS THE KNOWLEDGE OF CULTURES THROUGHOUT THE GALAXY. TECHNOLOGIES. MEDICINES.›
‹THERE IS MUCH WE CAN OFFER THE PEOPLE OF EARTH, IF THEY WILL OPEN THEIR ARMS TO US.›

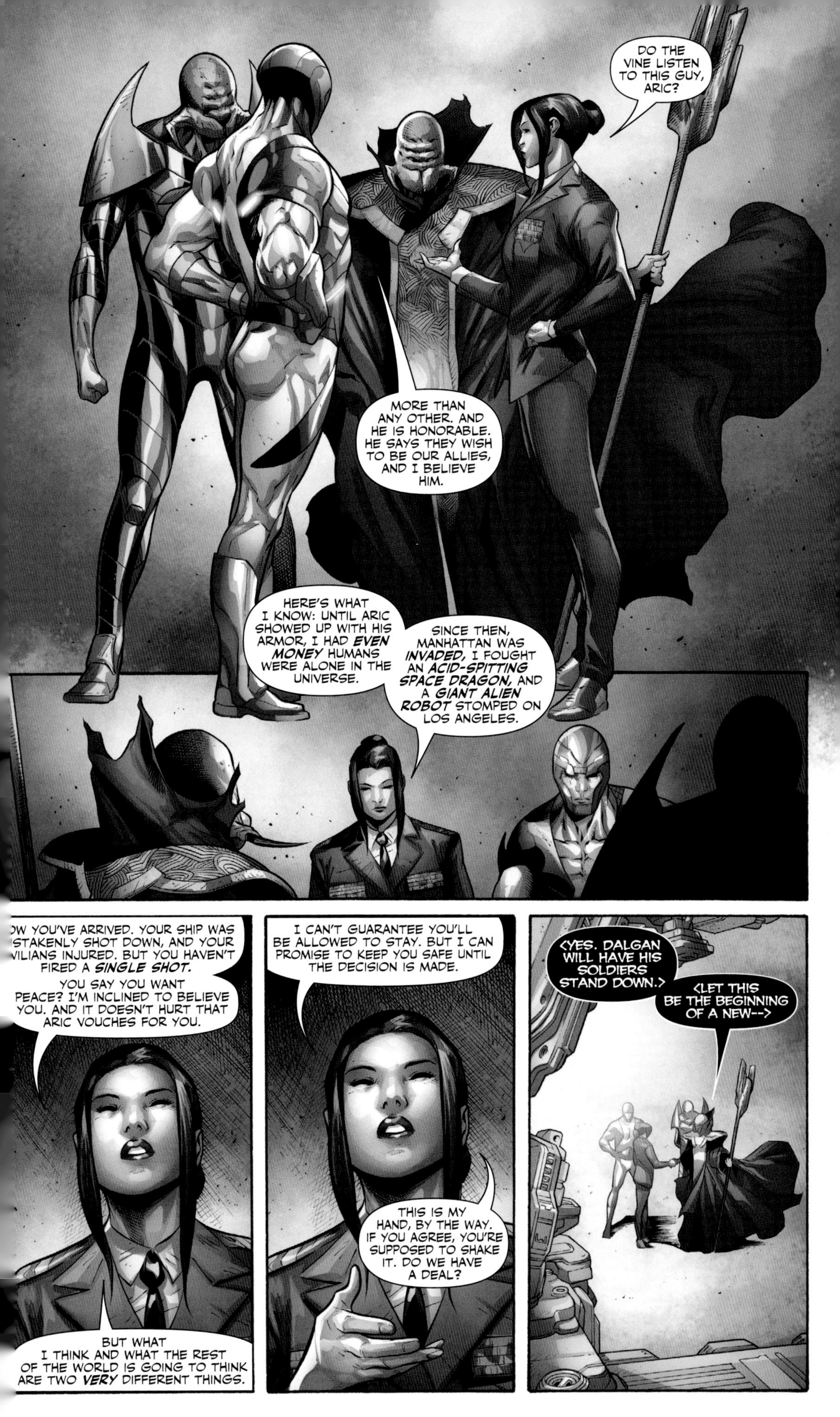
DO THE VINE LISTEN TO THIS GUY, ARIC?
MORE THAN ANY OTHER. AND HE IS HONORABLE. HE SAYS THEY WISH TO BE OUR ALLIES, AND I BELIEVE HIM.
HERE'S WHAT I KNOW: UNTIL ARIC SHOWED UP WITH HIS ARMOR, I HAD EVEN MONEY HUMANS WERE ALONE IN THE UNIVERSE.
SINCE THEN, MANHATTAN WAS INVADED, I FOUGHT AN ACID-SPITTING SPACE DRAGON, AND A GIANT ALIEN ROBOT STOMPED ON LOS ANGELES.
OW YOU'VE ARRIVED. YOUR SHIP WAS STAKENLY SHOT DOWN, AND YOUR VILIANS INJURED. BUT YOU HAVEN'T FIRED A SINGLE SHOT.
YOU SAY YOU WANT PEACE? I'M INCLINED TO BELIEVE YOU. AND IT DOESN'T HURT THAT ARIC VOUCHES FOR YOU.
BUT WHAT I THINK AND WHAT THE REST OF THE WORLD IS GOING TO THINK ARE TWO VERY DIFFERENT THINGS.
I CAN'T GUARANTEE YOU'LL BE ALLOWED TO STAY. BUT I CAN PROMISE TO KEEP YOU SAFE UNTIL THE DECISION IS MADE.
THIS IS MY HAND, BY THE WAY. IF YOU AGREE, YOU'RE SUPPOSED TO SHAKE IT. DO WE HAVE A DEAL?
<YES. DALGAN WILL HAVE HIS SOLDIERS STAND DOWN.>
<LET THIS BE THE BEGINNING OF A NEW-->

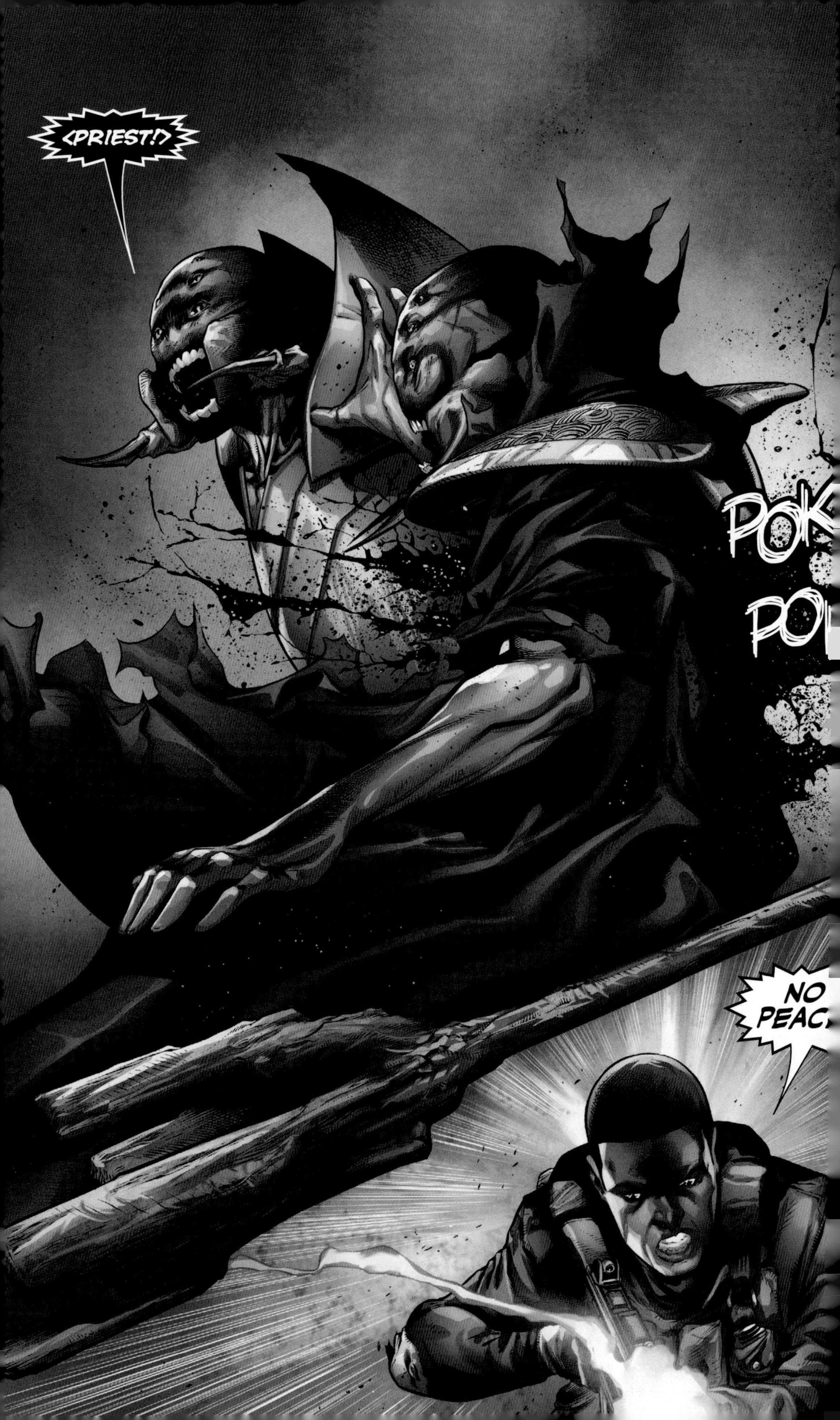
<PRIEST!?>
POK
PO
NO
PEAC

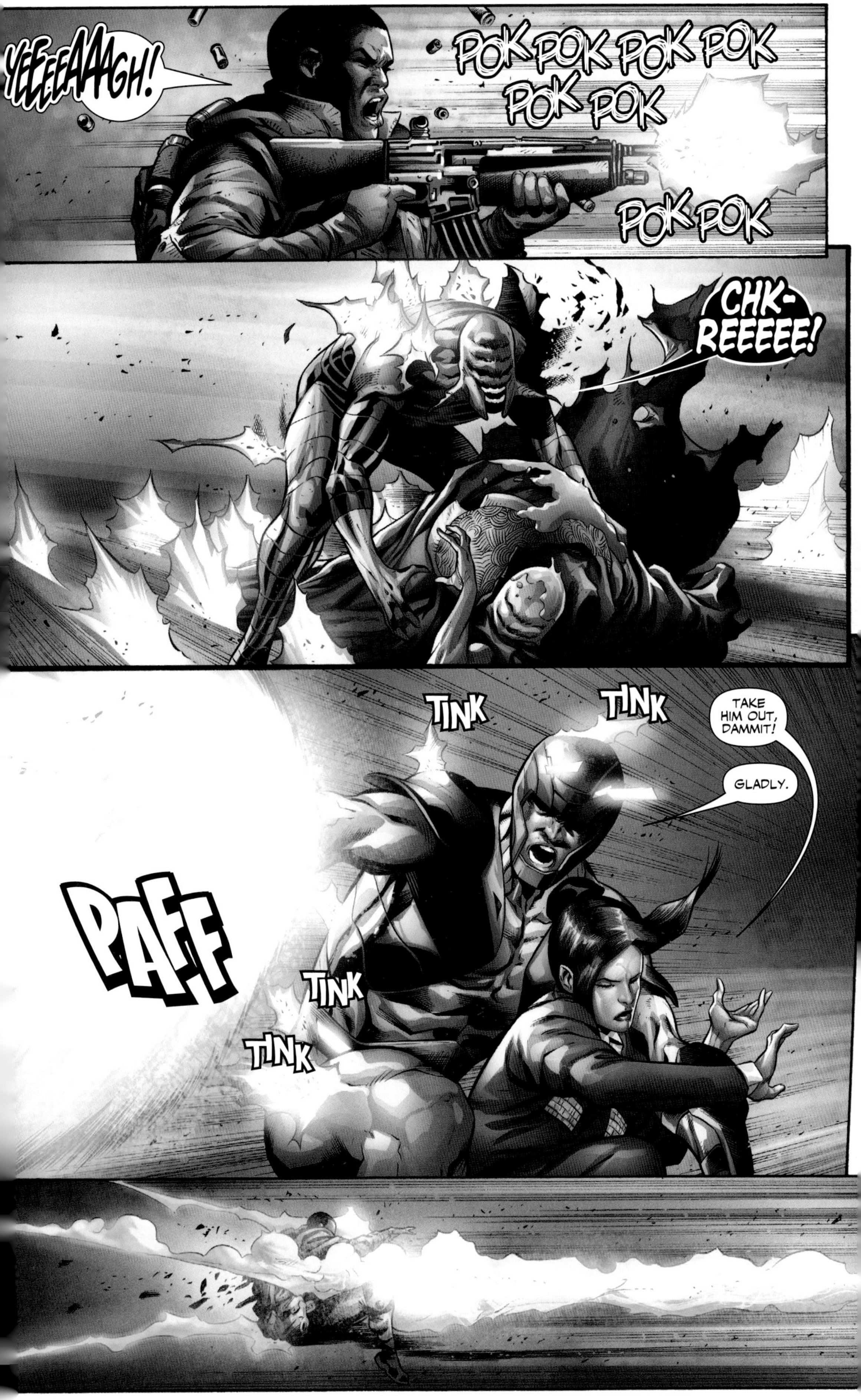
YEEEEAAAGH!
POK POK POK POK
POK POK
POK POK
CHK-REEEEEE!
TINK
TINK
TAKE HIM OUT, DAMMIT!
GLADLY.
PAFF
TINK
TINK

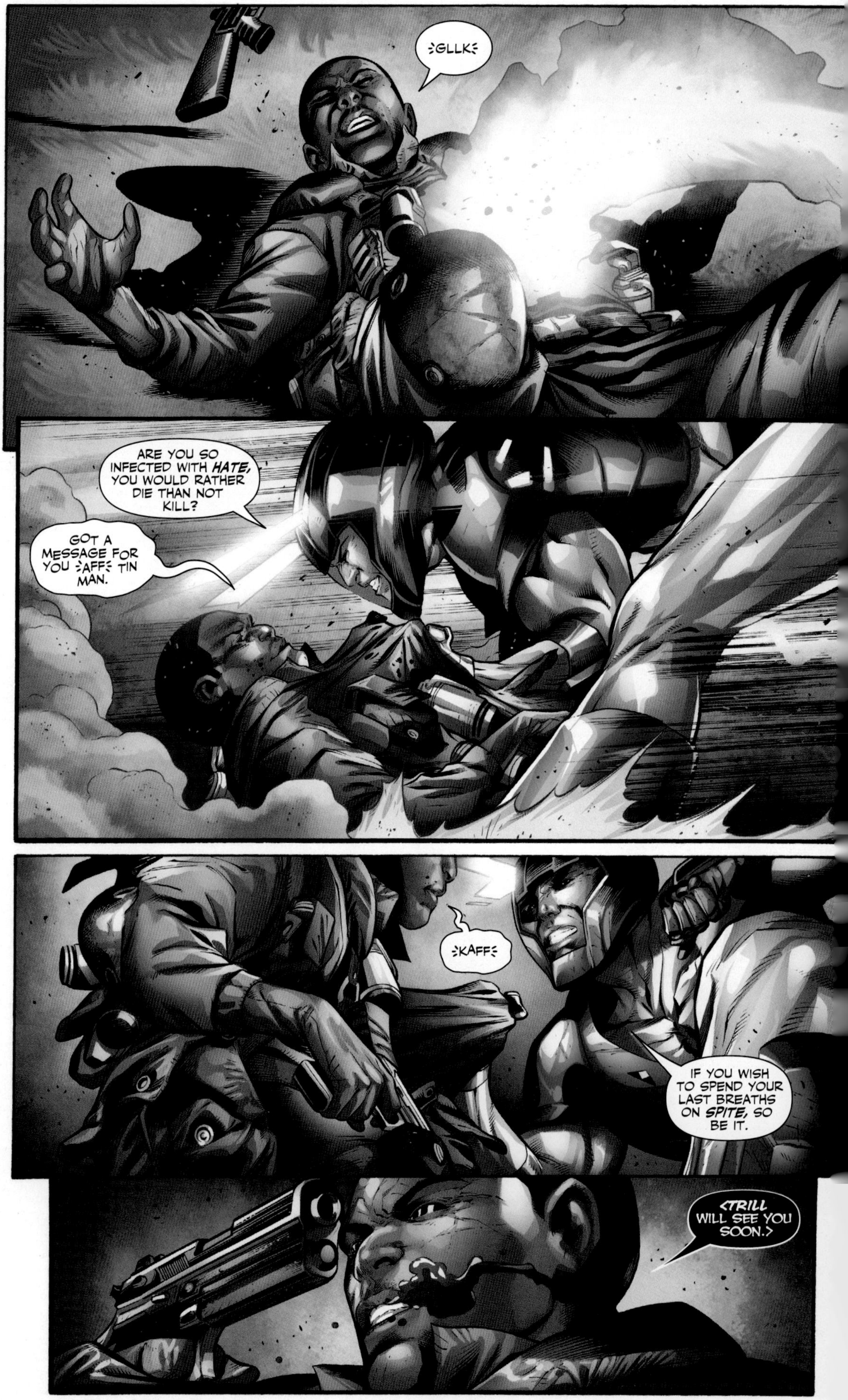
GLLK
ARE YOU SO INFECTED WITH *HATE*, YOU WOULD RATHER DIE THAN NOT KILL?
GOT A MESSAGE FOR YOU AFF TIN MAN.
KAFF
IF YOU WISH TO SPEND YOUR LAST BREATHS ON *SPITE*, SO BE IT.
<*TRILL* WILL SEE YOU SOON.>

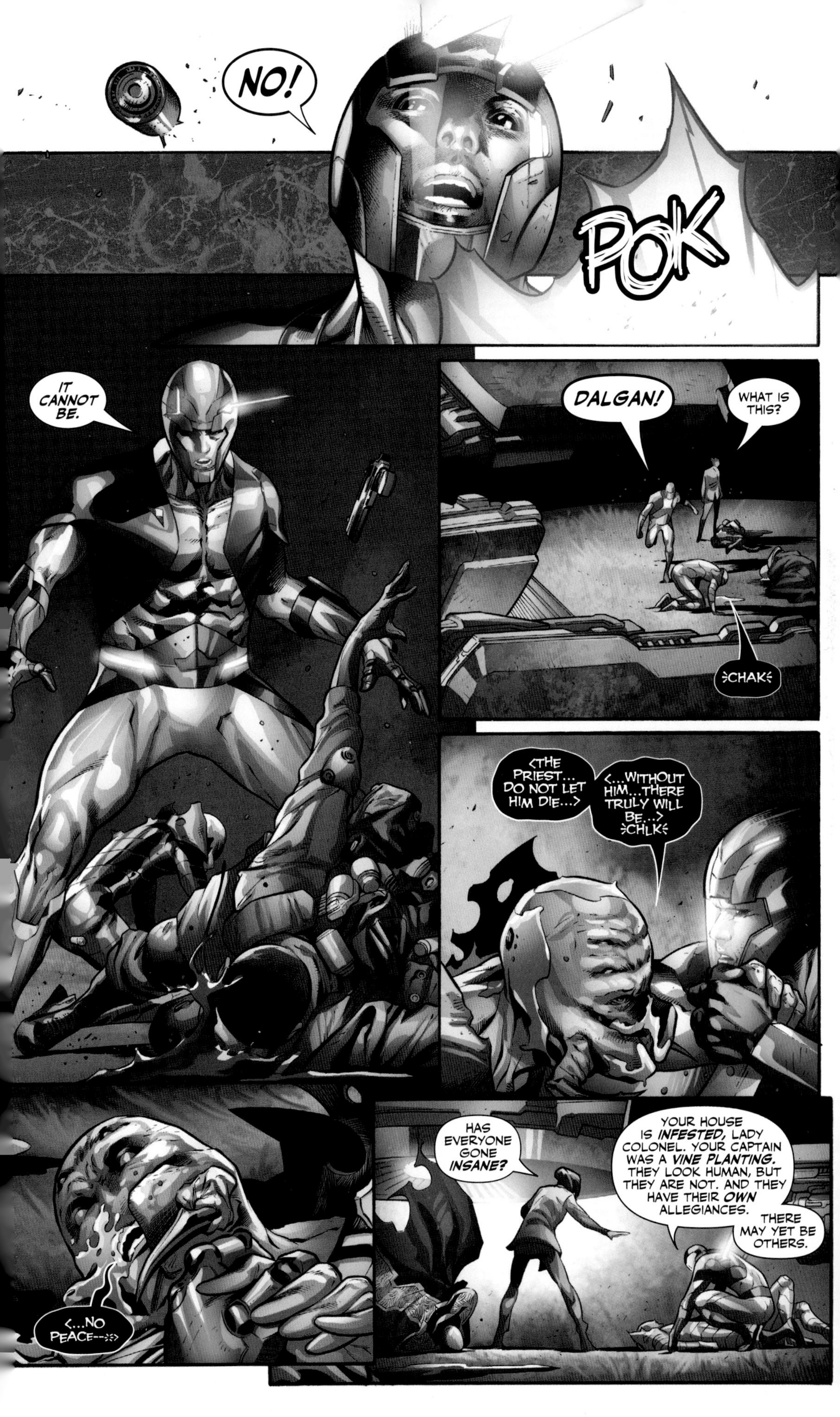
NO!
POK
IT CANNOT BE.
DALGAN!
WHAT IS THIS?
CHAK
<THE PRIEST... DO NOT LET HIM DIE...>
<...WITHOUT HIM...THERE TRULY WILL BE...> CHLK
<...NO PEACE-->
HAS EVERYONE GONE *INSANE?*
YOUR HOUSE IS *INFESTED,* LADY COLONEL. YOUR CAPTAIN WAS A *VINE PLANTING.* THEY LOOK HUMAN, BUT THEY ARE NOT. AND THEY HAVE THEIR *OWN* ALLEGIANCES.
THERE MAY YET BE OTHERS.

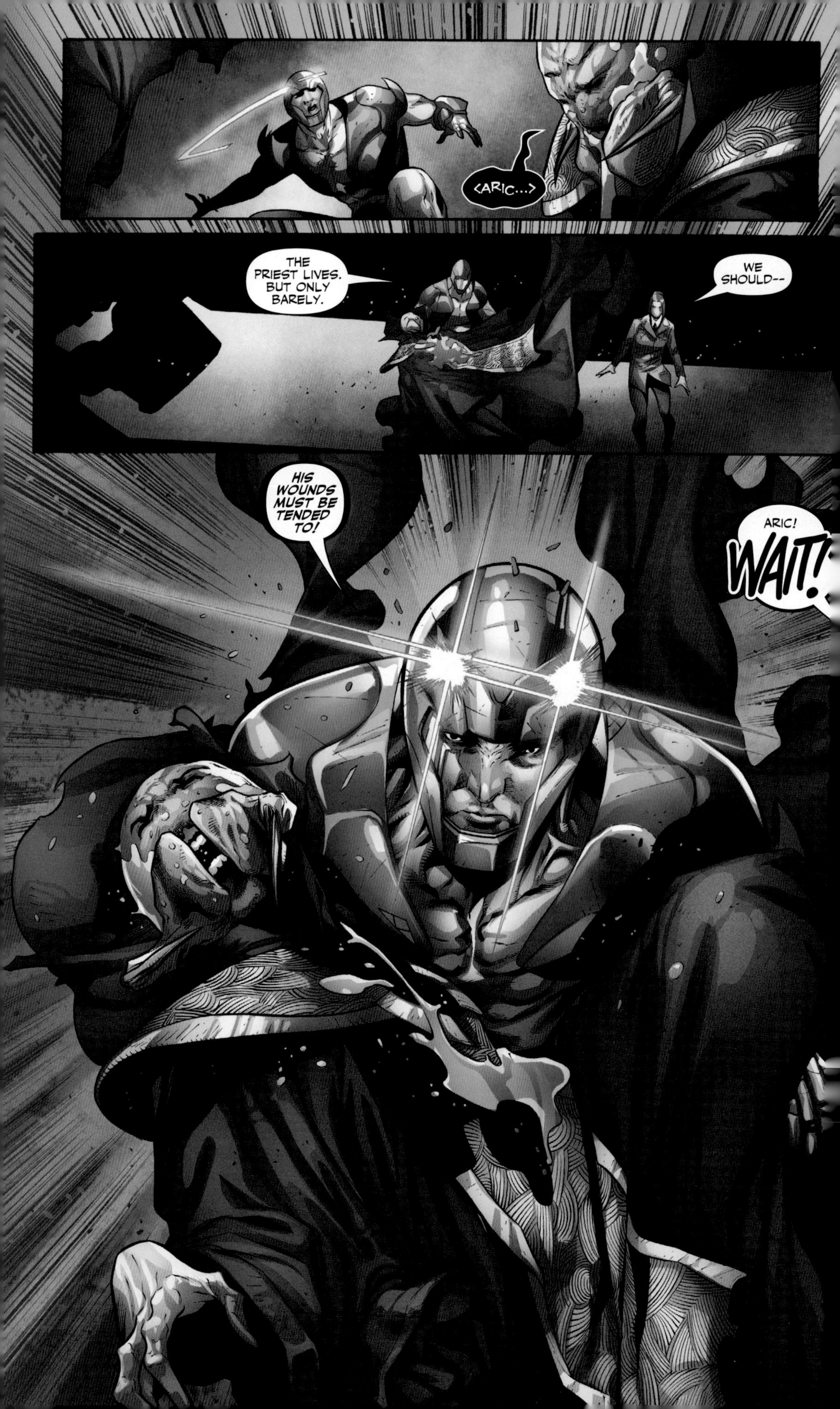
<ARIC...>
THE PRIEST LIVES. BUT ONLY BARELY.
WE SHOULD--
HIS WOUNDS MUST BE TENDED TO!
ARIC! WAIT!

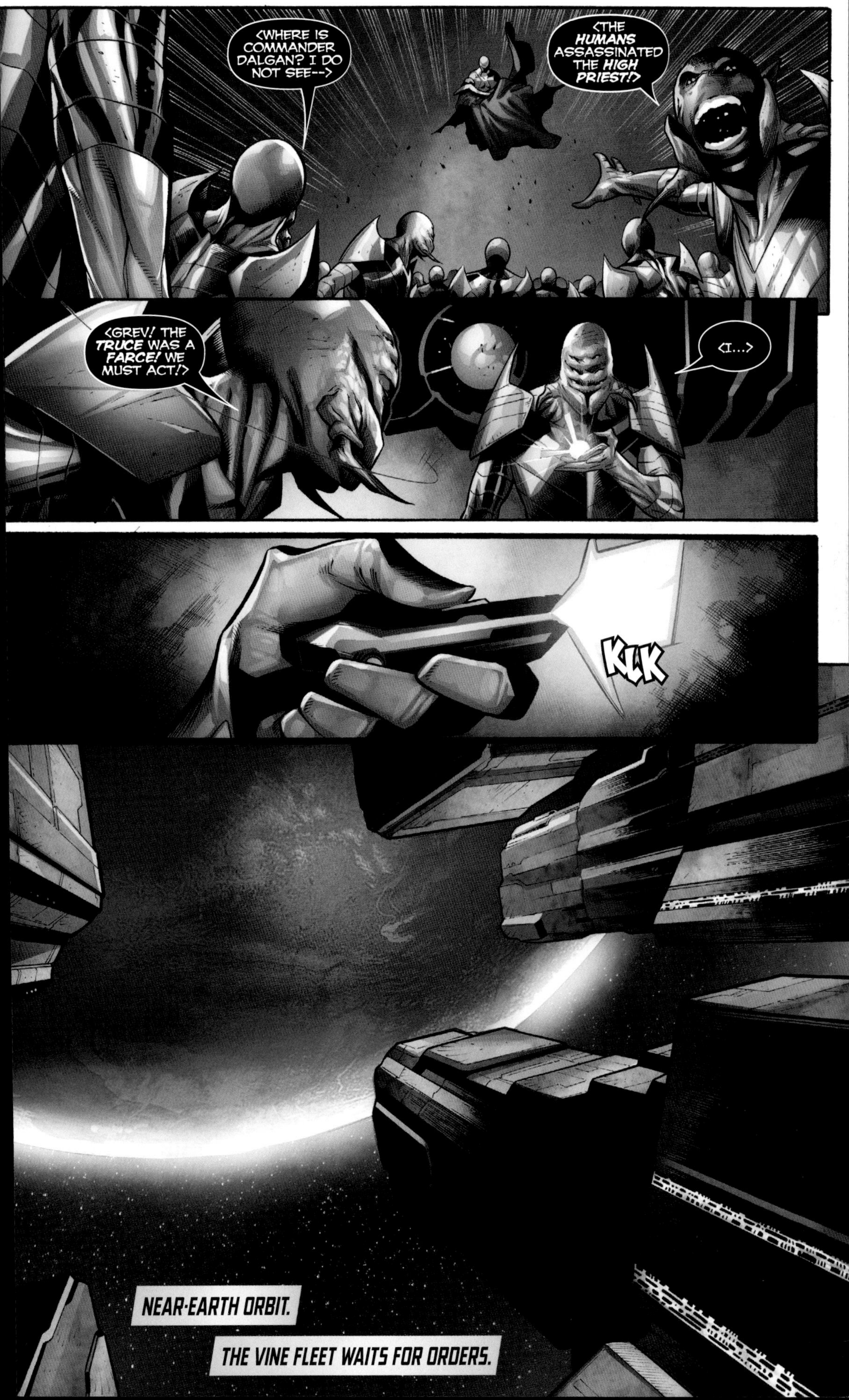
<WHERE IS COMMANDER DALGAN? I DO NOT SEE-->
<THE HUMANS ASSASSINATED THE HIGH PRIEST!>
<GREV! THE TRUCE WAS A FARCE! WE MUST ACT!>
<I...>
KLK
NEAR-EARTH ORBIT.
THE VINE FLEET WAITS FOR ORDERS.

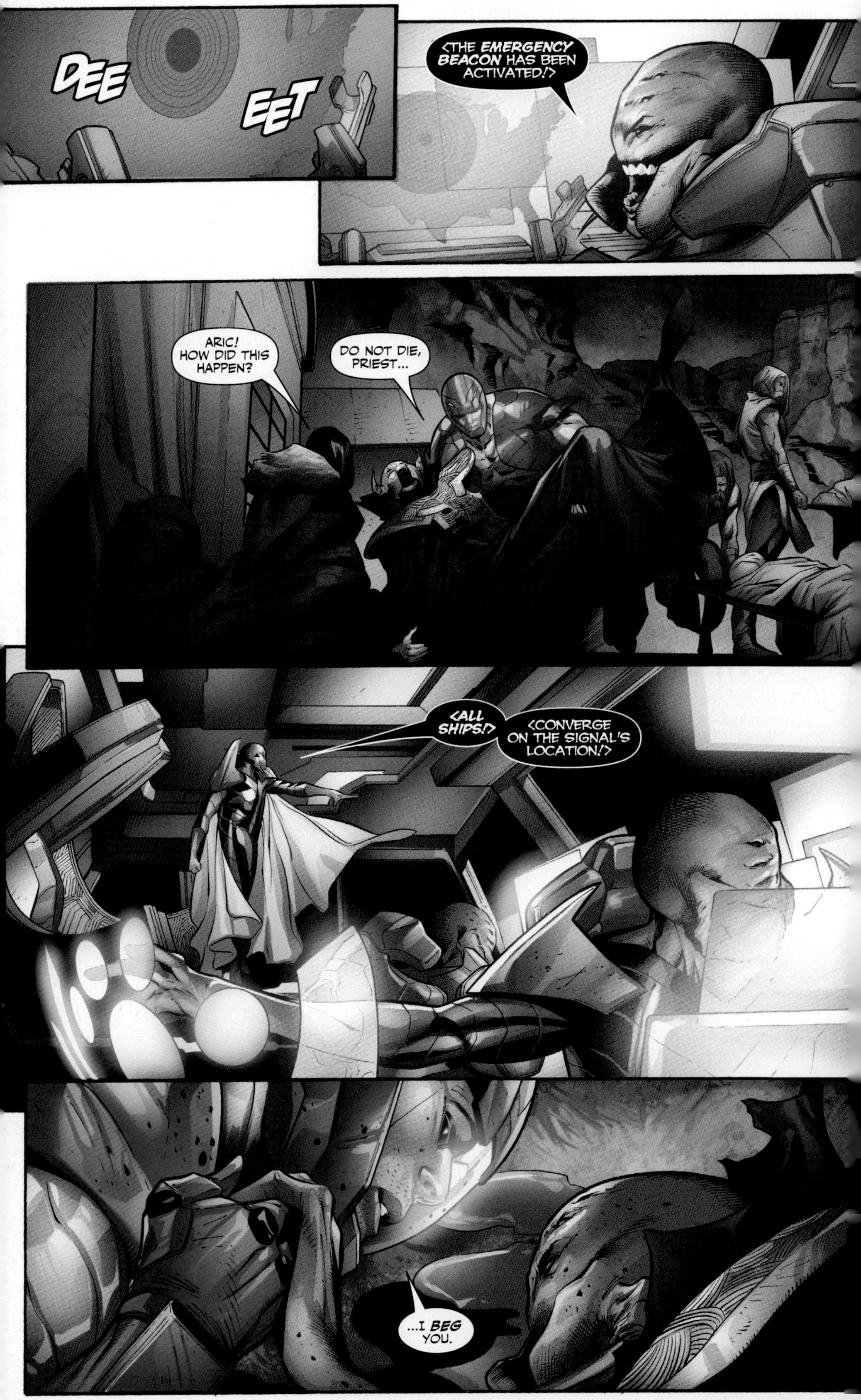
DEE
EET
<THE EMERGENCY BEACON HAS BEEN ACTIVATED!>
ARIC! HOW DID THIS HAPPEN?
DO NOT DIE, PRIEST...
<ALL SHIPS!>
<CONVERGE ON THE SIGNAL'S LOCATION!>
...I BEG YOU.

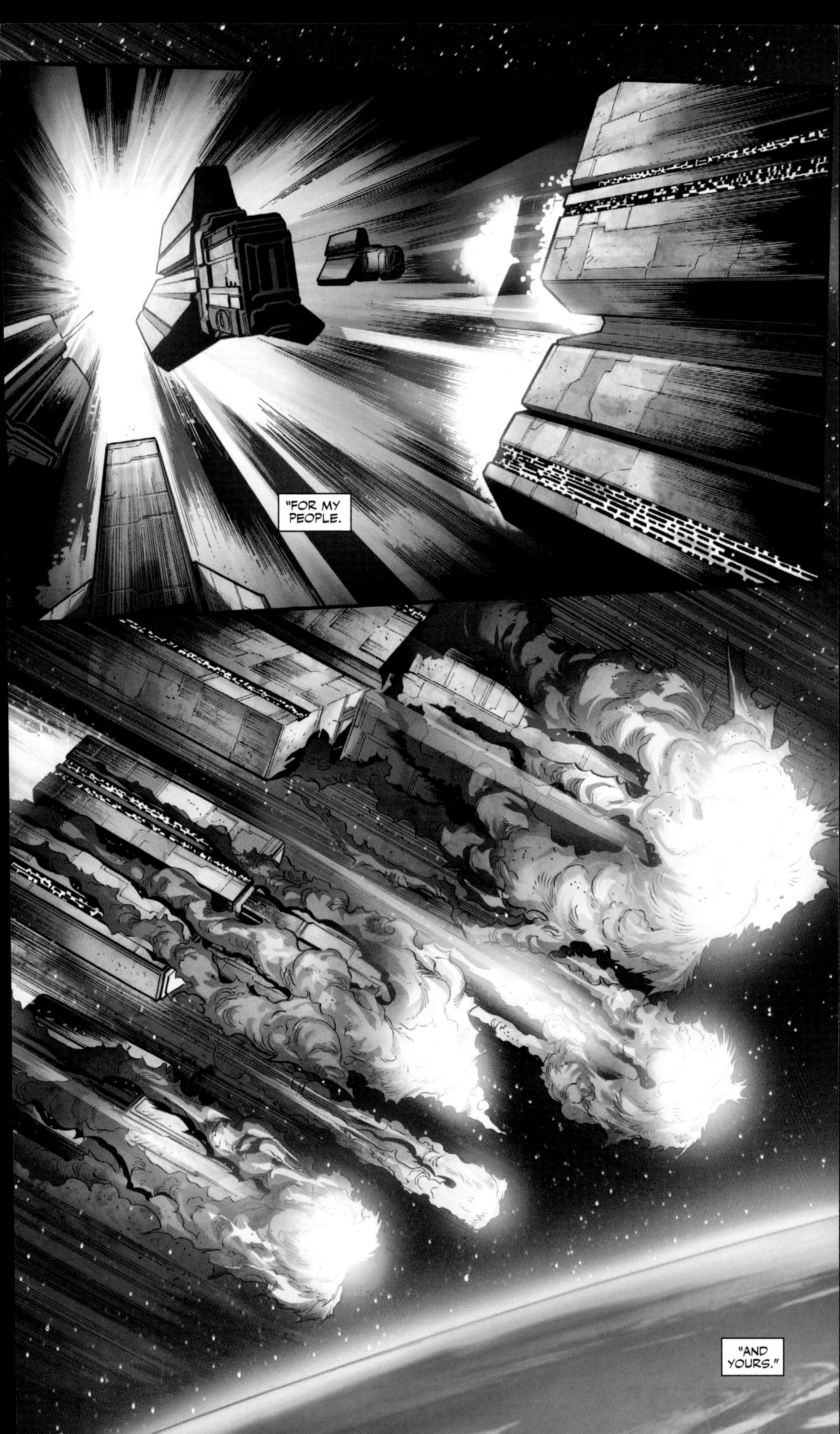
"FOR MY PEOPLE.
"AND YOURS."

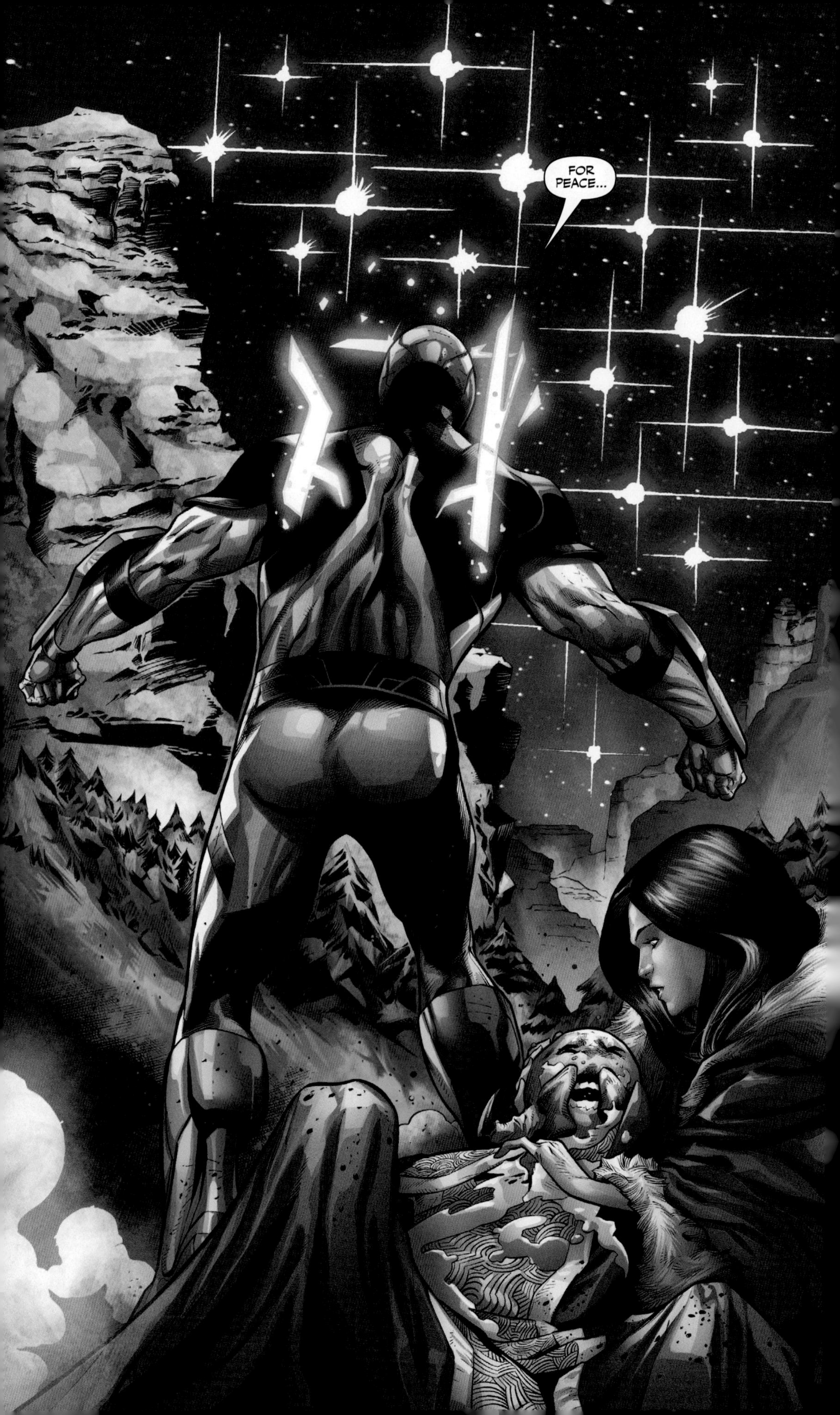
FOR PEACE...

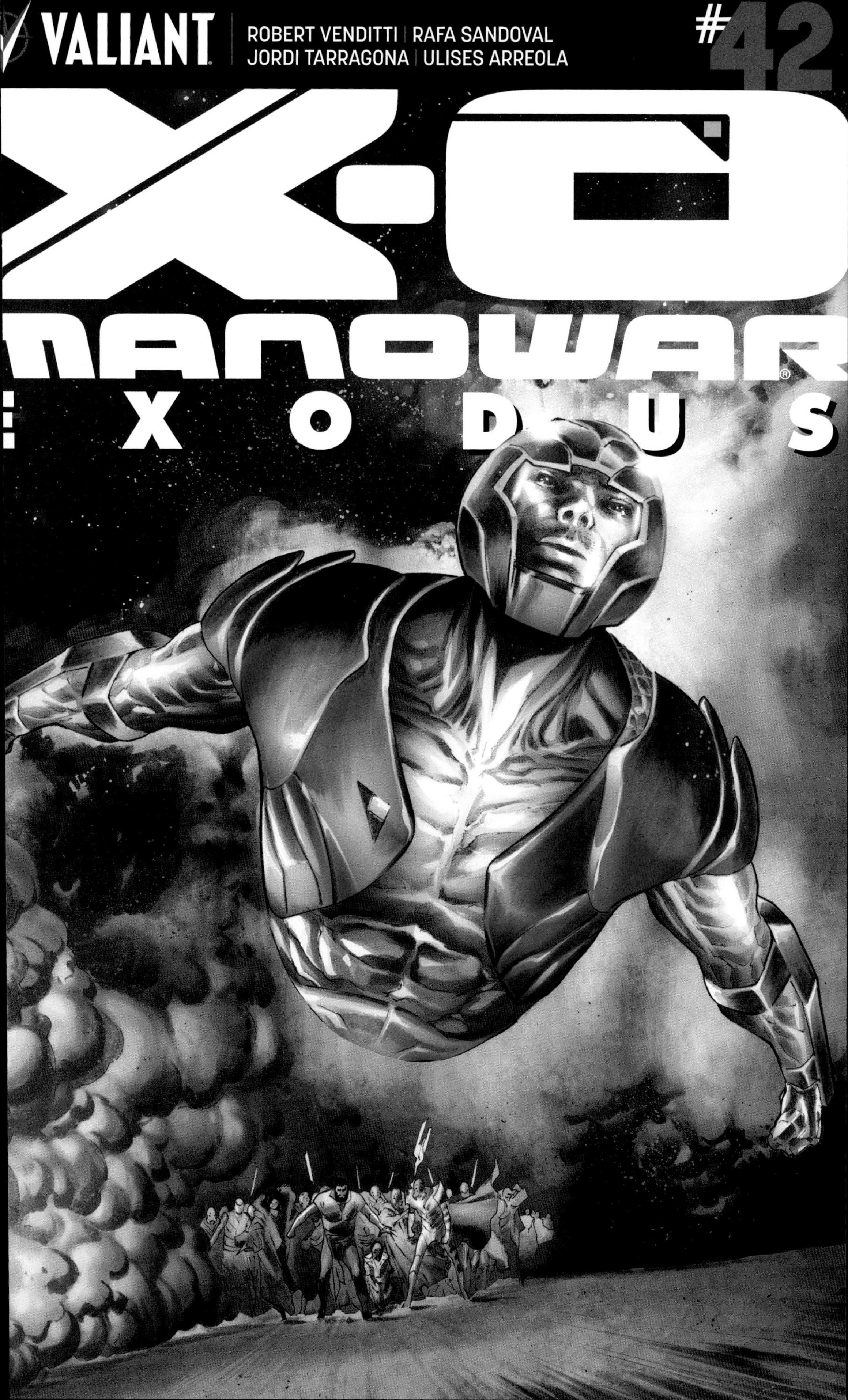
VALIANT
ROBERT VENDITTI | RAFA SANDOVAL
JORDI TARRAGONA | ULISES ARREOLA
#42
X-O
MANOWAR®
EXODUS

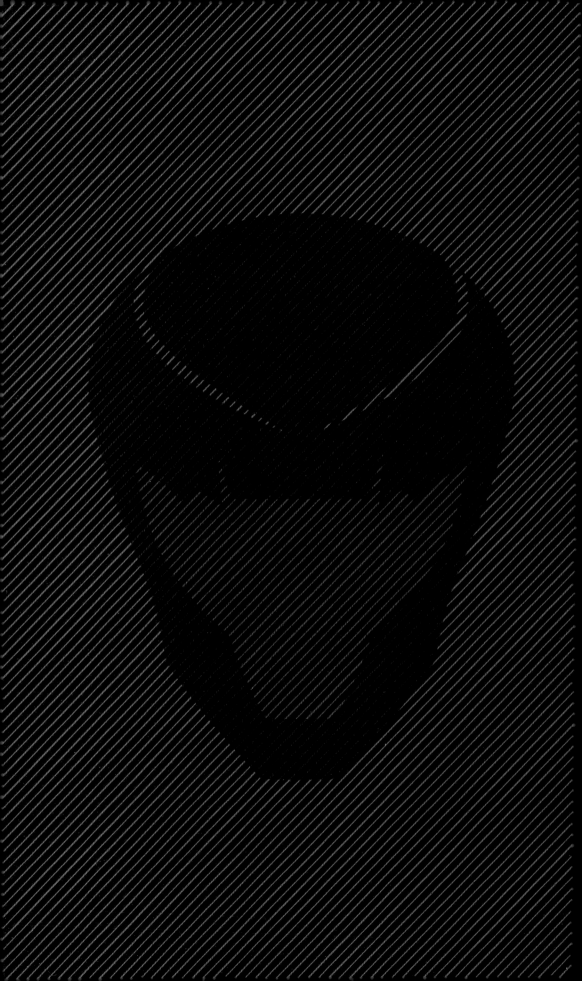

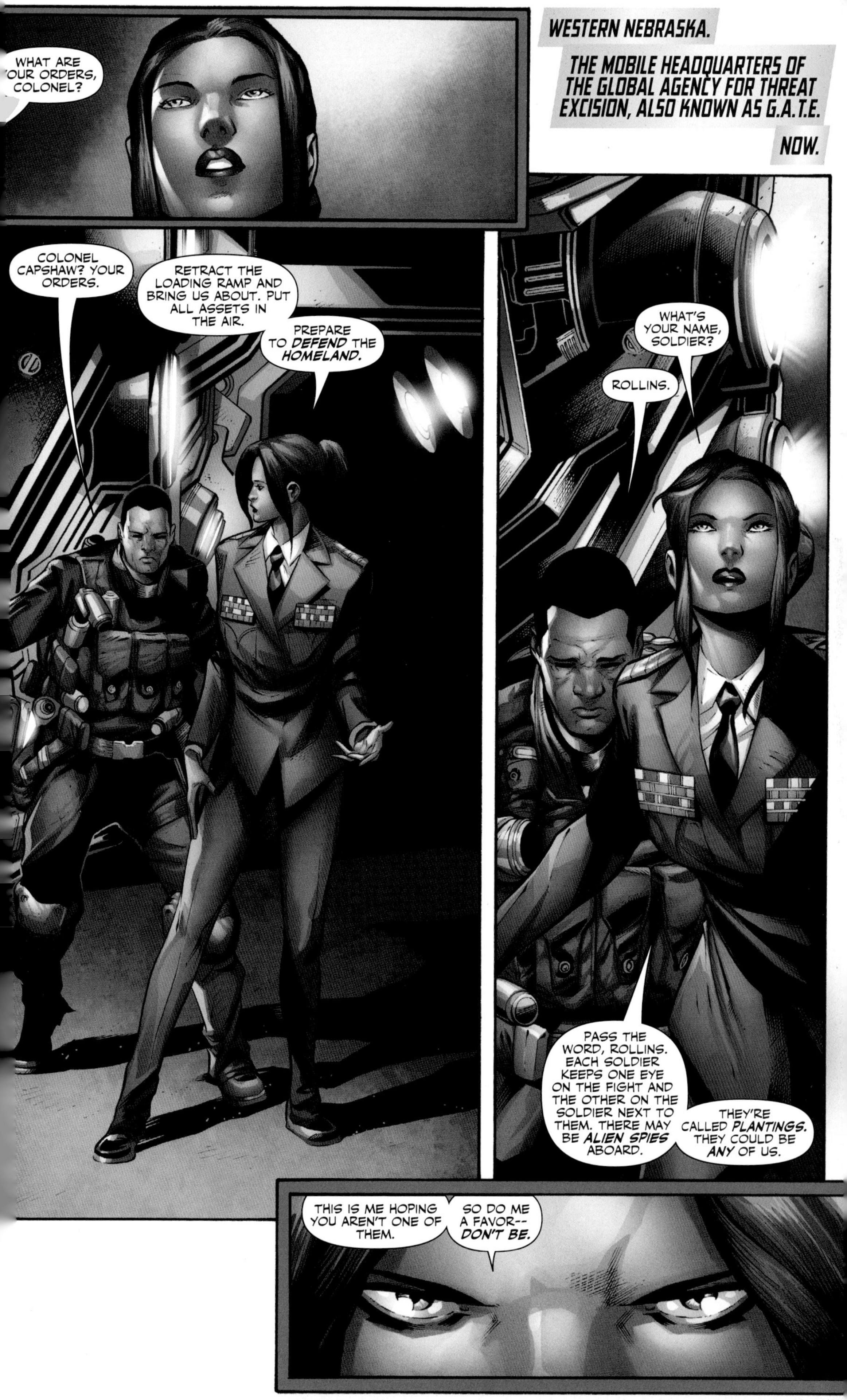

WESTERN NEBRASKA.
THE MOBILE HEADQUARTERS OF THE GLOBAL AGENCY FOR THREAT EXCISION, ALSO KNOWN AS G.A.T.E.
NOW.
WHAT ARE YOUR ORDERS, COLONEL?
COLONEL CAPSHAW? YOUR ORDERS.
RETRACT THE LOADING RAMP AND BRING US ABOUT. PUT ALL ASSETS IN THE AIR.
PREPARE TO DEFEND THE HOMELAND.
WHAT'S YOUR NAME, SOLDIER?
ROLLINS.
PASS THE WORD, ROLLINS. EACH SOLDIER KEEPS ONE EYE ON THE FIGHT AND THE OTHER ON THE SOLDIER NEXT TO THEM. THERE MAY BE ALIEN SPIES ABOARD.
THEY'RE CALLED PLANTINGS. THEY COULD BE ANY OF US.
THIS IS ME HOPING YOU AREN'T ONE OF THEM.
SO DO ME A FAVOR-- DON'T BE.

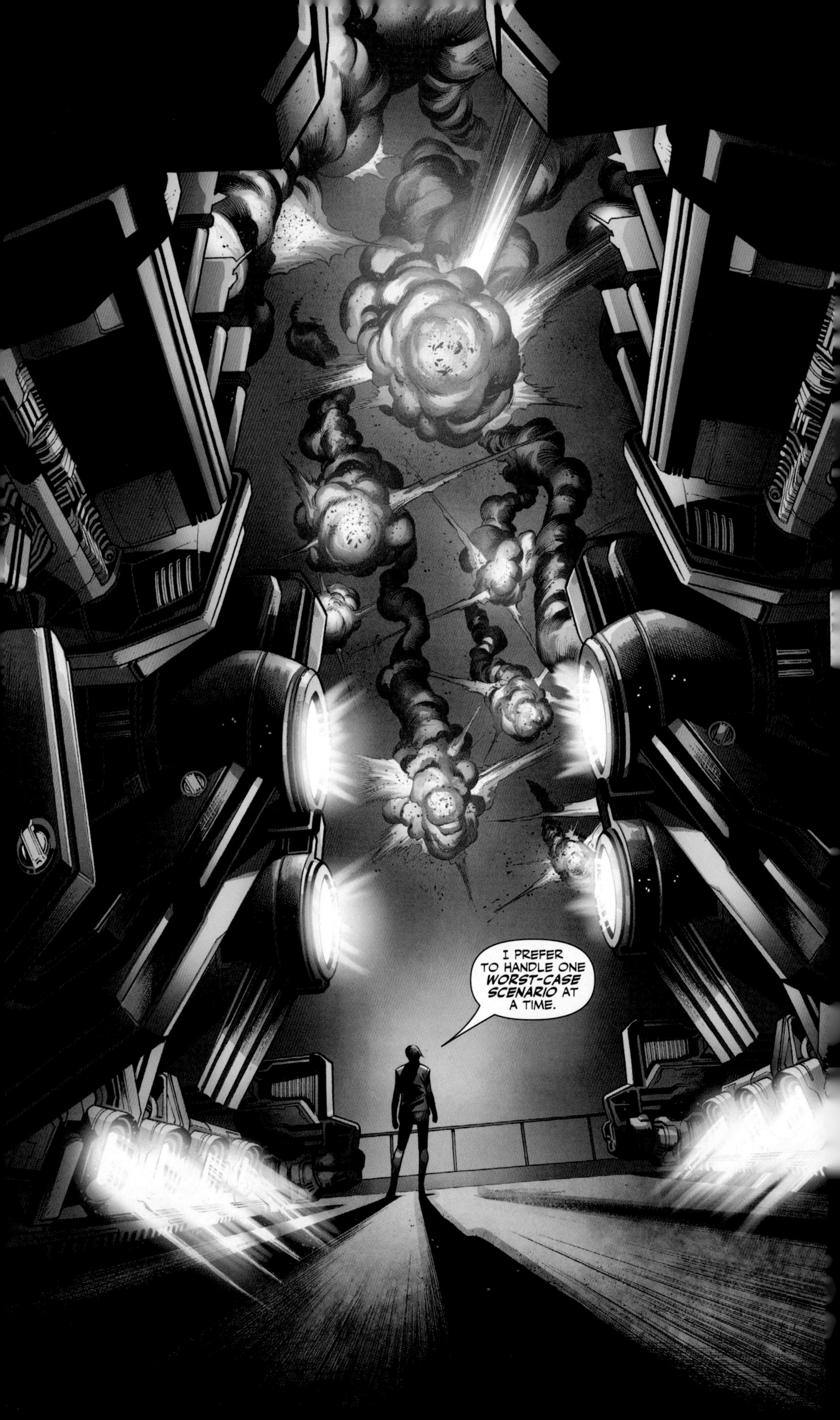
I PREFER TO HANDLE ONE *WORST-CASE SCENARIO* AT A TIME.

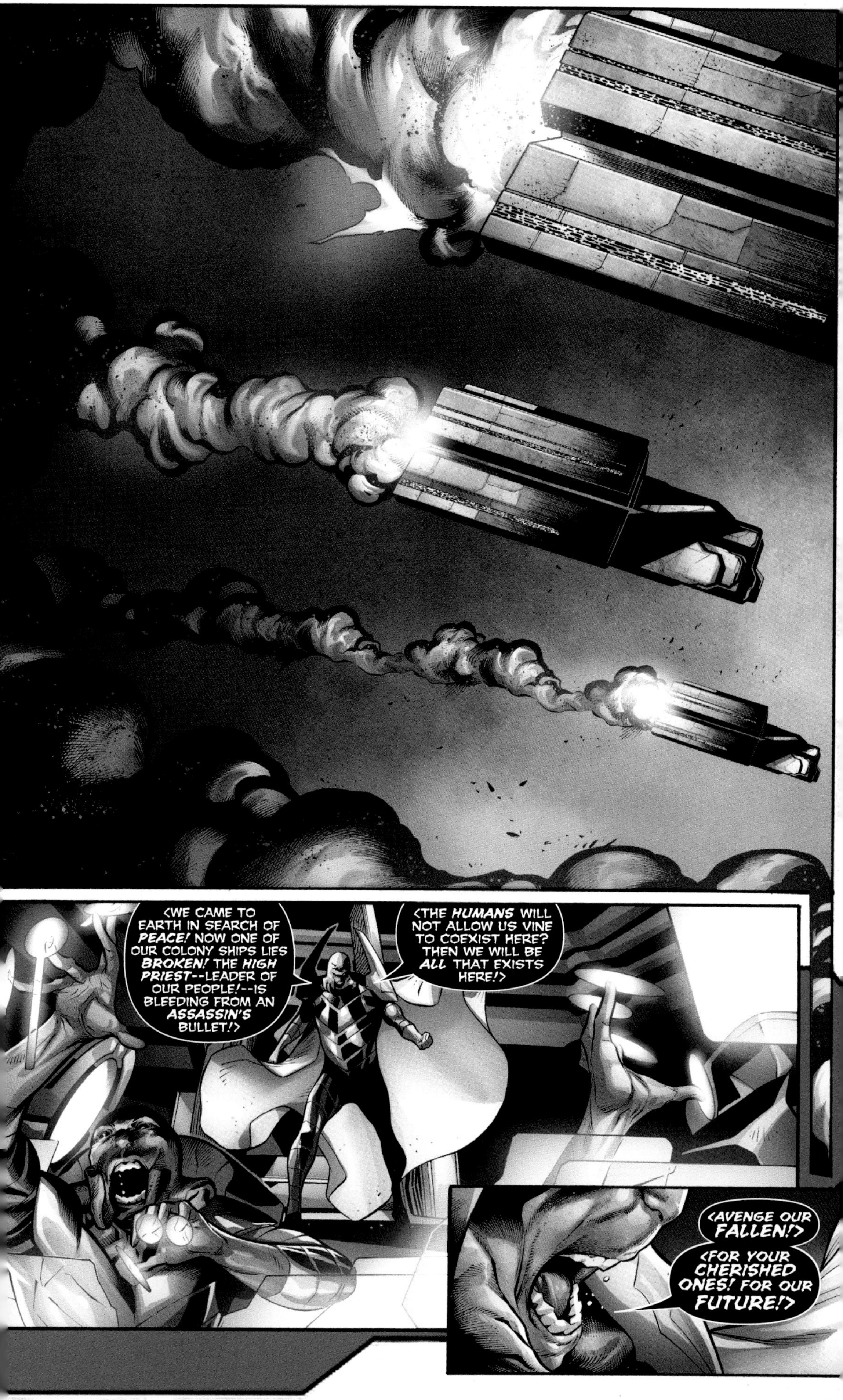
<WE CAME TO EARTH IN SEARCH OF PEACE! NOW ONE OF OUR COLONY SHIPS LIES BROKEN! THE HIGH PRIEST--LEADER OF OUR PEOPLE!--IS BLEEDING FROM AN ASSASSIN'S BULLET!>
<THE HUMANS WILL NOT ALLOW US VINE TO COEXIST HERE? THEN WE WILL BE ALL THAT EXISTS HERE!>
<AVENGE OUR FALLEN!>
<FOR YOUR CHERISHED ONES! FOR OUR FUTURE!>

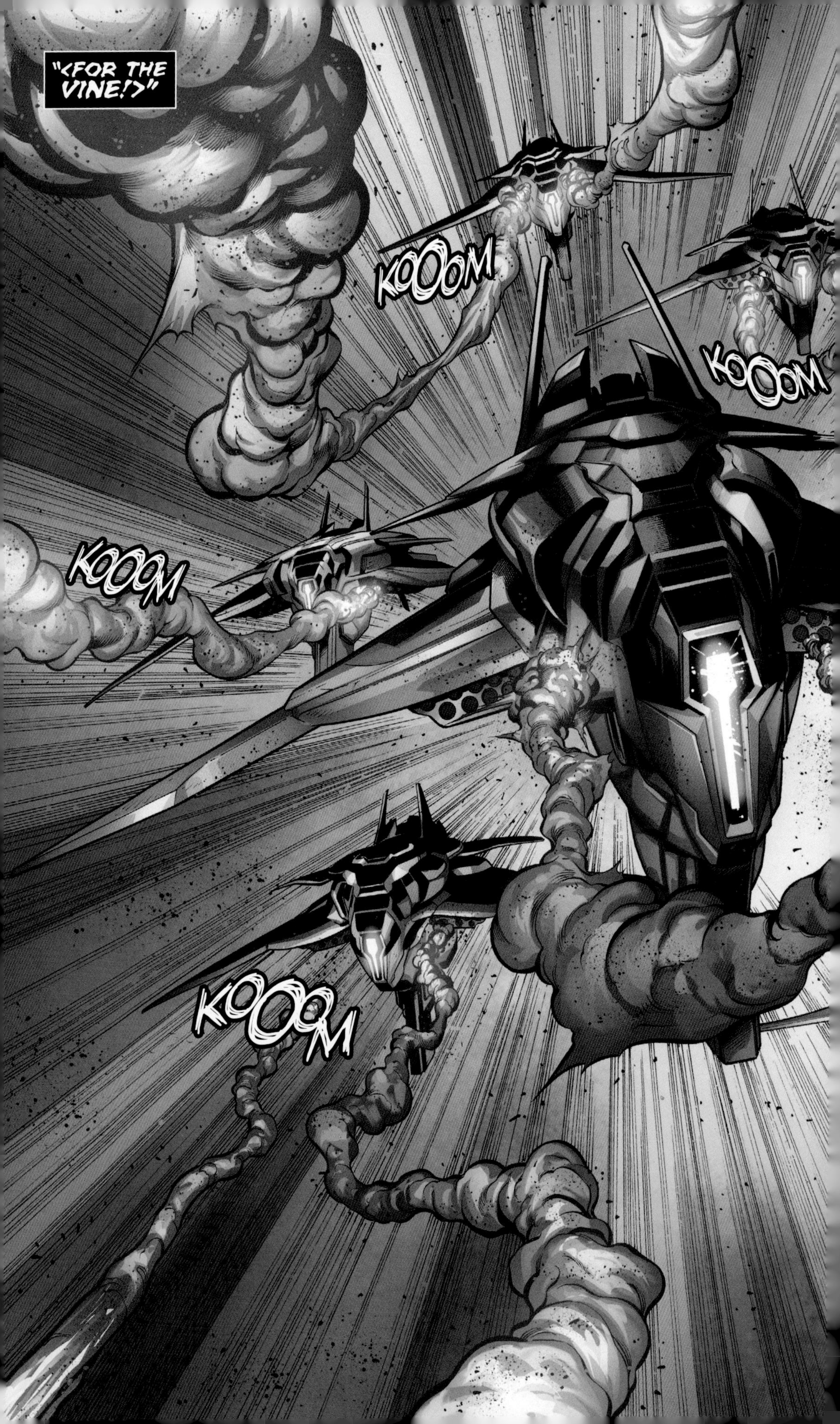
"<FOR THE VINE!>"
KOOOM
KOOOM
KOOOM
KOOOM

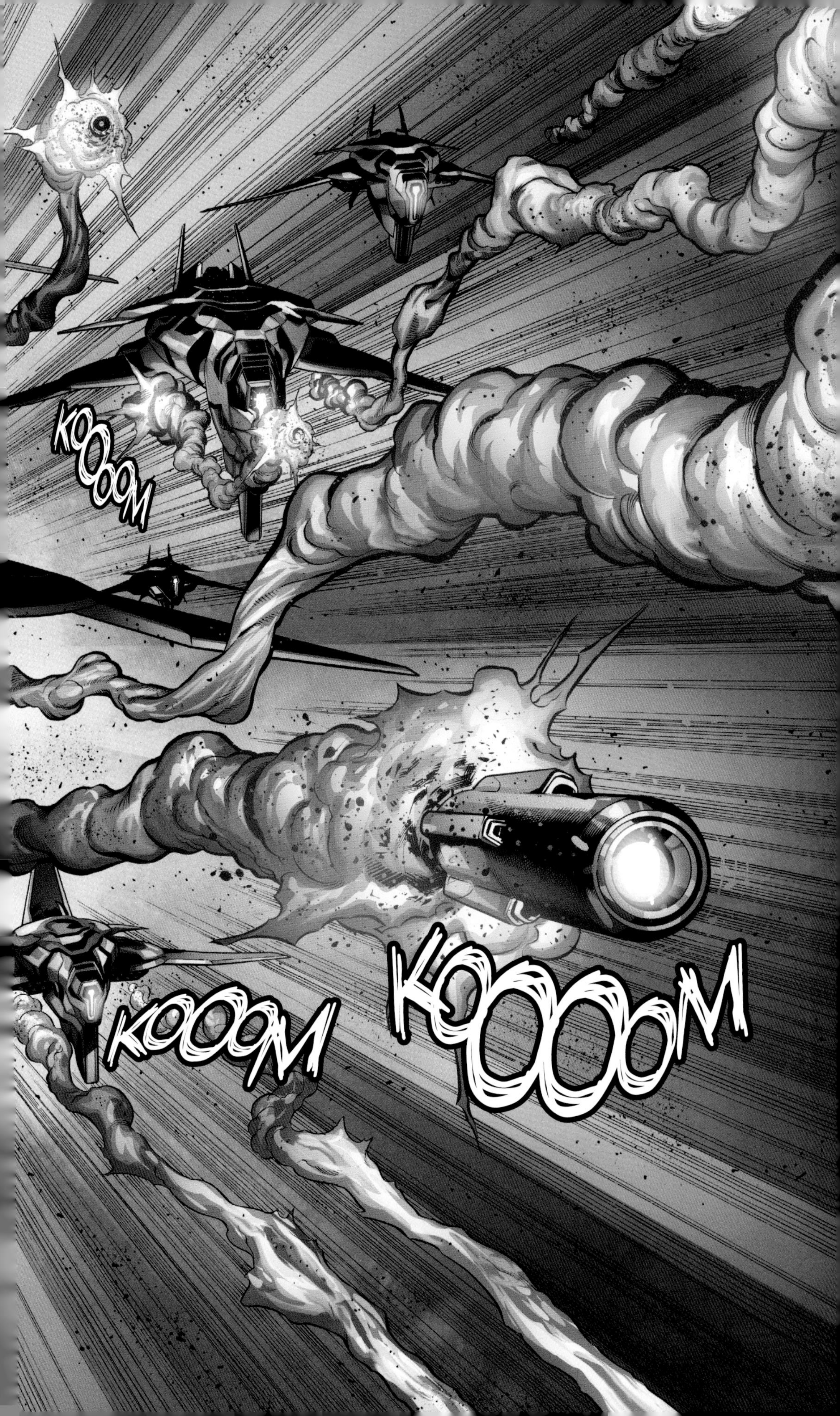
KOOOOM
KOOOM
KOOOOOM

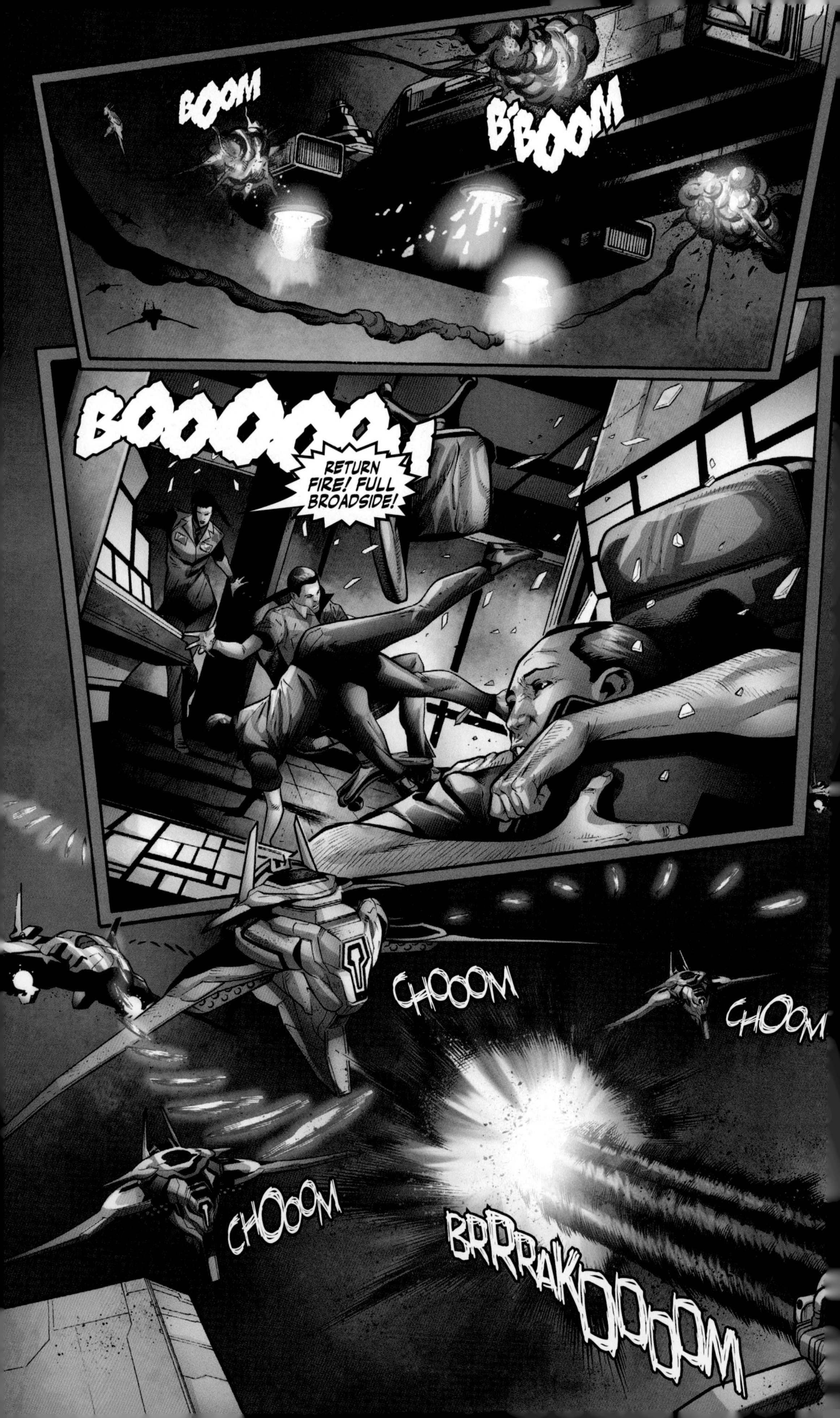
BOOM
B'BOOM
BOOOOOM
RETURN FIRE! FULL BROADSIDE!
CHOOOM
CHOOM
CHOOOM
BRRRAKOOOOM

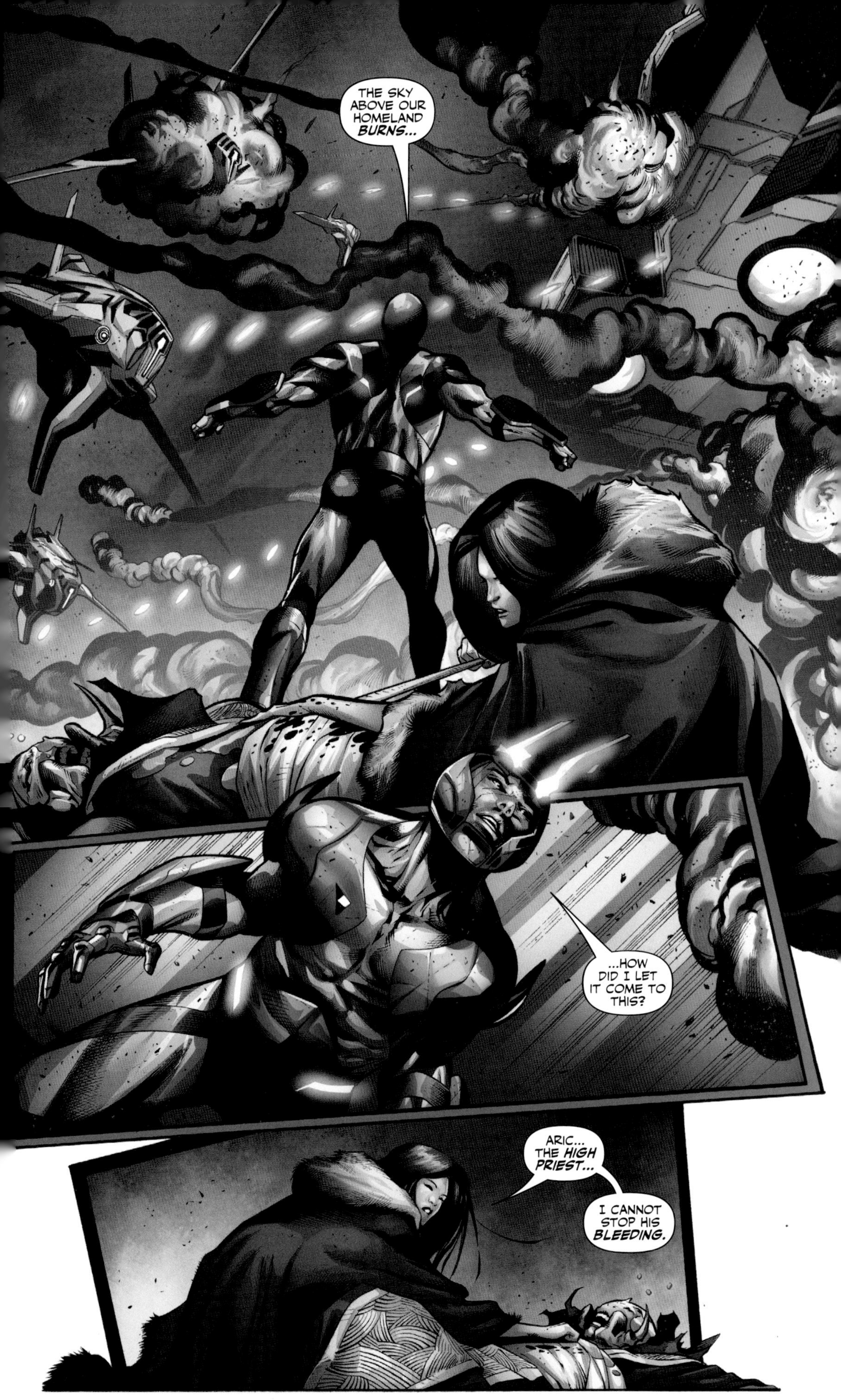
THE SKY ABOVE OUR HOMELAND *BURNS*...
...HOW DID I LET IT COME TO THIS?
ARIC... THE *HIGH PRIEST*...
I CANNOT STOP HIS *BLEEDING*.

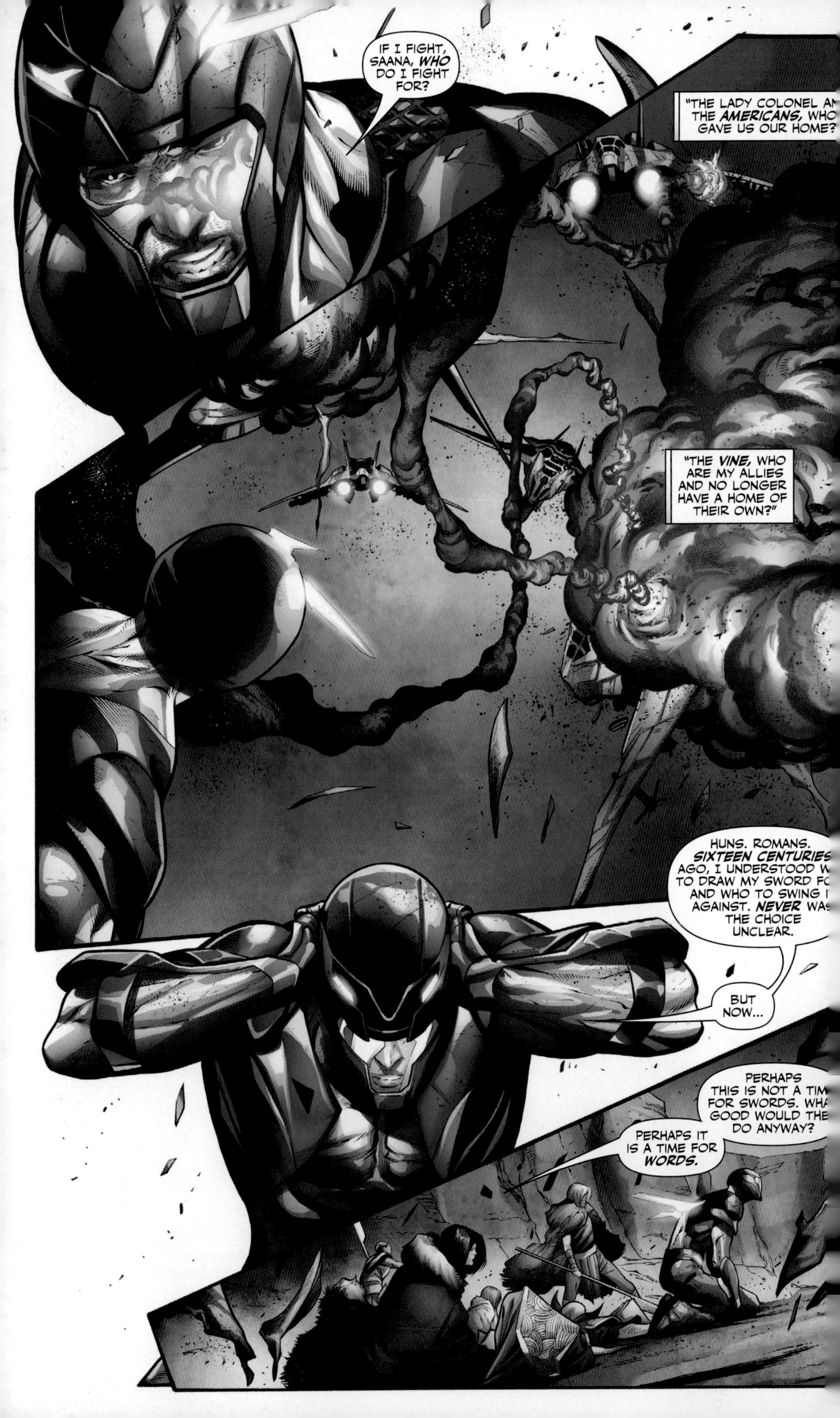
IF I FIGHT, SAANA, *WHO* DO I FIGHT FOR?
"THE LADY COLONEL A THE *AMERICANS,* WHO GAVE US OUR HOME?
"THE *VINE,* WHO ARE MY ALLIES AND NO LONGER HAVE A HOME OF THEIR OWN?"
HUNS. ROMANS. *SIXTEEN CENTURIES* AGO, I UNDERSTOOD TO DRAW MY SWORD FO AND WHO TO SWING AGAINST. *NEVER* WA THE CHOICE UNCLEAR.
BUT NOW...
PERHAPS THIS IS NOT A TIM FOR SWORDS. WHA GOOD WOULD THE DO ANYWAY?
PERHAPS IT IS A TIME FOR *WORDS.*

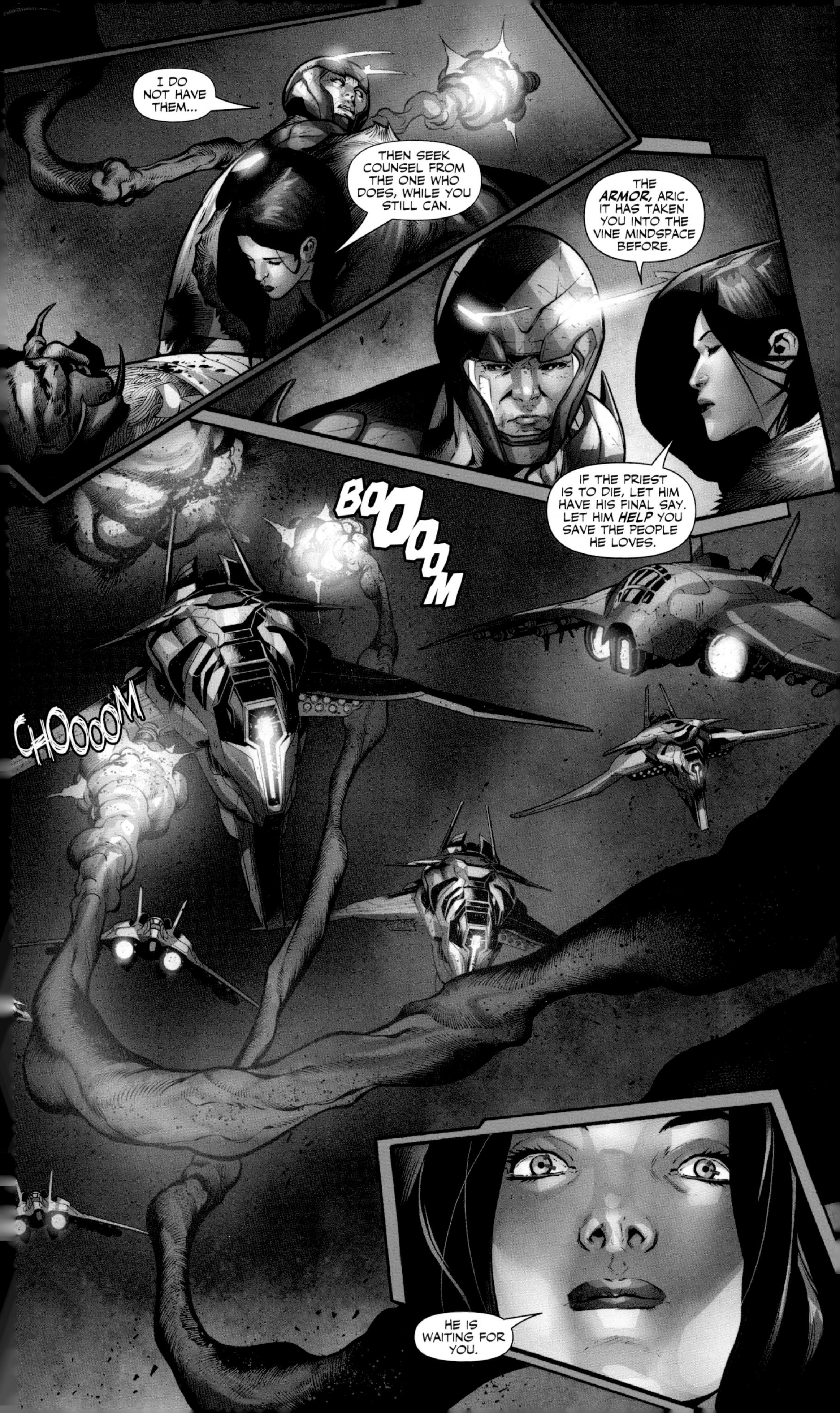
I DO NOT HAVE THEM...
THEN SEEK COUNSEL FROM THE ONE WHO DOES, WHILE YOU STILL CAN.
THE ARMOR, ARIC. IT HAS TAKEN YOU INTO THE VINE MINDSPACE BEFORE.
IF THE PRIEST IS TO DIE, LET HIM HAVE HIS FINAL SAY. LET HIM HELP YOU SAVE THE PEOPLE HE LOVES.
BOOOOOM
CHOOOOOM
HE IS WAITING FOR YOU.

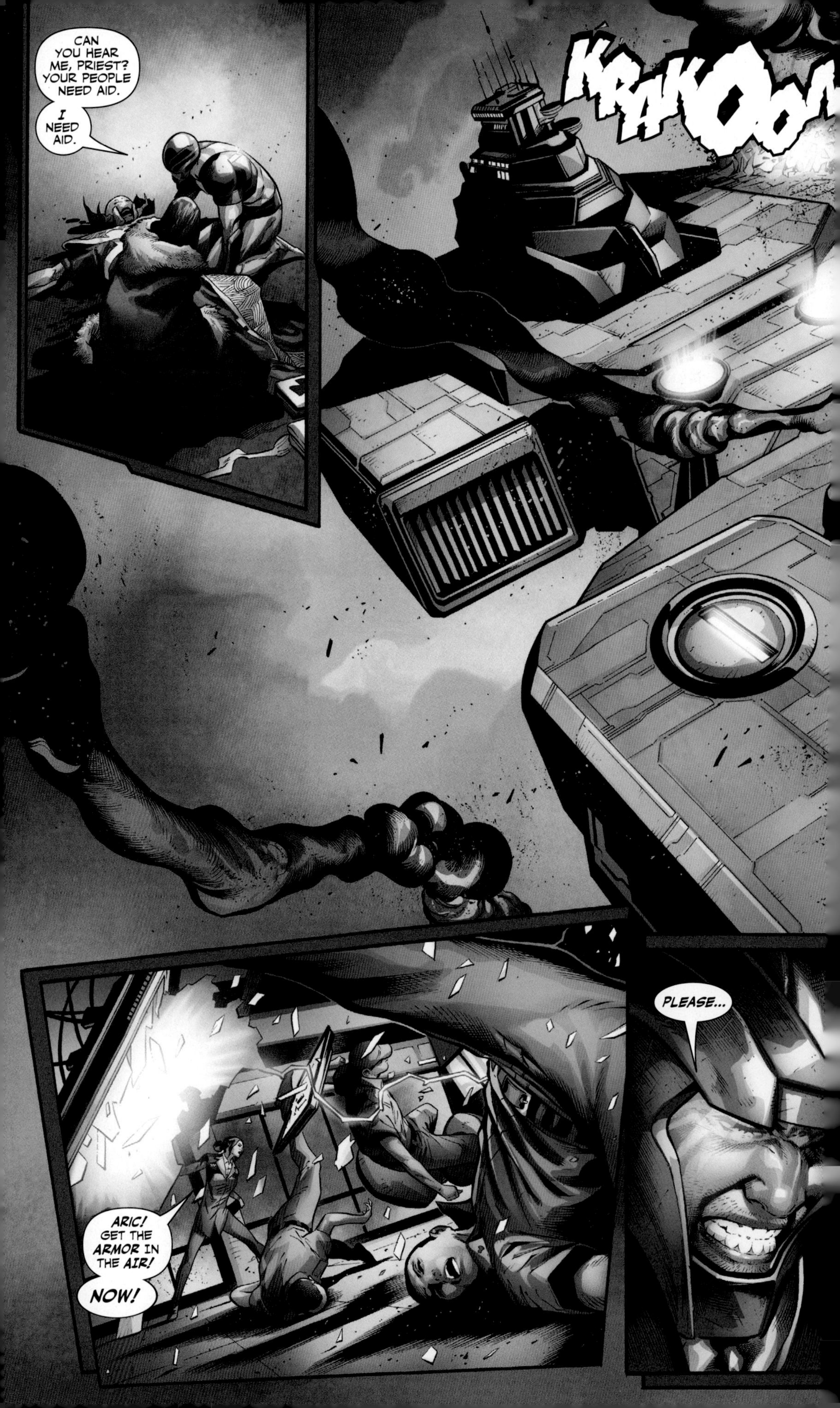
CAN YOU HEAR ME, PRIEST? YOUR PEOPLE NEED AID.
I NEED AID.
KRAKOOM
ARIC! GET THE ARMOR IN THE AIR!
NOW!
PLEASE...

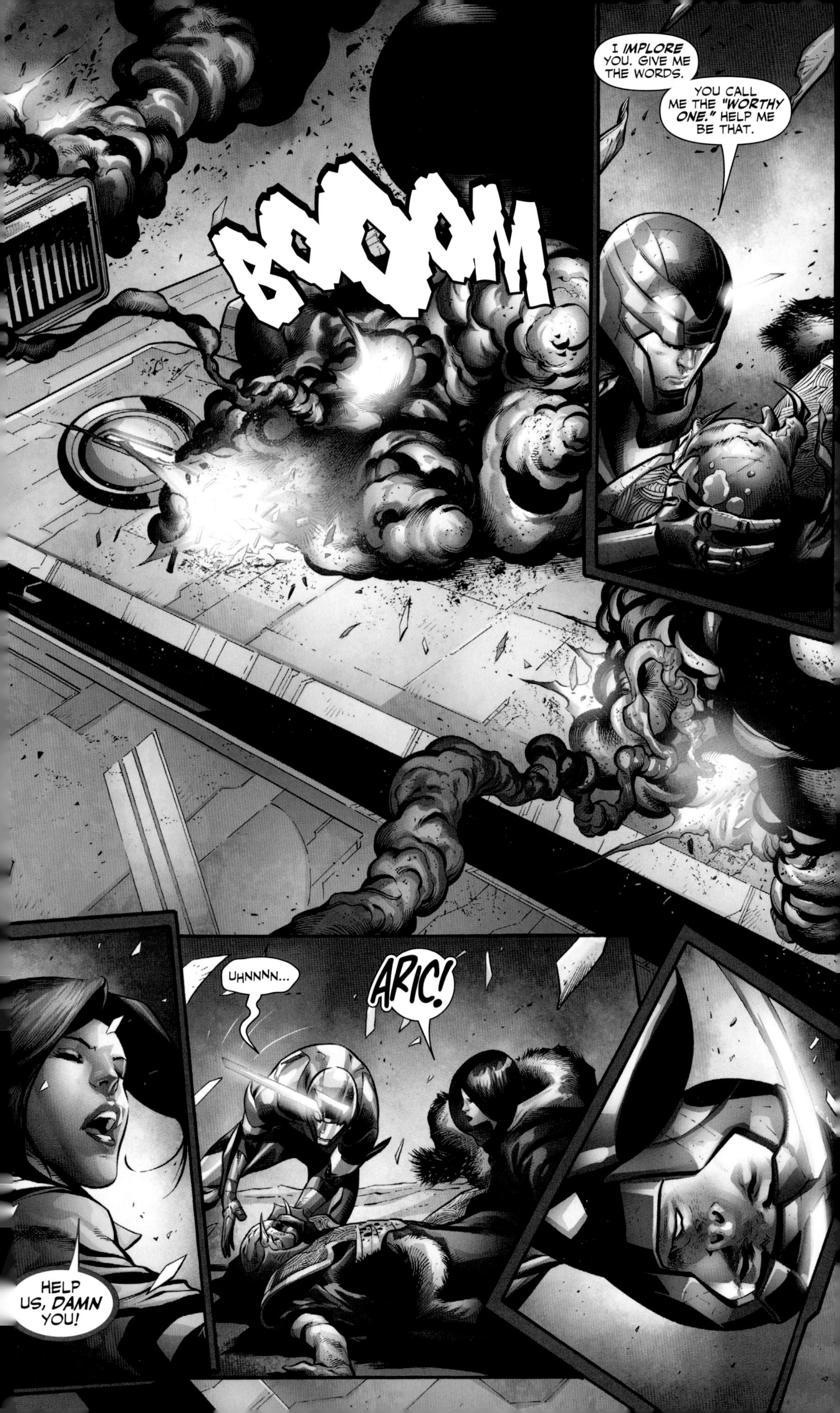

I *IMPLORE* YOU. GIVE ME THE WORDS.
YOU CALL ME THE *"WORTHY ONE."* HELP ME BE THAT.
BOOOM
HELP US, *DAMN* YOU!
UHNNNN...
ARIC!

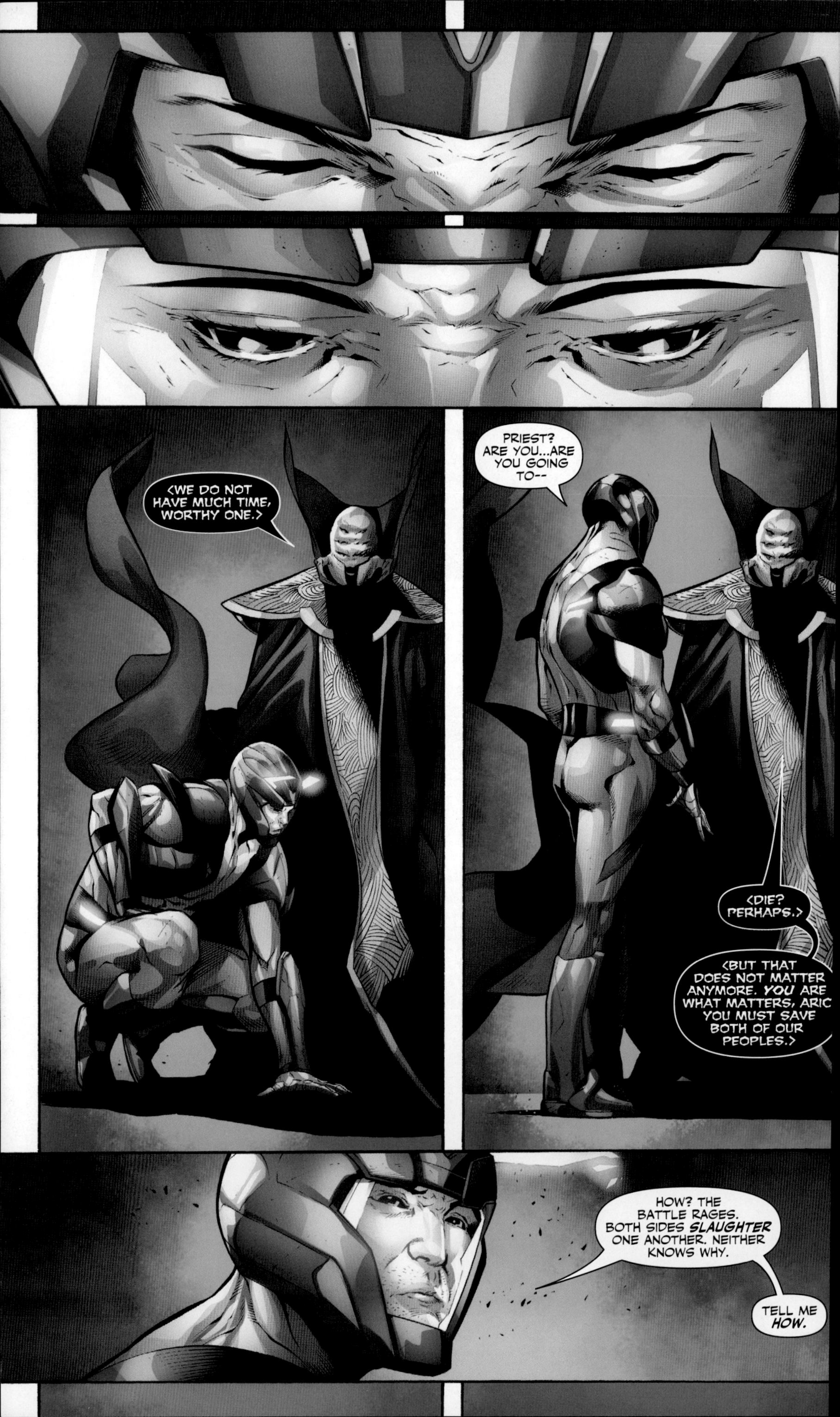

<WE DO NOT HAVE MUCH TIME, WORTHY ONE.>
PRIEST? ARE YOU...ARE YOU GOING TO--
<DIE? PERHAPS.>
<BUT THAT DOES NOT MATTER ANYMORE. *YOU* ARE WHAT MATTERS, ARIC. YOU MUST SAVE BOTH OF OUR PEOPLES.>
HOW? THE BATTLE RAGES. BOTH SIDES *SLAUGHTER* ONE ANOTHER. NEITHER KNOWS WHY.
TELL ME *HOW*.

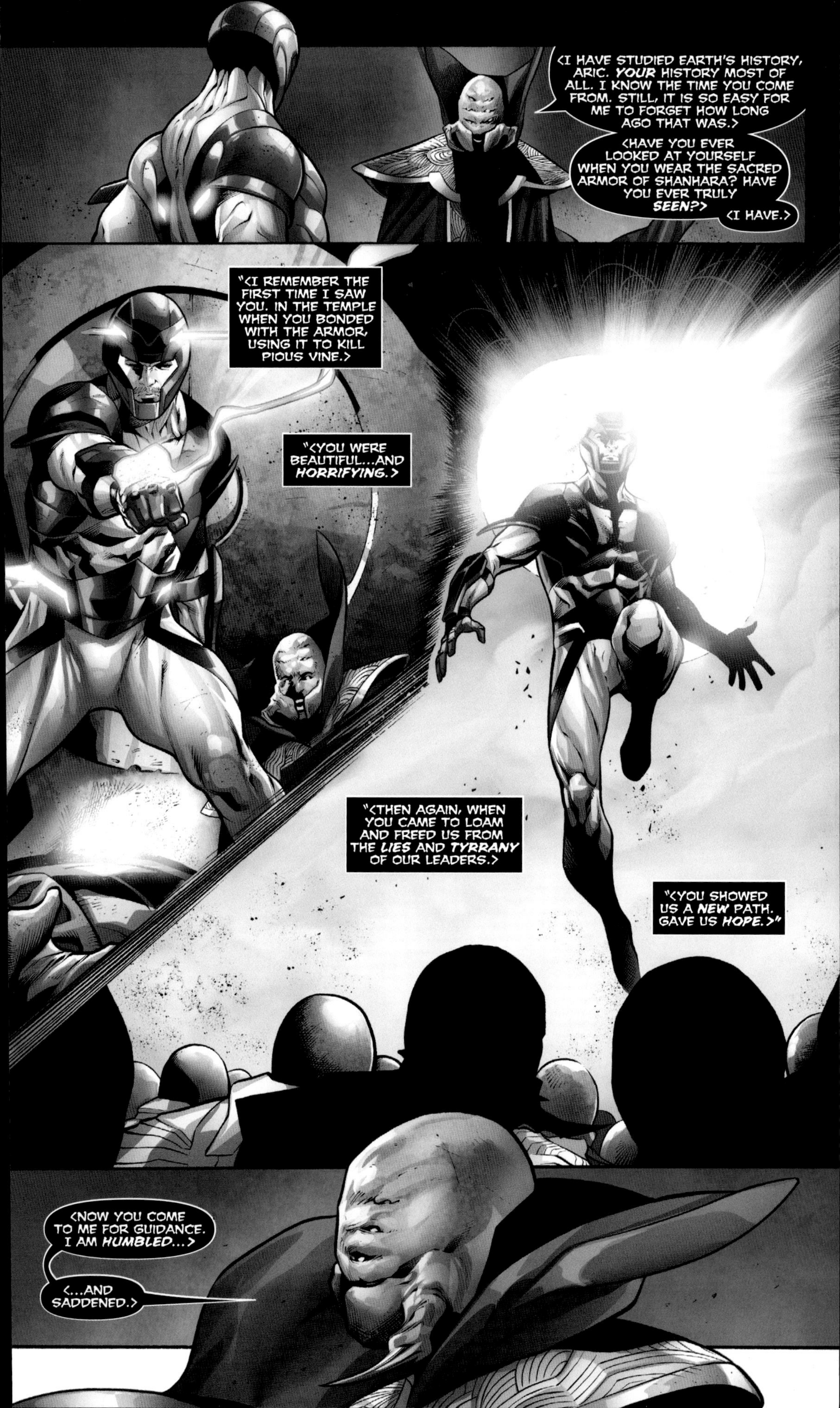

<I HAVE STUDIED EARTH'S HISTORY, ARIC. YOUR HISTORY MOST OF ALL. I KNOW THE TIME YOU COME FROM. STILL, IT IS SO EASY FOR ME TO FORGET HOW LONG AGO THAT WAS.>
<HAVE YOU EVER LOOKED AT YOURSELF WHEN YOU WEAR THE SACRED ARMOR OF SHANHARA? HAVE YOU EVER TRULY SEEN?>
<I HAVE.>
"<I REMEMBER THE FIRST TIME I SAW YOU. IN THE TEMPLE WHEN YOU BONDED WITH THE ARMOR, USING IT TO KILL PIOUS VINE.>
"<YOU WERE BEAUTIFUL...AND HORRIFYING.>
"<THEN AGAIN, WHEN YOU CAME TO LOAM AND FREED US FROM THE LIES AND TYRRANY OF OUR LEADERS.>
"<YOU SHOWED US A NEW PATH. GAVE US HOPE.>"
<NOW YOU COME TO ME FOR GUIDANCE. I AM HUMBLED...>
<...AND SADDENED.>

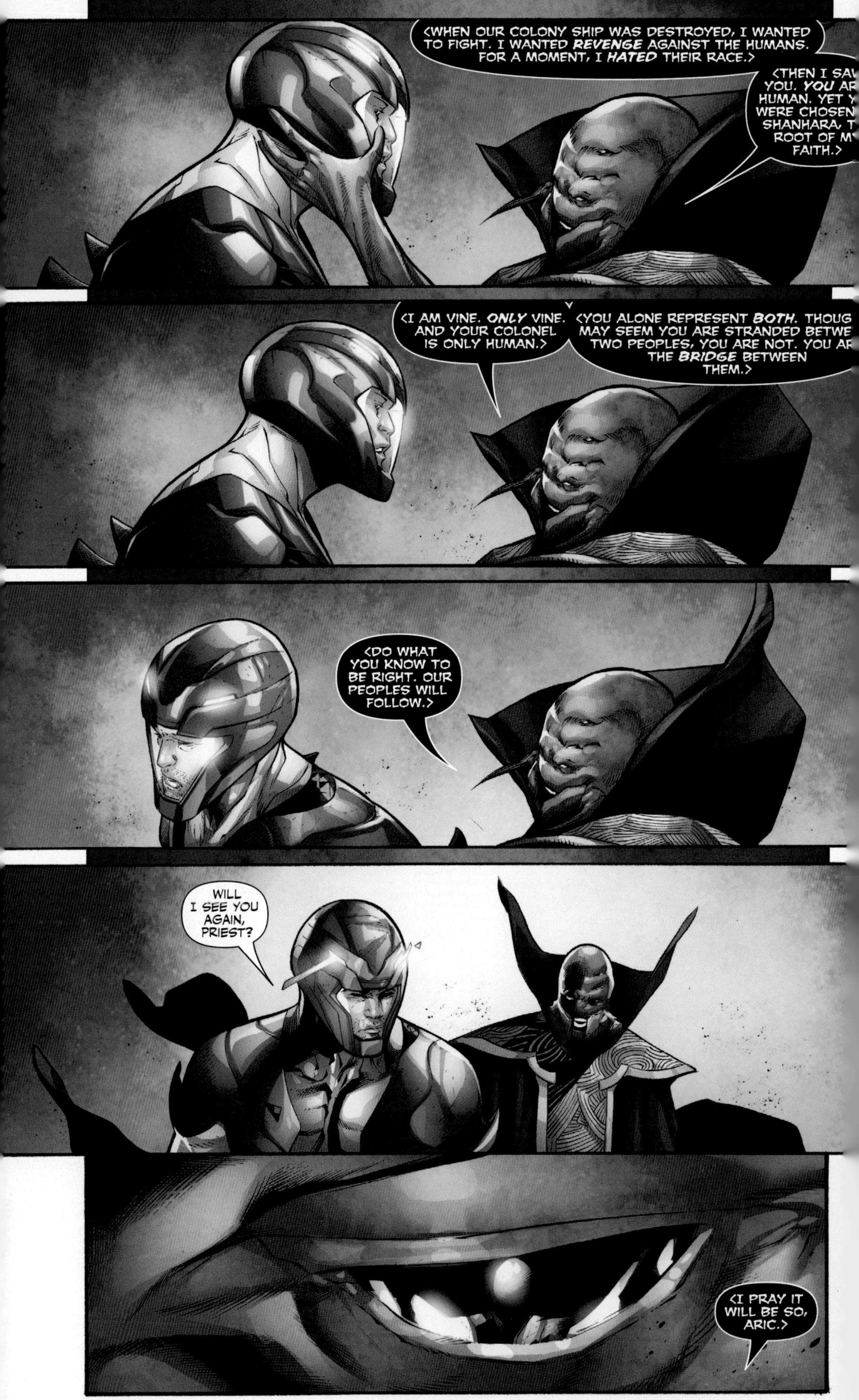
<WHEN OUR COLONY SHIP WAS DESTROYED, I WANTED TO FIGHT. I WANTED *REVENGE* AGAINST THE HUMANS. FOR A MOMENT, I *HATED* THEIR RACE.>
<THEN I SA YOU. *YOU* AR HUMAN. YET Y WERE CHOSEN SHANHARA, T ROOT OF M FAITH.>
<I AM VINE. *ONLY* VINE. AND YOUR COLONEL IS ONLY HUMAN.>
<YOU ALONE REPRESENT *BOTH*. THOUG MAY SEEM YOU ARE STRANDED BETWE TWO PEOPLES, YOU ARE NOT. YOU AR THE *BRIDGE* BETWEEN THEM.>
<DO WHAT YOU KNOW TO BE RIGHT. OUR PEOPLES WILL FOLLOW.>
WILL I SEE YOU AGAIN, PRIEST?
<I PRAY IT WILL BE SO, ARIC.>

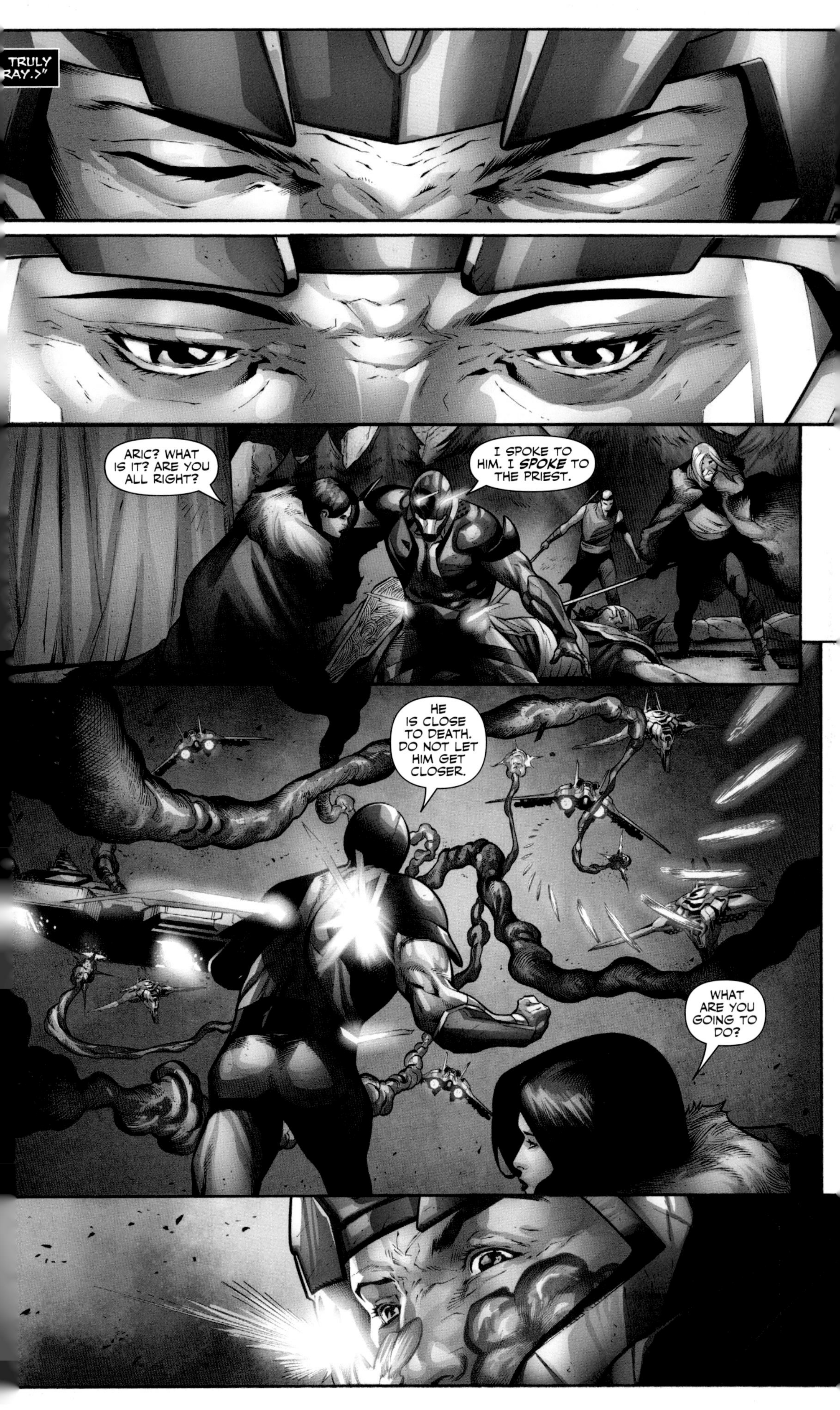
TRULY
RAY.>"
ARIC? WHAT IS IT? ARE YOU ALL RIGHT?
I SPOKE TO HIM. I SPOKE TO THE PRIEST.
HE IS CLOSE TO DEATH. DO NOT LET HIM GET CLOSER.
WHAT ARE YOU GOING TO DO?

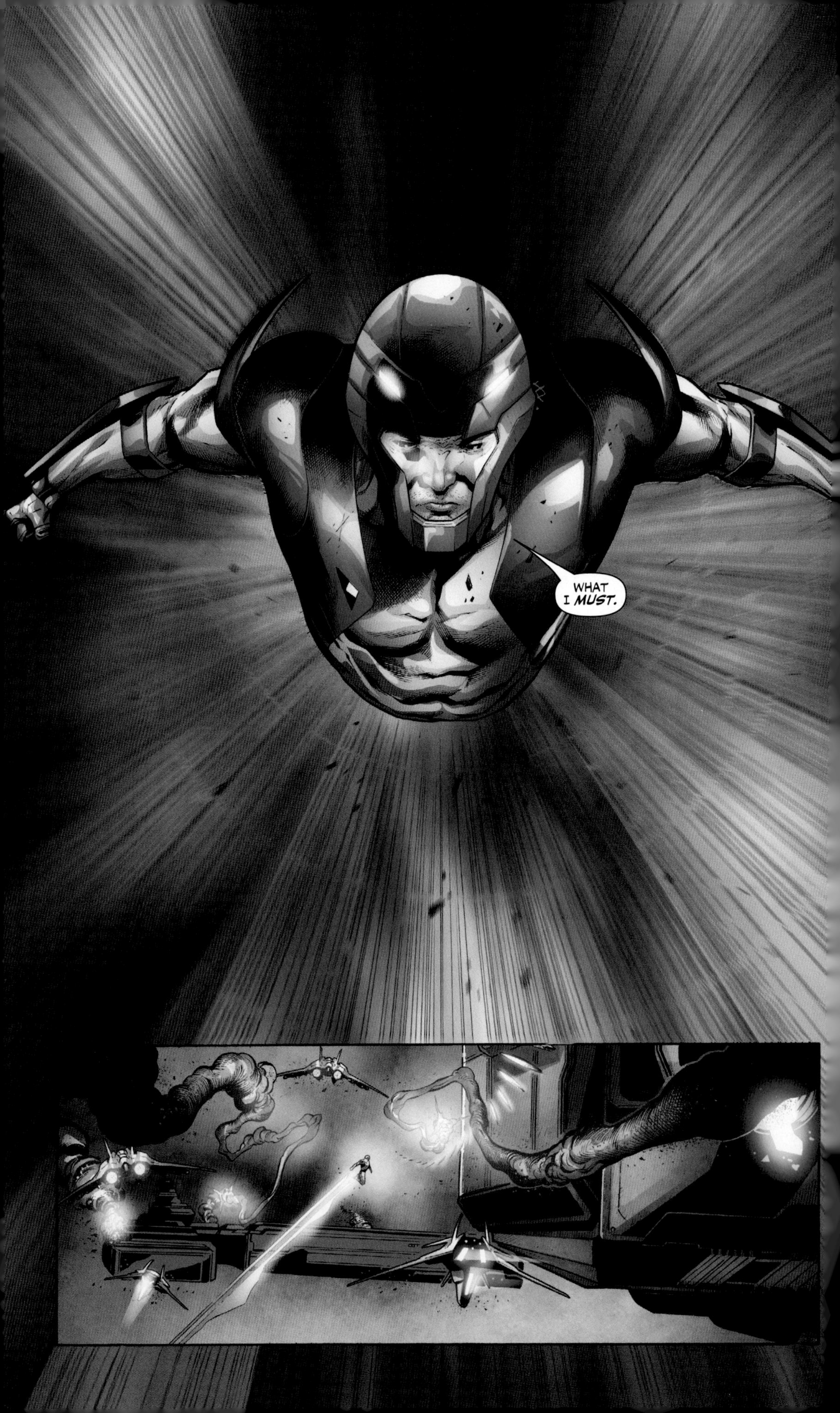
WHAT I MUST.

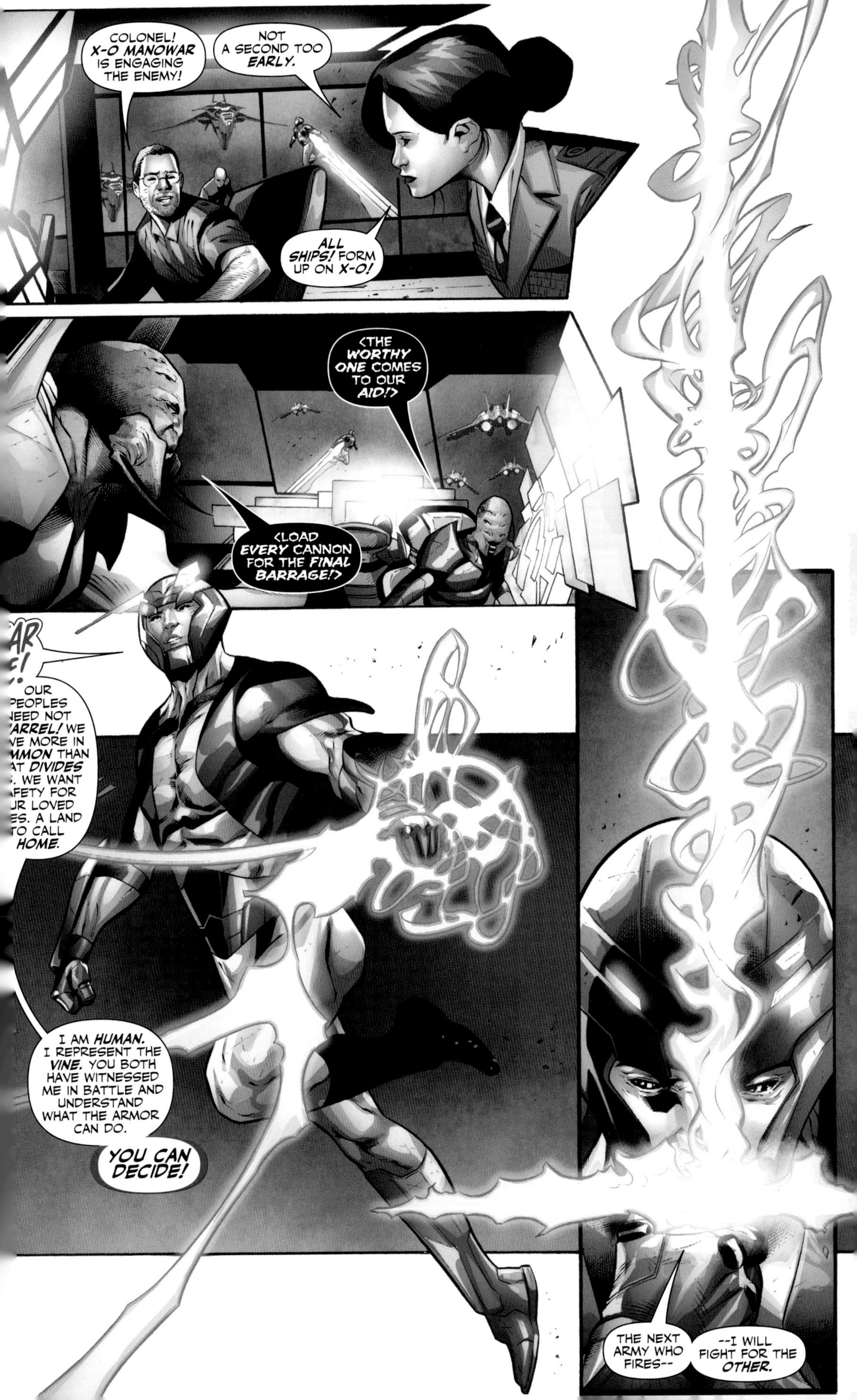
COLONEL! X-O MANOWAR IS ENGAGING THE ENEMY!
NOT A SECOND TOO EARLY.
ALL SHIPS! FORM UP ON X-O!
<THE WORTHY ONE COMES TO OUR AID!>
<LOAD EVERY CANNON FOR THE FINAL BARRAGE!>
OUR PEOPLES NEED NOT ...ARREL! WE ...VE MORE IN ...MMON THAN ...AT DIVIDES ... WE WANT ...AFETY FOR ...UR LOVED ...ES. A LAND TO CALL HOME.
I AM HUMAN. I REPRESENT THE VINE. YOU BOTH HAVE WITNESSED ME IN BATTLE AND UNDERSTAND WHAT THE ARMOR CAN DO.
YOU CAN DECIDE!
THE NEXT ARMY WHO FIRES--
--I WILL FIGHT FOR THE OTHER.

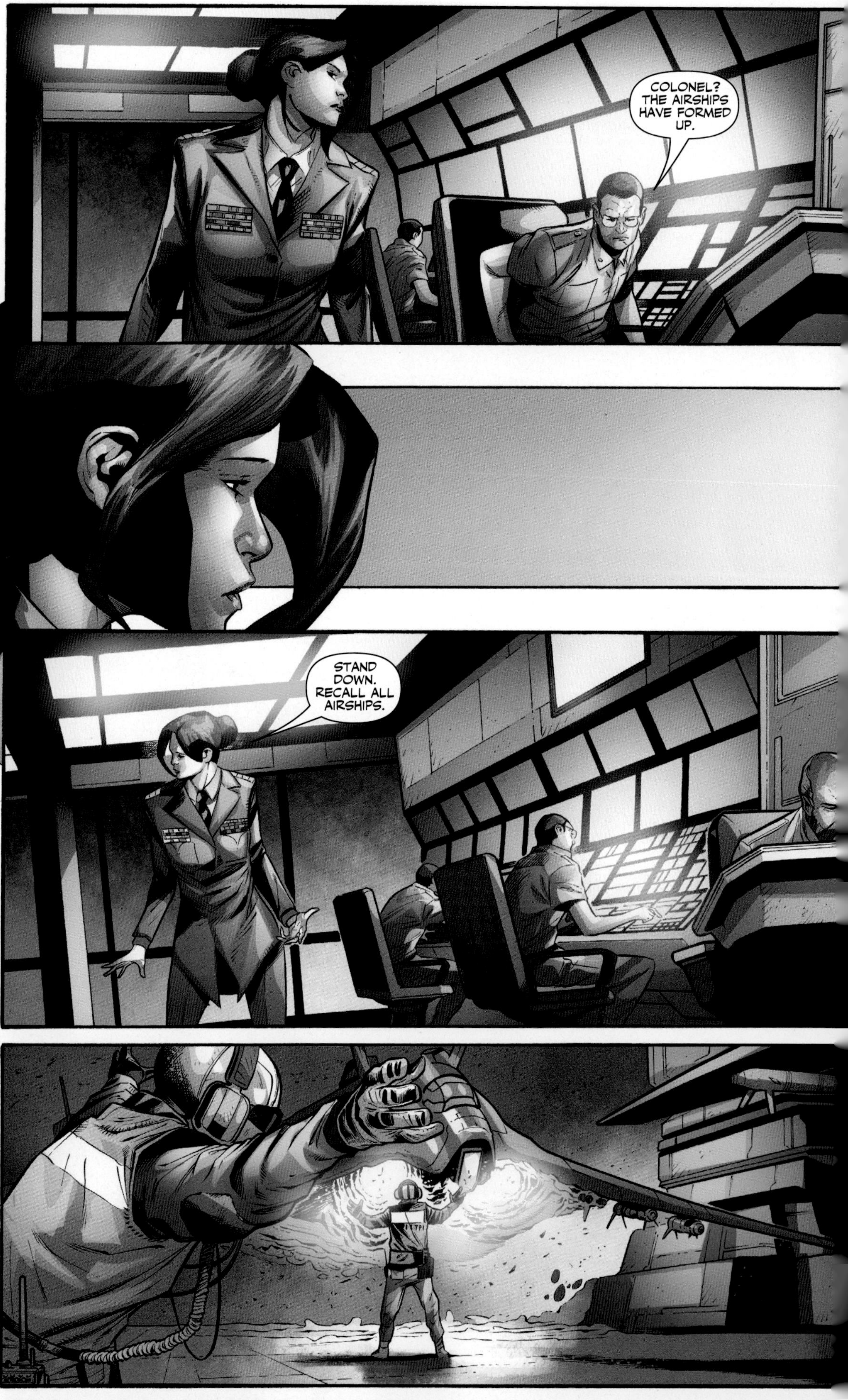
COLONEL? THE AIRSHIPS HAVE FORMED UP.
STAND DOWN. RECALL ALL AIRSHIPS.

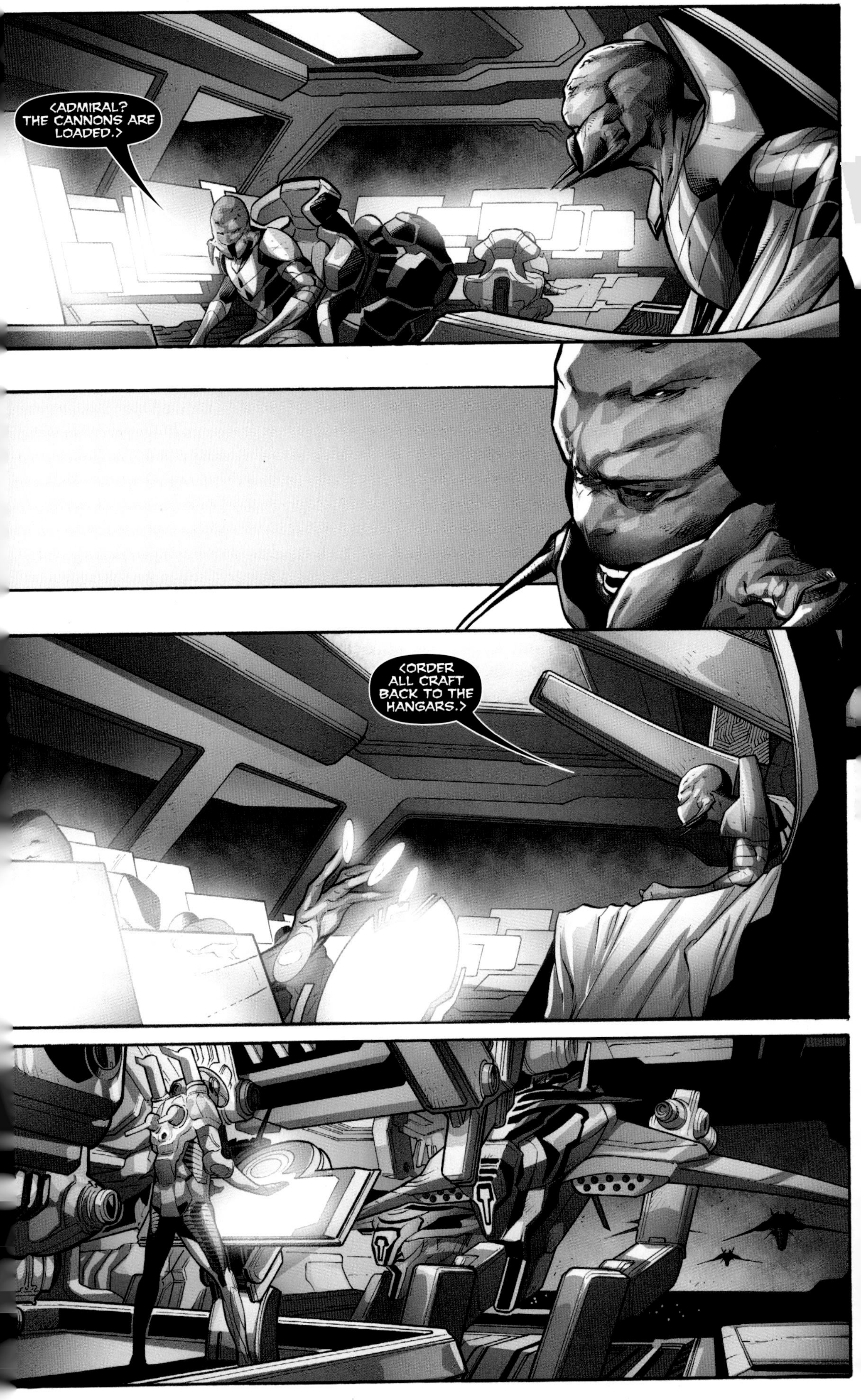
<ADMIRAL? THE CANNONS ARE LOADED.>
<ORDER ALL CRAFT BACK TO THE HANGARS.>

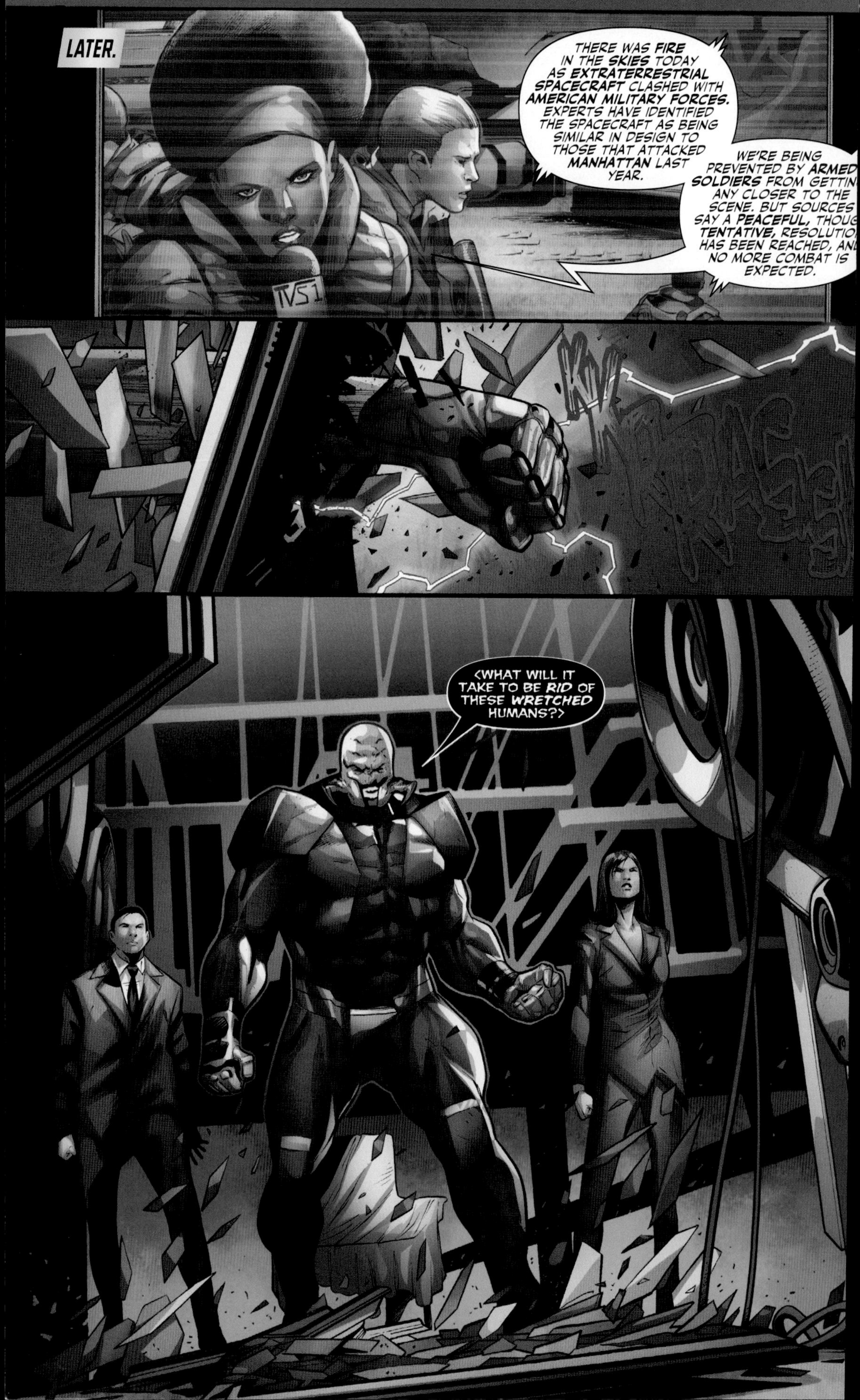
LATER.
THERE WAS FIRE IN THE SKIES TODAY AS EXTRATERRESTRIAL SPACECRAFT CLASHED WITH AMERICAN MILITARY FORCES. EXPERTS HAVE IDENTIFIED THE SPACECRAFT AS BEING SIMILAR IN DESIGN TO THOSE THAT ATTACKED MANHATTAN LAST YEAR.
WE'RE BEING PREVENTED BY ARMED SOLDIERS FROM GETTIN ANY CLOSER TO THE SCENE. BUT SOURCES SAY A PEACEFUL, THOUG TENTATIVE, RESOLUTIO HAS BEEN REACHED, AN NO MORE COMBAT IS EXPECTED.
TVS1
<WHAT WILL IT TAKE TO BE RID OF THESE WRETCHED HUMANS?>

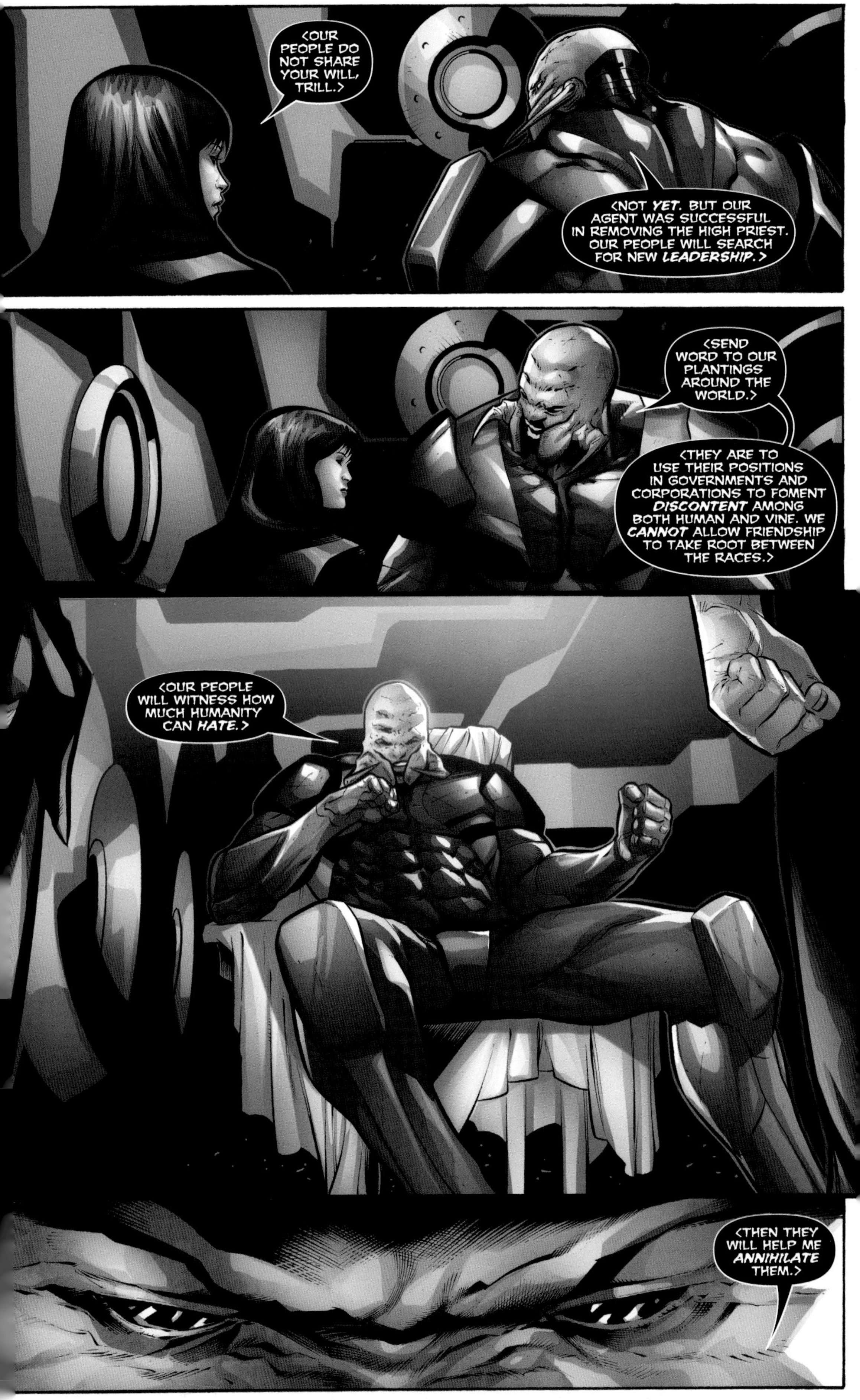
<OUR PEOPLE DO NOT SHARE YOUR WILL, TRILL.>
<NOT *YET*. BUT OUR AGENT WAS SUCCESSFUL IN REMOVING THE HIGH PRIEST. OUR PEOPLE WILL SEARCH FOR NEW *LEADERSHIP*.>
<SEND WORD TO OUR PLANTINGS AROUND THE WORLD.>
<THEY ARE TO USE THEIR POSITIONS IN GOVERNMENTS AND CORPORATIONS TO FOMENT *DISCONTENT* AMONG BOTH HUMAN AND VINE. WE *CANNOT* ALLOW FRIENDSHIP TO TAKE ROOT BETWEEN THE RACES.>
<OUR PEOPLE WILL WITNESS HOW MUCH HUMANITY CAN *HATE*.>
<THEN THEY WILL HELP ME *ANNIHILATE* THEM.>

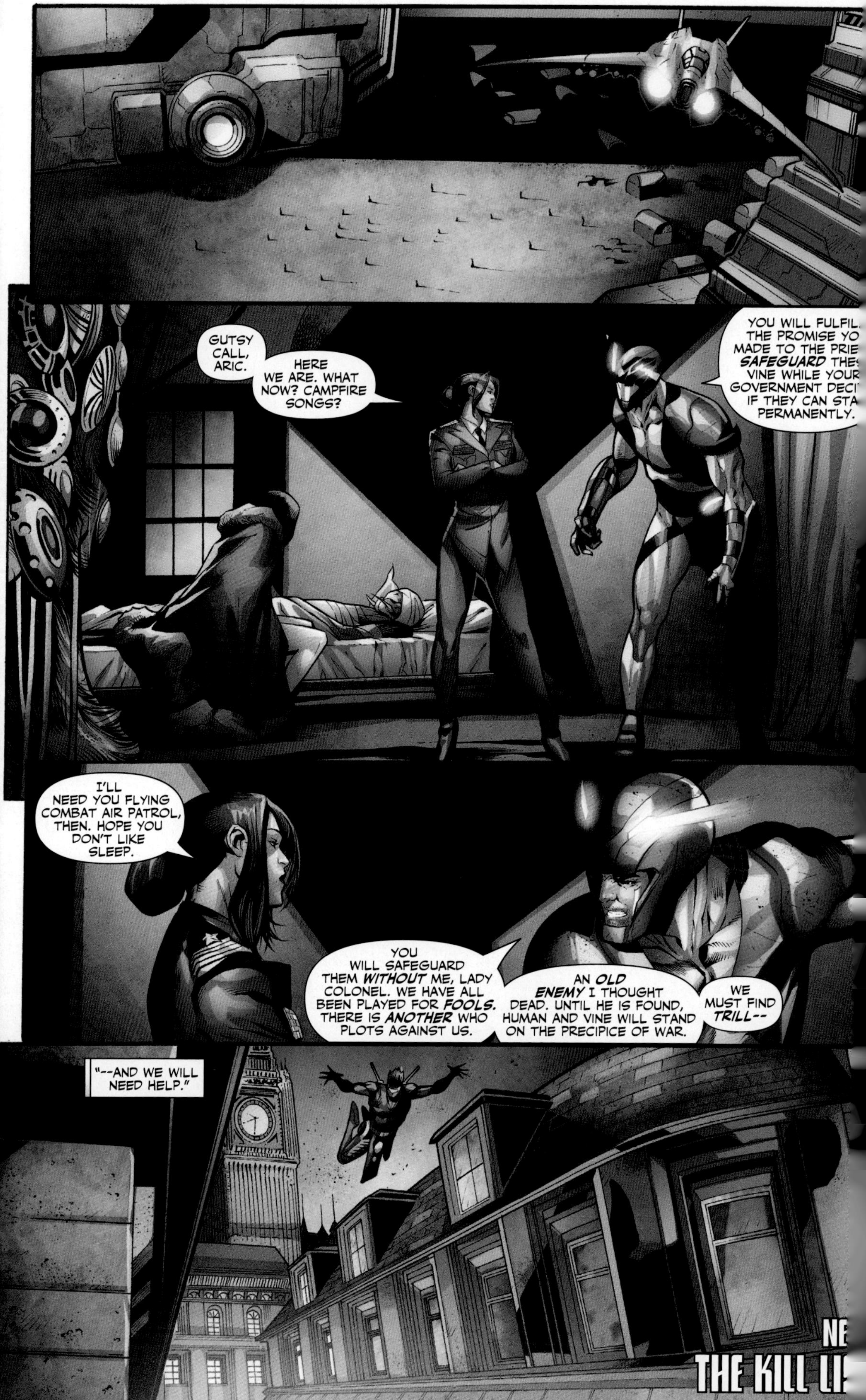

YOU WILL FULFIL THE PROMISE YO MADE TO THE PRIE SAFEGUARD THES VINE WHILE YOUR GOVERNMENT DECI IF THEY CAN STA PERMANENTLY.
GUTSY CALL, ARIC.
HERE WE ARE. WHAT NOW? CAMPFIRE SONGS?
I'LL NEED YOU FLYING COMBAT AIR PATROL, THEN. HOPE YOU DON'T LIKE SLEEP.
YOU WILL SAFEGUARD THEM WITHOUT ME, LADY COLONEL. WE HAVE ALL BEEN PLAYED FOR FOOLS. THERE IS ANOTHER WHO PLOTS AGAINST US.
AN OLD ENEMY I THOUGHT DEAD. UNTIL HE IS FOUND, HUMAN AND VINE WILL STAND ON THE PRECIPICE OF WAR.
WE MUST FIND TRILL--
"--AND WE WILL NEED HELP."
NE
THE KILL LI

GALLERY

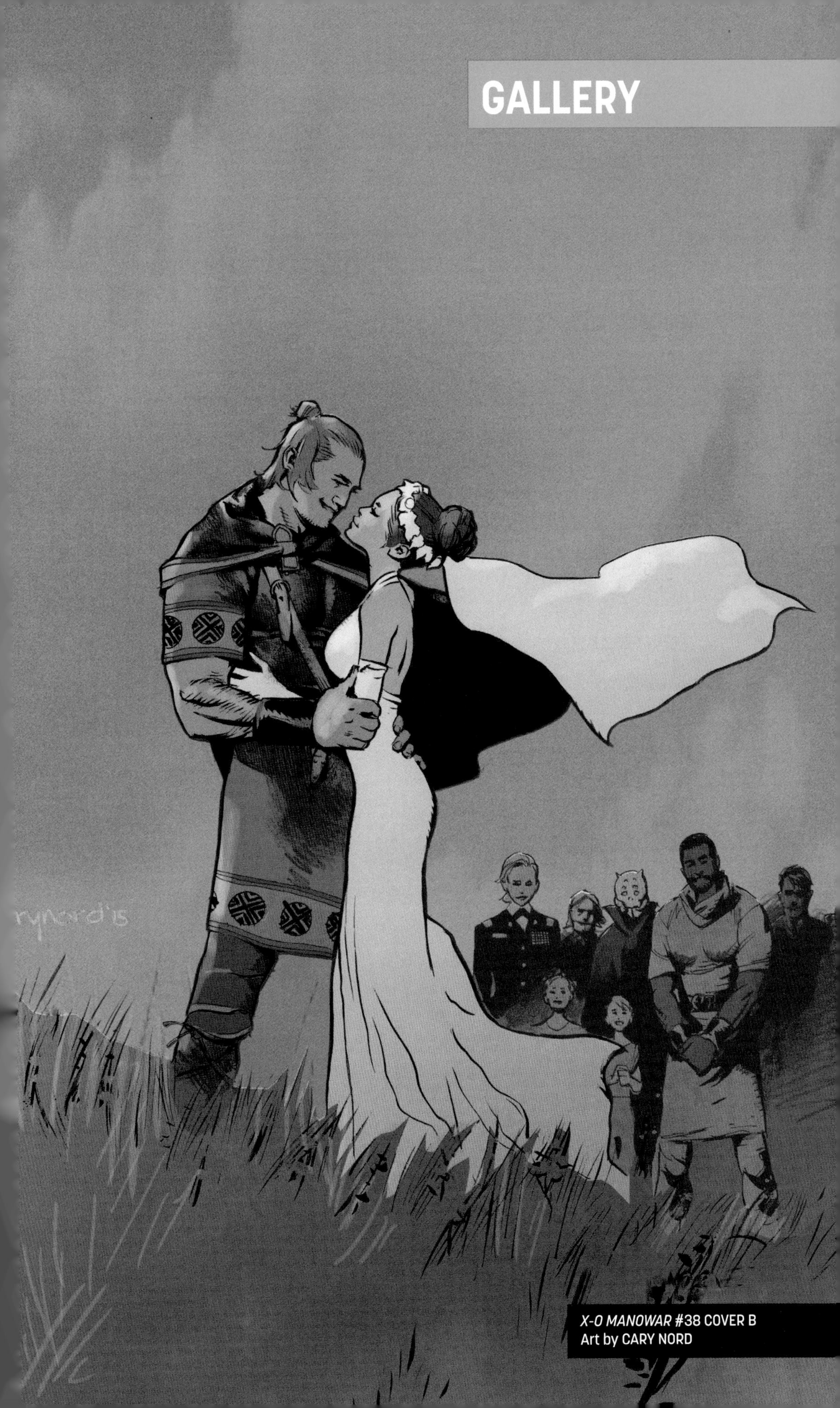

X-O MANOWAR #38 COVER B
Art by CARY NORD

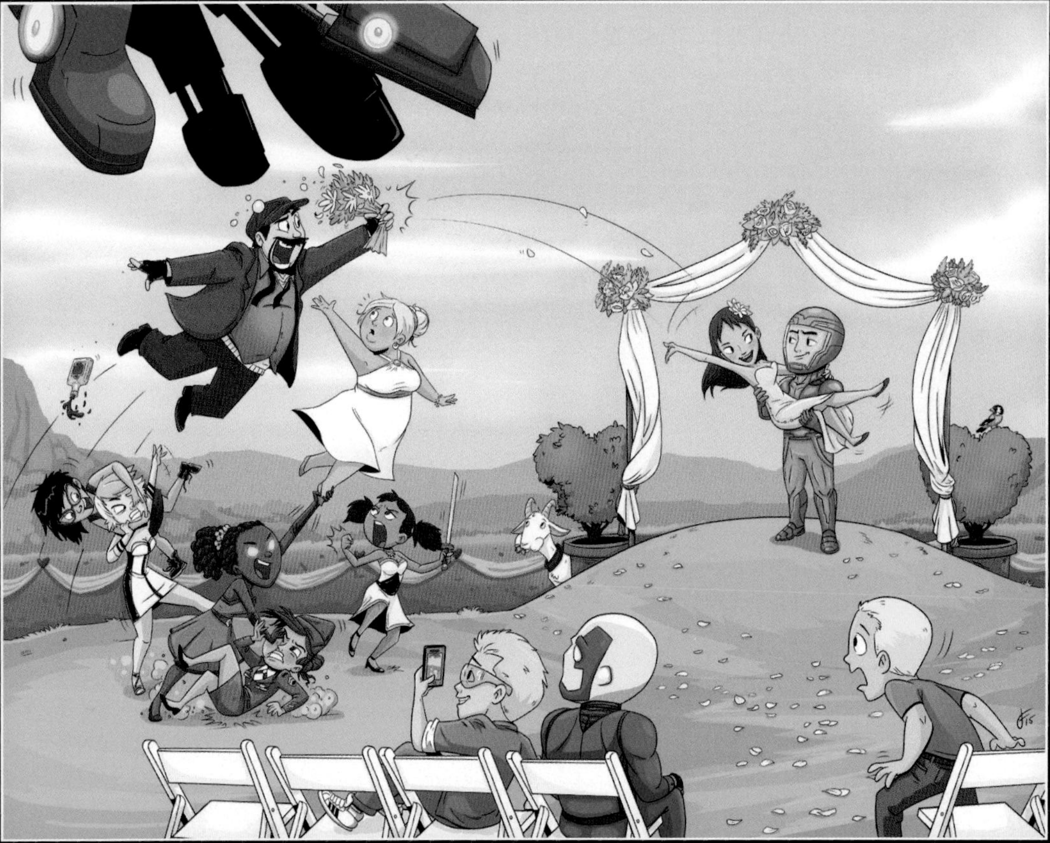

X-O MANOWAR #38
VARIANT WRAPAROUND COVER
Art by JAY FABARES

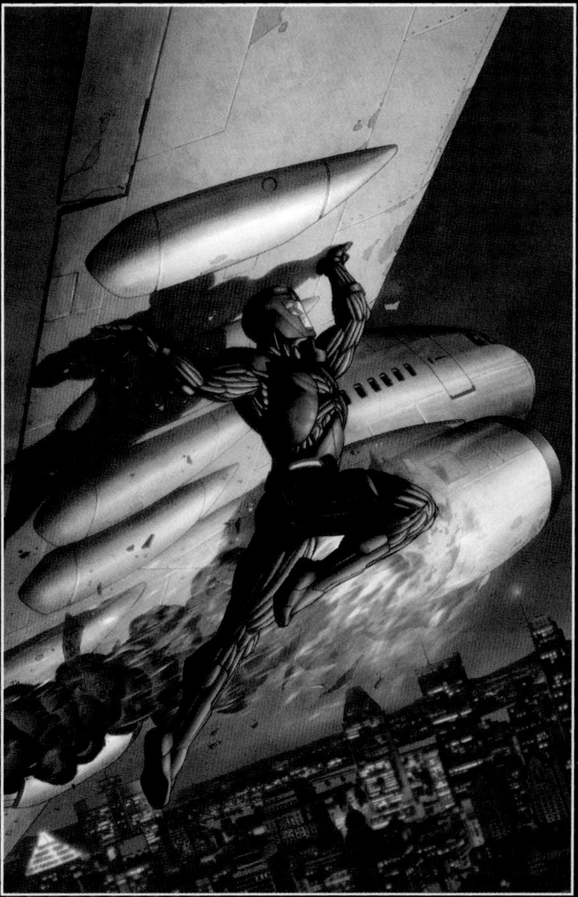

X-O MANOWAR #39 VARIANT COVER
Art by CAFU

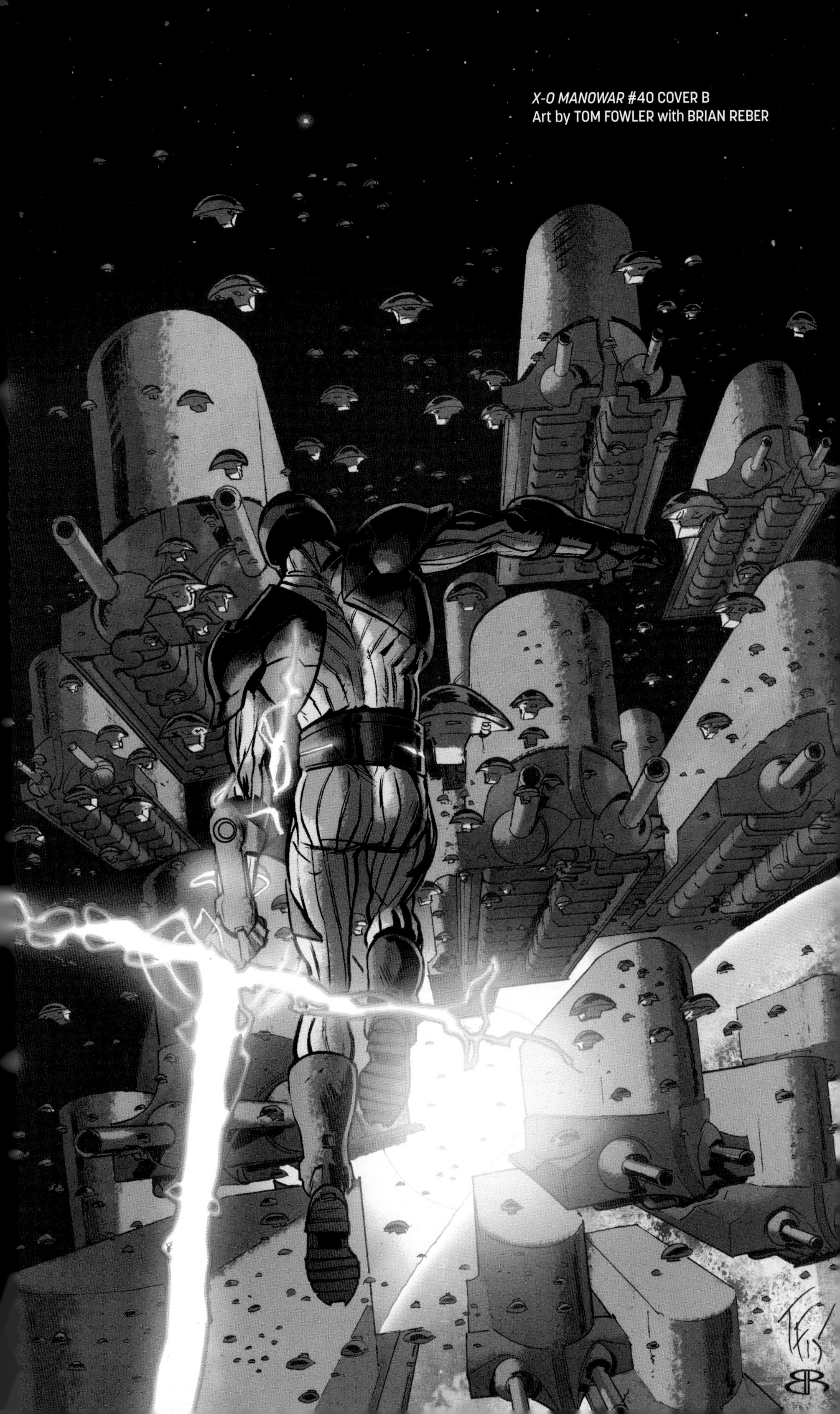

X-O MANOWAR #40 COVER B
Art by TOM FOWLER with BRIAN REBER

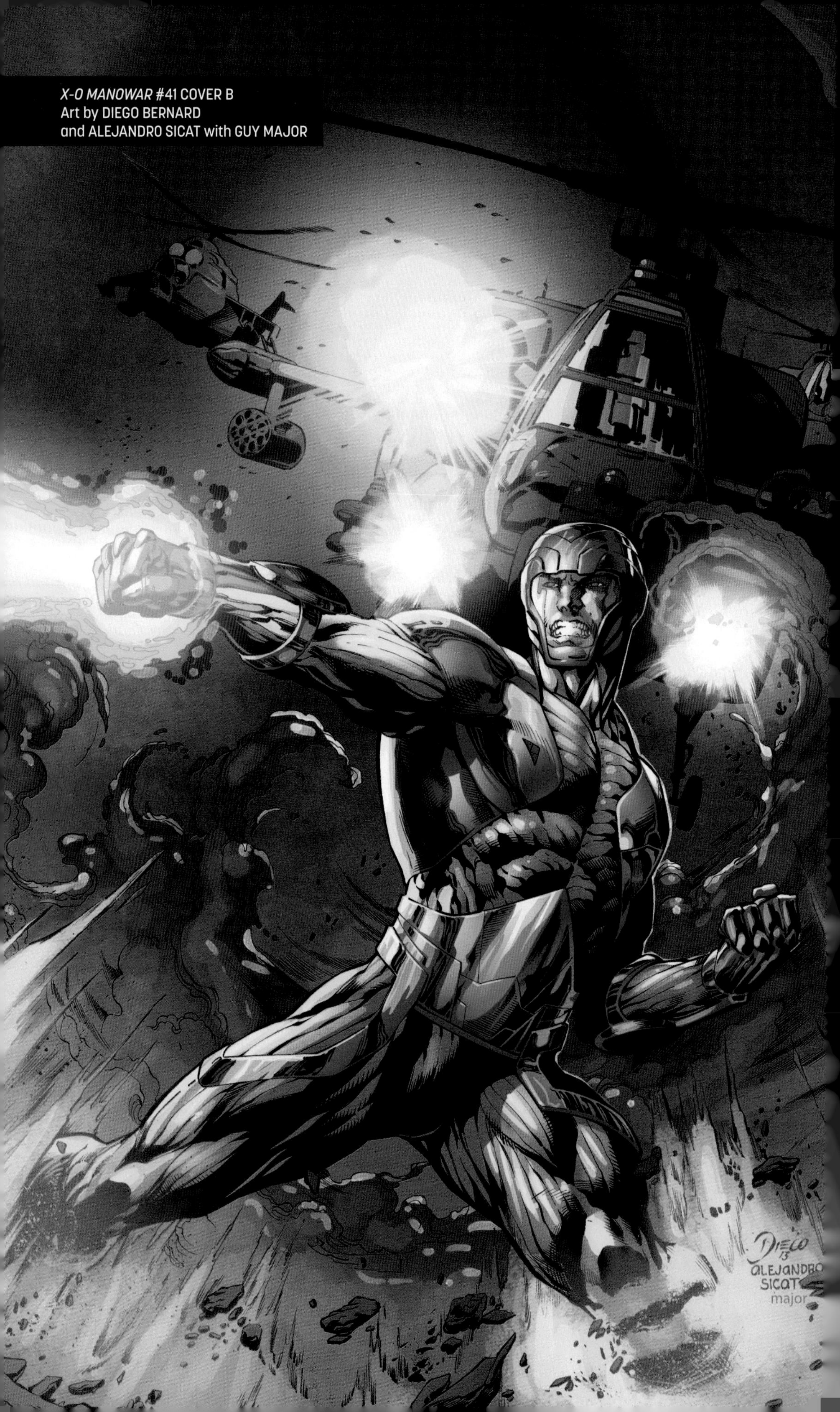
alejandro
sicat
major

X-O MANOWAR #41 COVER B
Art by DIEGO BERNARD
and ALEJANDRO SICAT with GUY MAJOR

X-O MANOWAR #42 COVER B
Art by STEVE LIEBER with RON CHAN

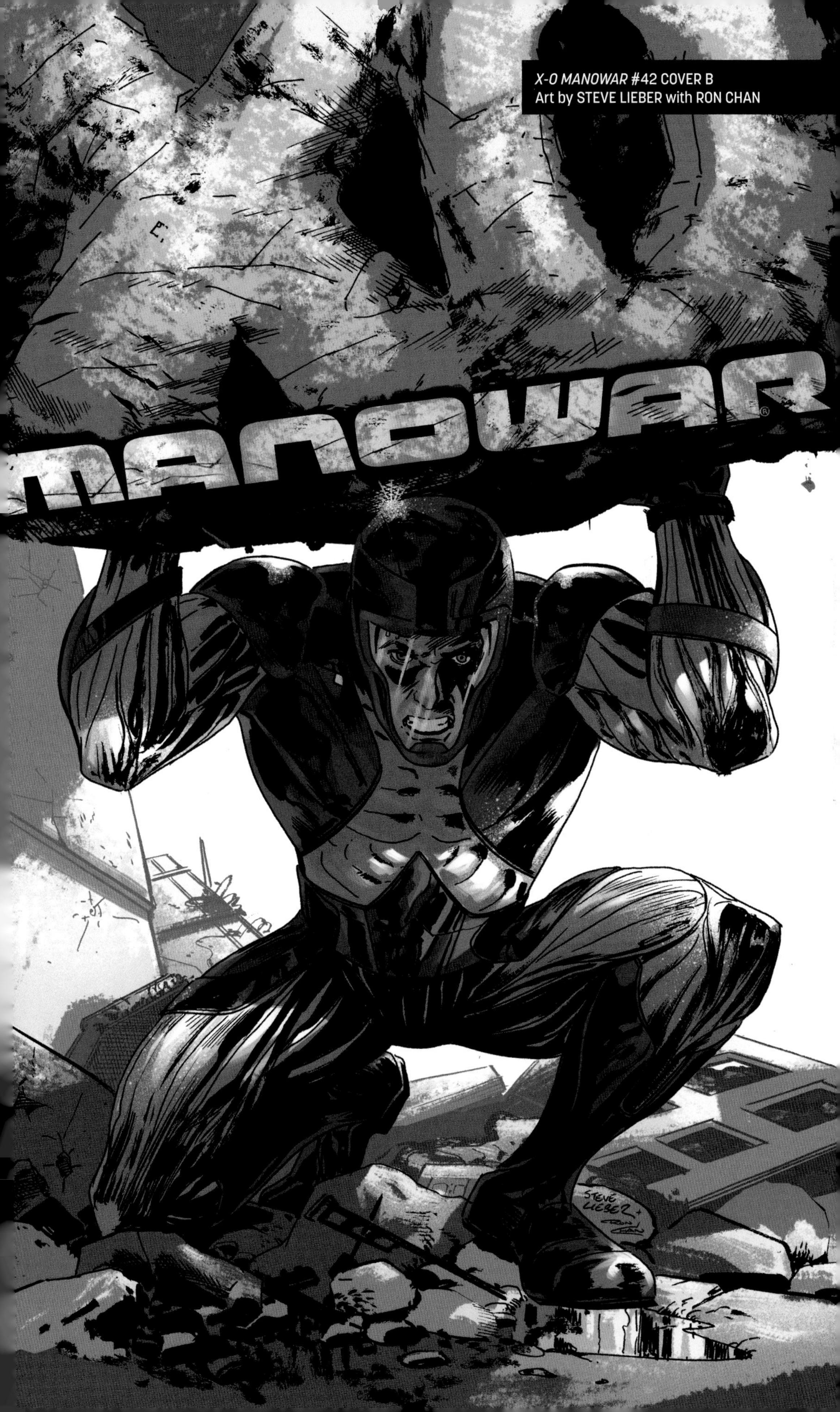
MANOWAR
STEVE LIEBER + RON CHAN

X-O MANOWAR #38, p. 5
Pencils by RAFA SANDOVAL
Inks by JORDI TARRAGONA

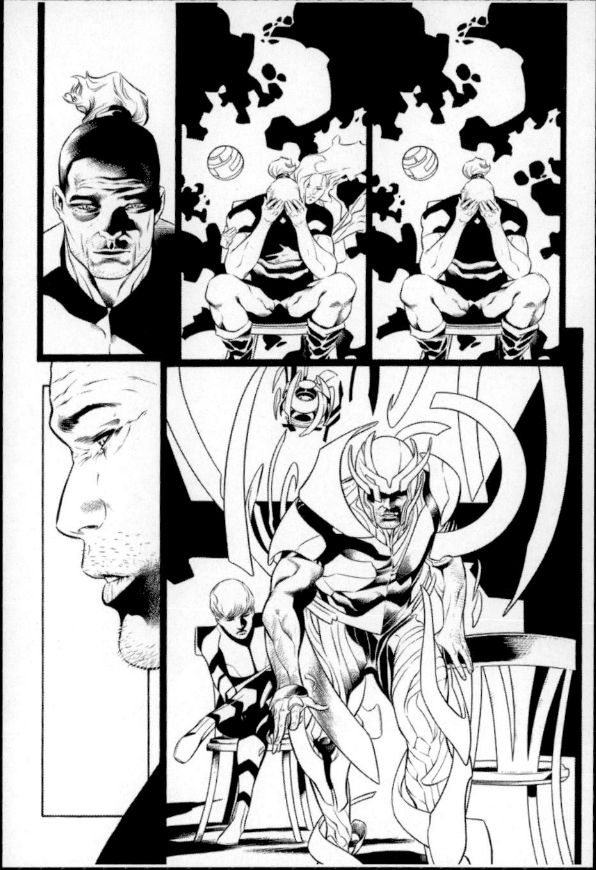

X-O MANOWAR #38, p. 8
Pencils by RAFA SANDOVAL
Inks by JORDI TARRAGONA

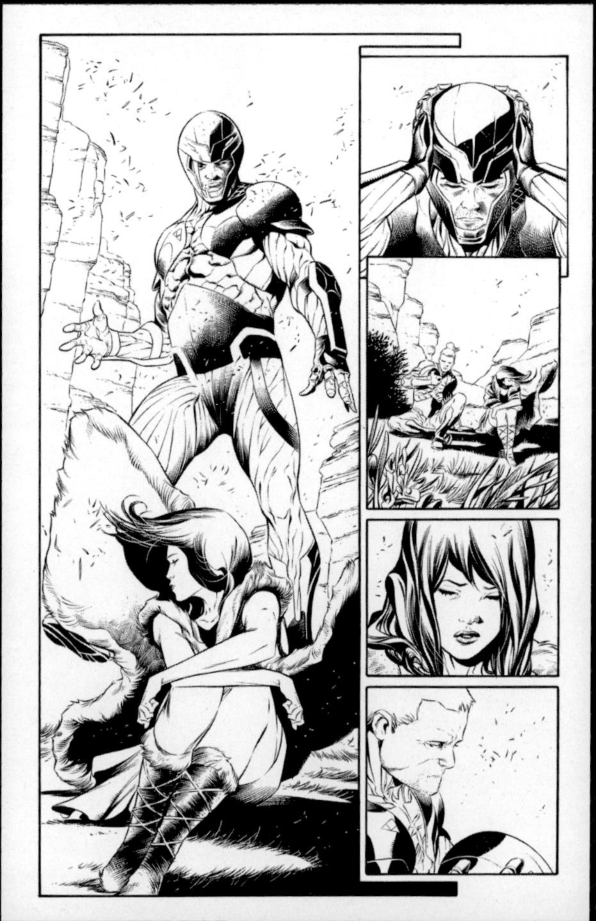

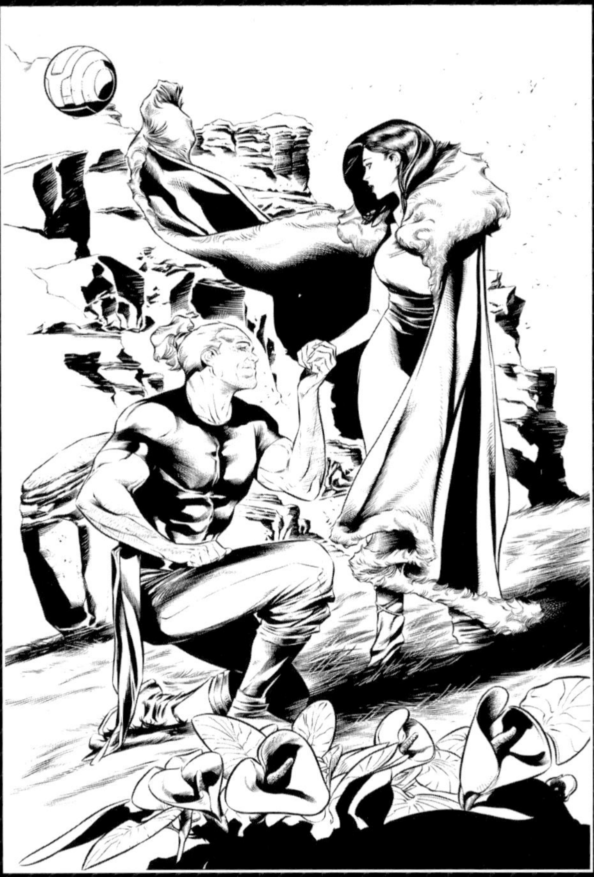

X-O MANOWAR #38, p. 11
Pencils by RAFA SANDOVAL
Inks by JORDI TARRAGONA

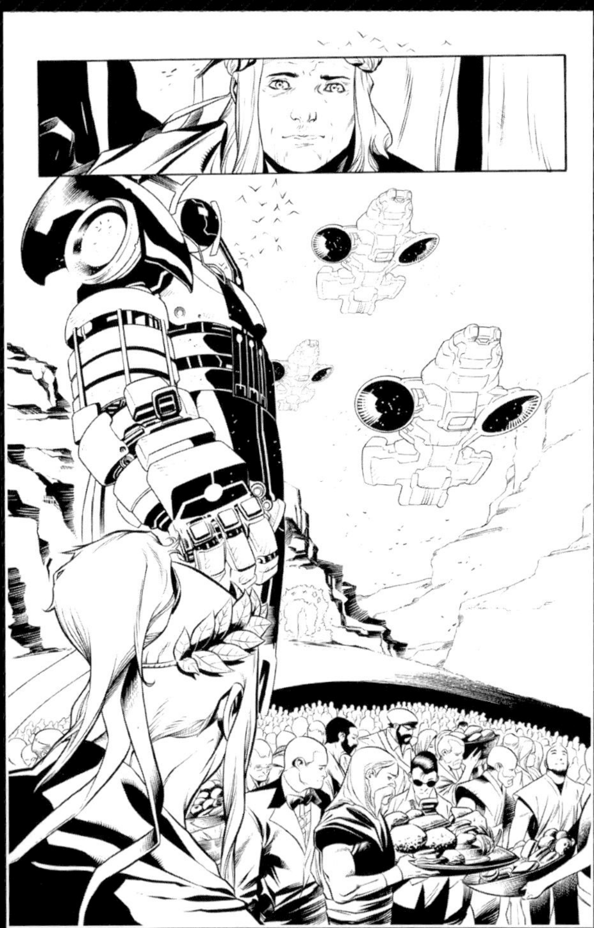

X-O MANOWAR #38, p. 15
Pencils by RAFA SANDOVAL
Inks by JORDI TARRAGONA

X-O MANOWAR #39, p. 5
Pencils by RAFA SANDOVAL
Inks by JORDI TARRAGONA

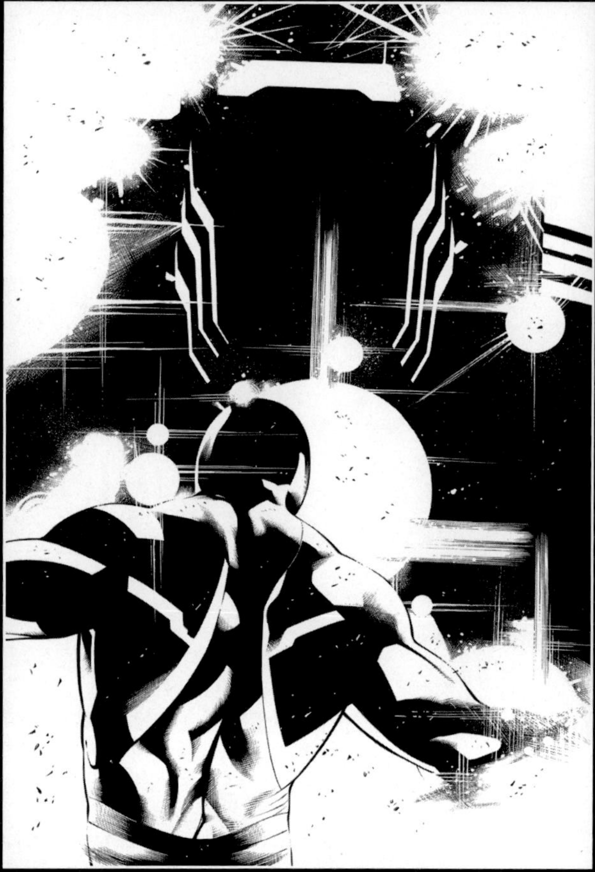

X-O MANOWAR #39, p. 7
Pencils by RAFA SANDOVAL
Inks by JORDI TARRAGONA

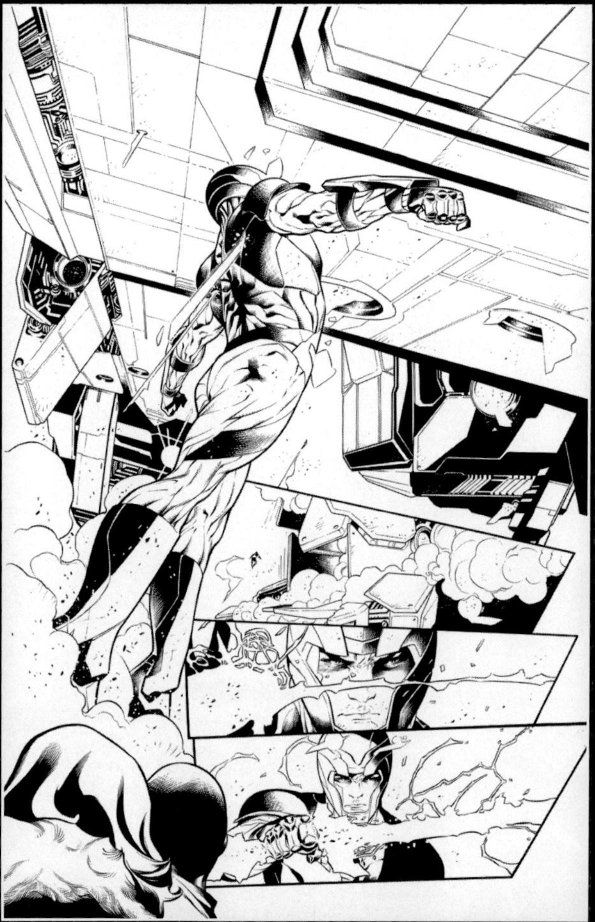

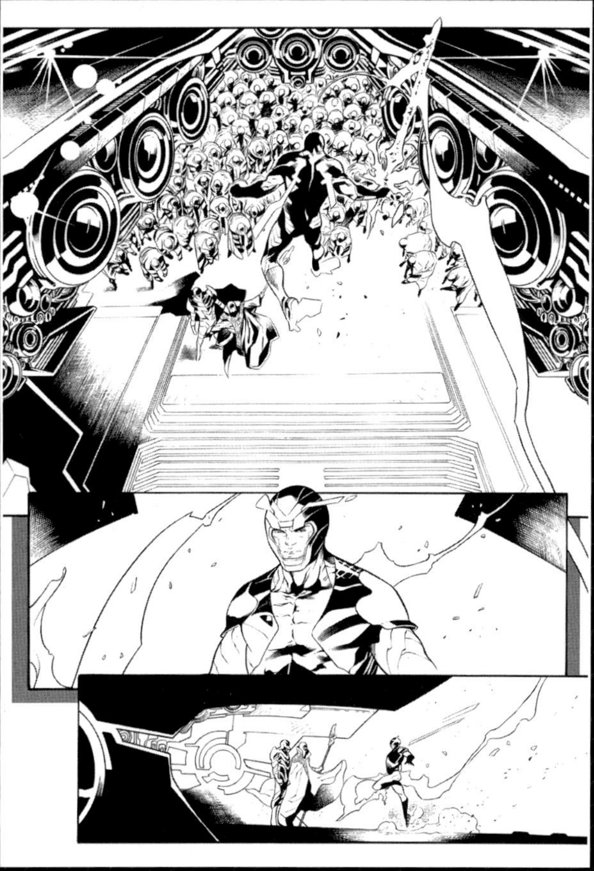

X-O MANOWAR #39, p. 8
Pencils by RAFA SANDOVAL
Inks by JORDI TARRAGONA

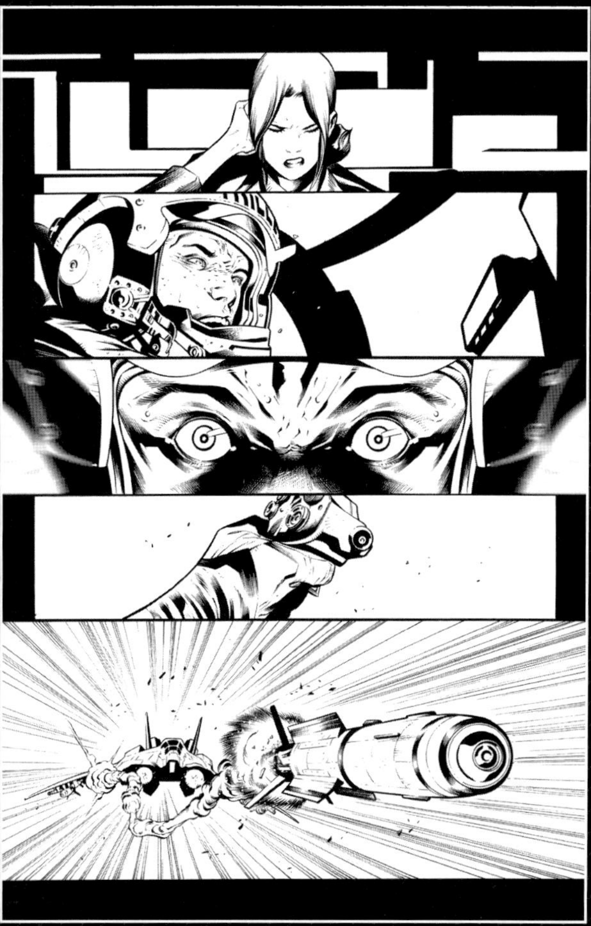

X-O MANOWAR #39, p. 12
Pencils by RAFA SANDOVAL
Inks by JORDI TARRAGONA

X-O MANOWAR #40, pages 4-5
Pencils by RAFA SANDOVAL
nks by JORDI TARRAGONA

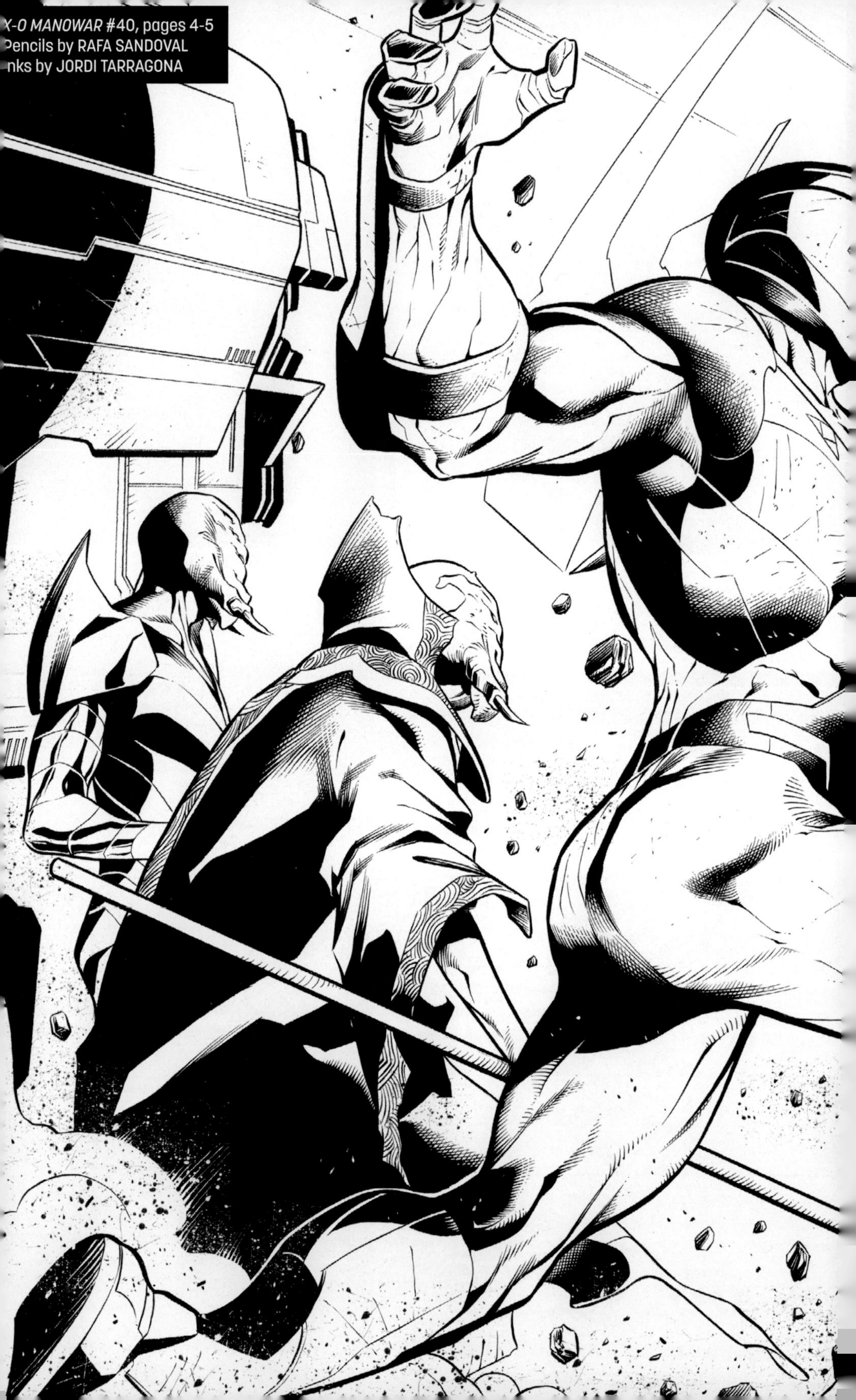

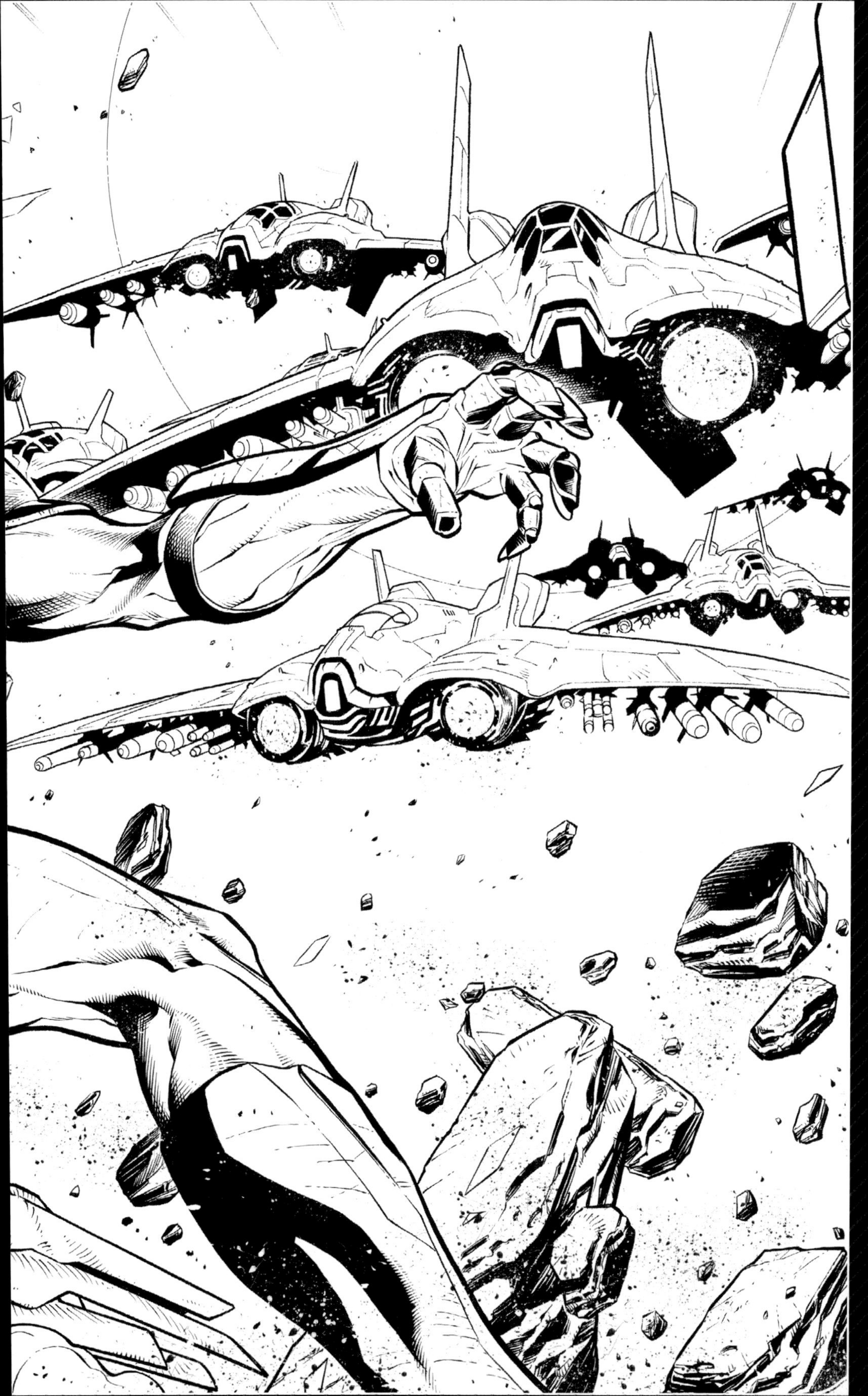

X-O MANOWAR #41, p.2
Pencils by RAFA SANDOVAL
Inks by JORDI TARRAGONA

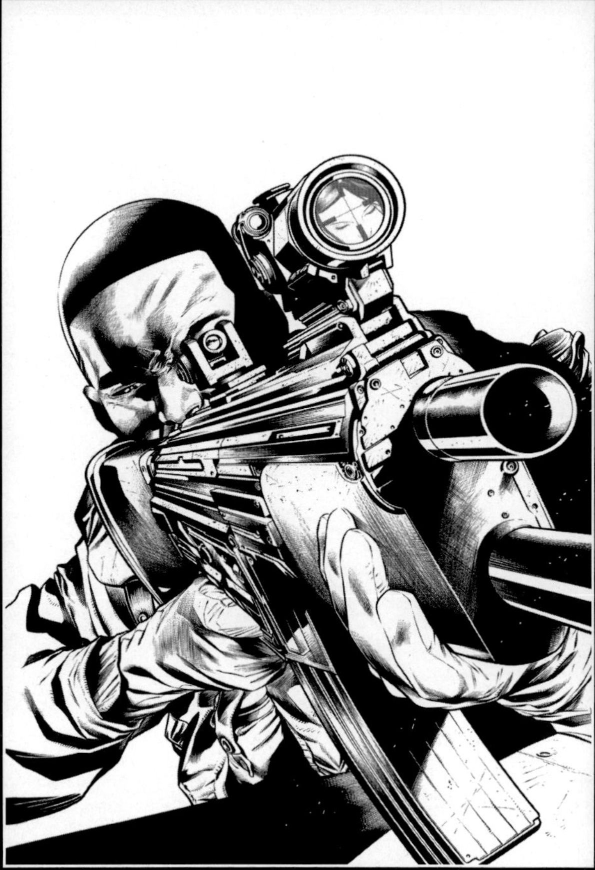

X-O MANOWAR #41, p.17
Pencils by RAFA SANDOVAL
Inks by JORDI TARRAGONA

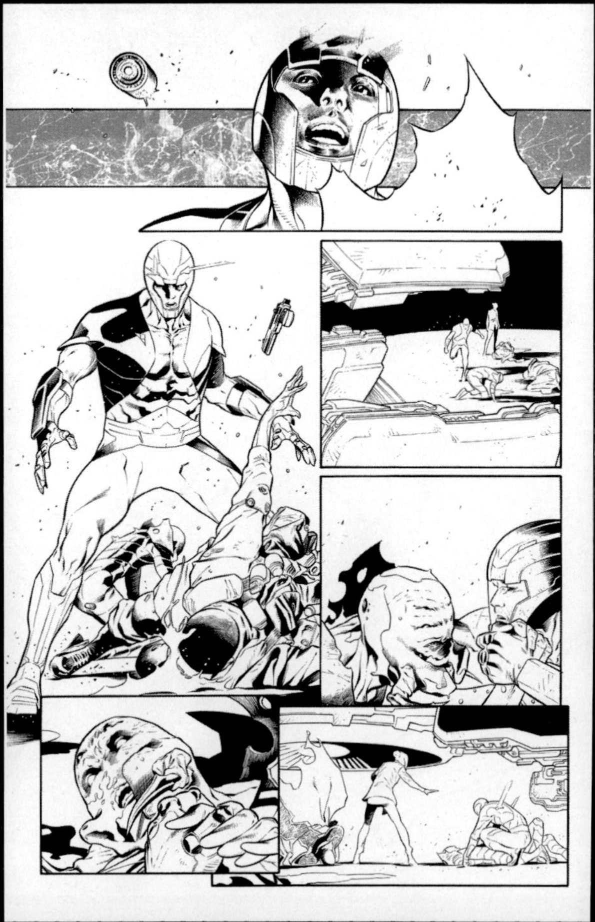

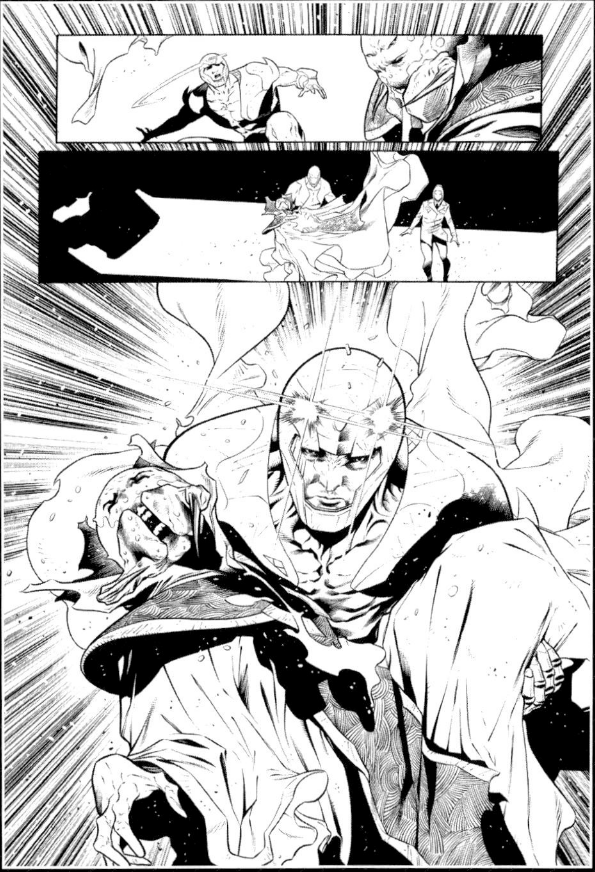

X-O MANOWAR #41, p. 18
Pencils by RAFA SANDOVAL
Inks by JORDI TARRAGONA

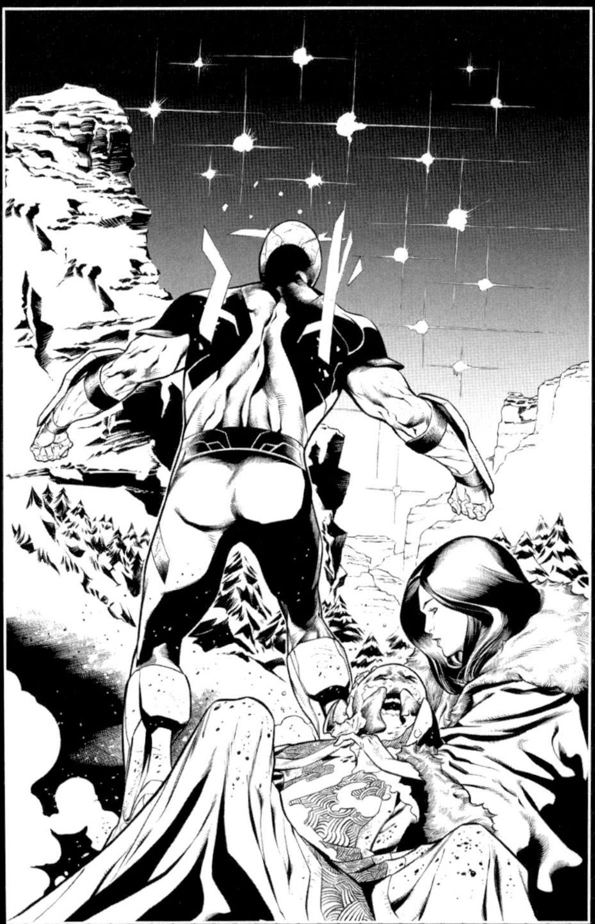

X-O MANOWAR #41, p. 22
Pencils by RAFA SANDOVAL
Inks by JORDI TARRAGONA

EXPLORE THE VALIANT UNIVERSE

THE MICHELANGELO CODE
ARCHER & ARMSTRONG
SETTING THE WORLD ON FIRE
BLOODSHOT
OMEGA RISING
HARBINGER
BY THE SWORD
X-O MANOWAR
THE WORLD'S WORST SUPERHERO TEA
QUANTUM AND WOODY!

ARCHER & ARMSTRONG

Volume 1: The Michelangelo Code
ISBN: 9780979640988

Volume 2: Wrath of the Eternal Warrior
ISBN: 9781939346049

Volume 3: Far Faraway
ISBN: 9781939346148

Volume 4: Sect Civil War
ISBN: 9781939346254

Volume 5: Mission: Improbable
ISBN: 9781939346353

Volume 6: American Wasteland
ISBN: 9781939346421

Volume 7: The One Percent and Other Tales
ISBN: 9781939346537

ARMOR HUNTERS

Armor Hunters
ISBN: 9781939346452

Armor Hunters: Bloodshot
ISBN: 9781939346469

Armor Hunters: Harbinger
ISBN: 9781939346506

Unity Vol. 3: Armor Hunters
ISBN: 9781939346445

X-O Manowar Vol. 7: Armor Hunters
ISBN: 9781939346476

BLOODSHOT

Volume 1: Setting the World on Fire
ISBN: 9780979640964

Volume 2: The Rise and the Fall
ISBN: 9781939346032

Volume 3: Harbinger Wars
ISBN: 9781939346124

Volume 4: H.A.R.D. Corps
ISBN: 9781939346193

Volume 5: Get Some!
ISBN: 9781939346315

Volume 6: The Glitch and Other Tales
ISBN: 9781939346711

BLOODSHOT REBORN

Volume 1: Colorado
ISBN: 9781939346674

Volume 2: The Hunt
ISBN: 9781939346827

DEAD DROP

ISBN: 9781939346858

THE DEATH-DEFYING DOCTOR MIRAGE

ISBN: 9781939346490

THE DELINQUENTS

ISBN: 9781939346513

DIVINITY

ISBN: 9781939346766

ETERNAL WARRIOR

Volume 1: Sword of the Wild
ISBN: 9781939346209

Volume 2: Eternal Emperor
ISBN: 9781939346292

Volume 3: Days of Steel
ISBN: 9781939346742

HARBINGER

Volume 1: Omega Rising
ISBN: 9780979640957

Volume 2: Renegades
ISBN: 9781939346025

Volume 3: Harbinger Wars
ISBN: 9781939346117

Volume 4: Perfect Day
ISBN: 9781939346155

Volume 5: Death of a Renegade
ISBN: 9781939346339

Volume 6: Omegas
ISBN: 9781939346384

HARBINGER WARS

Harbinger Wars
ISBN: 9781939346094

Bloodshot Vol. 3: Harbinger Wars
ISBN: 9781939346124

Harbinger Vol. 3: Harbinger Wars
ISBN: 9781939346117

EXPLORE THE VALIANT UNIVERSE

IMPERIUM
インピリアム

Volume 1: Collecting Monsters
ISBN: 9781939346759

Volume 2: Broken Angels
ISBN: 9781939346896

NINJAK

Volume 1: Weaponeer
ISBN: 9781939346667

Volume 2: The Shadow Wars
ISBN: 9781939346940

QUANTUM AND WOODY!

Volume 1: The World's Worst Superhero Team
ISBN: 9781939346186

Volume 2: In Security
ISBN: 9781939346230

Volume 3: Crooked Pasts, Present Tense
ISBN: 9781939346391

Volume 4: Quantum and Woody Must Die!
ISBN: 9781939346629

QUANTUM AND WOODY
BY PRIEST & BRIGHT

Volume 1: Klang
ISBN: 9781939346780

Volume 2: Switch
ISBN: 9781939346803

Volume 3: And So...
ISBN: 9781939346865

Volume 4: The Return
ISBN: 9781682151099

RAI

Volume 1: Welcome to New Japan
ISBN: 9781939346414

Volume 2: Battle for New Japan
ISBN: 9781939346612

Volume 3: The Orphan
ISBN: 9781939346841

SHADOWMAN

Volume 1: Birth Rites
ISBN: 9781939346001

Volume 2: Darque Reckoning
ISBN: 9781939346056

Volume 3: Deadside Blues
ISBN: 9781939346162

Volume 4: Fear, Blood, And Shadows
ISBN: 9781939346278

Volume 5: End Times
ISBN: 9781939346377

Ivar, Timewalker

Volume 1: Making History
ISBN: 9781939346636

Volume 2: Breaking History
ISBN: 9781939346834

UNITY

Volume 1: To Kill a King
ISBN: 9781939346261

Volume 2: Trapped by Webnet
ISBN: 9781939346346

Volume 3: Armor Hunters
ISBN: 9781939346445

Volume 4: The United
ISBN: 9781939346544

UNITY (Continued)

Volume 5: Homefront
ISBN: 9781939346797

Volume 6: The War-Monger
ISBN: 9781939346902

THE VALIANT

ISBN: 9781939346605

VALIANT ZEROES AND ORIGINS

ISBN: 9781939346582

X-O MANOWAR

Volume 1: By the Sword
ISBN: 9780979640940

Volume 2: Enter Ninjak
ISBN: 9780979640995

Volume 3: Planet Death
ISBN: 9781939346087

Volume 4: Homecoming
ISBN: 9781939346179

Volume 5: At War With Unity
ISBN: 9781939346247

Volume 6: Prelude to Armor Hunters
ISBN: 9781939346407

Volume 7: Armor Hunters
ISBN: 9781939346476

Volume 8: Enter: Armorines
ISBN: 9781939346551

Volume 9: Dead Hand
ISBN: 9781939346650

Volume 10: Exodus
ISBN: 9781939346933

EXPLORE THE VALIANT UNIVERSE

Omnibuses

**Archer & Armstrong:
The Complete Classic Omnibus**
ISBN: 9781939346872
Collecting ARCHER & ARMSTRONG (1992) #0-26,
ETERNAL WARRIOR (1992) #25 along with ARCHER &
ARMSTRONG: THE FORMATION OF THE SECT.

**Quantum and Woody:
The Complete Classic Omnibus**
ISBN: 9781939346360
Collecting QUANTUM AND WOODY (1997) #0, 1-21
and #32, THE GOAT: H.A.E.D.U.S. #1,
and X-O MANOWAR (1996) #16

X-O Manowar Classic Omnibus Vol. 1
ISBN: 9781939346308
Collecting X-O MANOWAR (1992) #0-30,
ARMORINES #0, X-O DATABASE #1, as well
as material from SECRETS OF THE
VALIANT UNIVERSE #1

Deluxe Editions

Archer & Armstrong Deluxe Edition Book 1
ISBN: 9781939346223
Collecting ARCHER & ARMSTRONG #0-13

Archer & Armstrong Deluxe Edition Book 2
ISBN: 9781939346957
Collecting ARCHER & ARMSTRONG #14-25, ARCHER
& ARMSTRONG: ARCHER #0 and BLOODSHOT AND
H.A.R.D. CORPS #20-21.

Armor Hunters Deluxe Edition
ISBN: 9781939346728
Collecting Armor Hunters #1-4, Armor Hunters:
Aftermath #1, Armor Hunters: Bloodshot #1-3,
Armor Hunters: Harbinger #1-3, Unity #8-11, and
X-O MANOWAR #23-29

Bloodshot Deluxe Edition Book 1
ISBN: 9781939346216
Collecting BLOODSHOT #1-13

Bloodshot Deluxe Edition Book 2
ISBN: 9781939346810
Collecting BLOODSHOT AND H.A.R.D. CORPS #14-23,
BLOODSHOT #24-25, BLOODSHOT #0, BLOODSHOT
AND H.A.R.D. CORPS: H.A.R.D. CORPS #0, along
with ARCHER & ARMSTRONG #18-19

Divinity Deluxe Edition
ISBN: 9781939346993
Collecting DIVNITY #1-4

Harbinger Deluxe Edition Book 1
ISBN: 9781939346131
Collecting HARBINGER #0-14

Harbinger Deluxe Edition Book 2
SBN: 9781939346773
Collecting HARBINGER #15-25, HARBINGER: OMEGAS
#1-3, and HARBINGER: BLEEDING MONK #0

Harbinger Wars Deluxe Edition
ISBN: 9781939346322
Collecting HARBINGER WARS #1-4, HARBINGER #11-14,
and BLOODSHOT #10-13

Quantum and Woody Deluxe Edition Book 1
ISBN: 9781939346681
Collecting QUANTUM AND WOODY #1-12 and
QUANTUM AND WOODY: THE GOAT #0

**Q2: The Return of Quantum and
Woody Deluxe Edition**
ISBN: 9781939346568
Collecting Q2: THE RETURN OF QUANTUM
AND WOODY #1-5

Shadowman Deluxe Edition Book 1
ISBN: 9781939346438
Collecting SHADOWMAN #0-10

Shadowman Deluxe Edition Book 2
ISBN: 9781682151075
Collecting SHADOWMAN #11-16, SHADOWMAN #13X,
SHADOWMAN: END TIMES #1-3 and PUNK MAMBO #0

Unity Deluxe Edition Book 1
ISBN: 9781939346575
Collecting UNITY #0-14

The Valiant Deluxe Edition
ISBN: 9781939460986
Collecting THE VALIANT #1-4

X-O Manowar Deluxe Edition Book 1
ISBN: 9781939346100
Collecting X-O MANOWAR #1-14

X-O Manowar Deluxe Edition Book 2
ISBN: 9781939346520
Collecting X-O MANOWAR #15-22, and UNITY #1-4

Valiant Masters

Bloodshot Vol. 1 - Blood of the Machine
ISBN: 9780979640933

H.A.R.D. Corps Vol. 1 - Search and Destroy
ISBN: 9781939346285

Harbinger Vol. 1 - Children of the Eighth Day
ISBN: 9781939346483

Ninjak Vol. 1 - Black Water
ISBN: 9780979640971

Rai Vol. 1 - From Honor to Strength
ISBN: 9781939346070

Shadowman Vol. 1 - Spirits Within
ISBN: 9781939346018

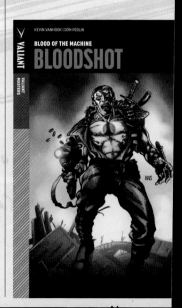

X-O MANOWAR READING ORDER

ROBERT VENDITTI | CARY NORD | STEFANO GAUDIANO | MOOSE BAUMANN
BY THE SWORD
VALIANT
X-O MANOWAR

X-O Manowar Vol. 1: By the Sword

ENTER: NINJAK
VALIANT
X-O MANOWAR

X-O Manowar Vol. 2:
Enter Ninjak

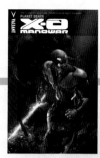

PLANET DEATH
VALIANT
X-O MANOWAR

X-O Manowar Vol. 3:
Planet Death

HOMECOMING
VALIANT
X-O MANOWAR

X-O Manowar Vol. 4:
Homecoming

AT WAR WITH UNITY
VALIANT
X-O MANOWAR

X-O Manowar Vol. 5:
At War With Unity

UNITY

Unity Vol. 1: To Kill a King
(OPTIONAL)

PRELUDE TO ARMOR HUNTERS
VALIANT
X-O MANOWAR

X-O Manowar Vol. 6:
Prelude to Armor Hunters

ARMOR HUNTERS
VALIANT
X-O MANOWAR

X-O Manowar Vol. 7:
Armor Hunters

ARMOR HUNTERS

Armor Hunters
(OPTIONAL)

ENTER: ARMORINES
VALIANT
X-O MANOWAR

X-O Manowar Vol. 8:
Enter: Armorines

DEAD HAND
VALIANT
X-O MANOWAR

X-O Manowar Vol. 9:
Dead Hand

EXODUS
VALIANT
X-O MANOWAR

X-O Manowar Vol. 10:
Exodus

BOOK OF DEATH

Book of Death
(OPTIONAL)

BOOK OF DEATH

Book of Death: The Fall of
the Valiant Universe
(OPTIONAL)

THE KILL LIST
VALIANT
X-O MANOWAR

X-O Manowar Vol. 11:
The Kill List

VALIANT

X-O MANOWAR

VOLUME ELEVEN: THE KILL LIST

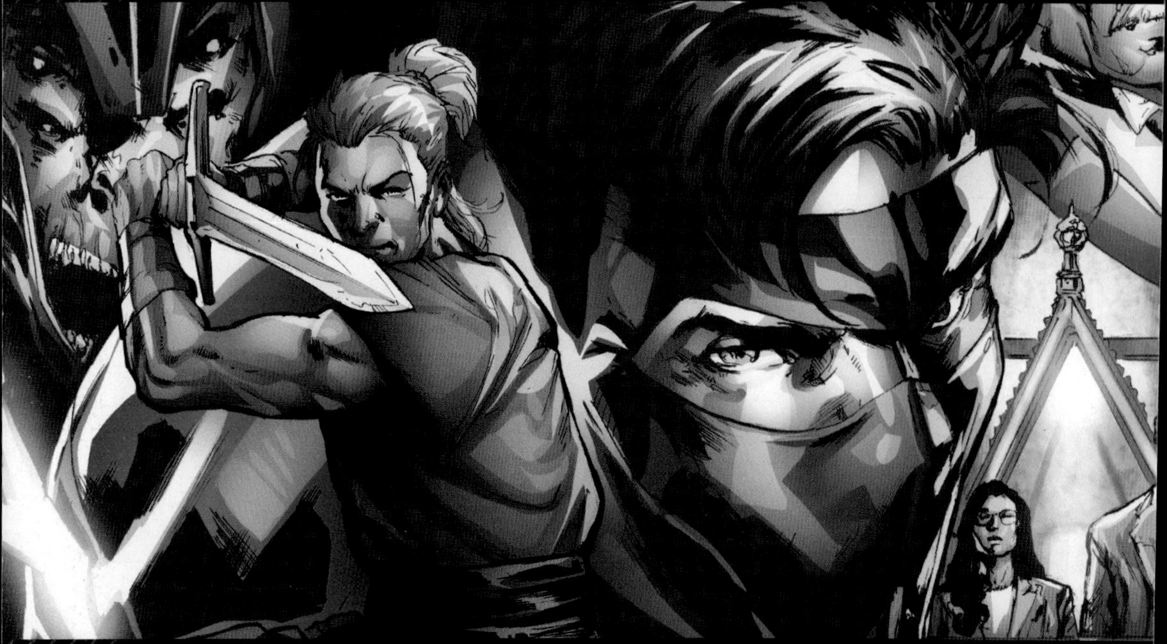

X-O MANOWAR AND NINJAK GO DEEP UNDERCOVER FOR... "THE KILL LIST"!

With two kingdoms now under his command, Aric of Dacia has pledged loyalty to his adopted nation - the United States of America - and now America has given him a new mission: destroy The Vine's network of humanoid alien agents, once and for all. To do it, he'll have to turn to the one man among us he can trust...his own former enemy, the deadly MI-6 operative called Ninjak!

Meanwhile, The Vine's most militant warrior, Commander Trill, is readying a counterattack...and what happens next will shake the Valiant Universe to its core. Can X-O Manowar and Ninjak cut their way to the source of this stealth attack before all is lost?

New York Times best-selling writer Robert Venditti (WRATH OF THE ETERNAL WARRIOR) and explosive artists Robert Gill (BOOK OF DEATH) and Francis Portela (*Green Lantern*) prepare the next salvo in X-O MANOWAR's unfolding epic!

Collecting X-O MANOWAR #43-46 and X-O MANOWAR: COMMANDER TRILL #0.

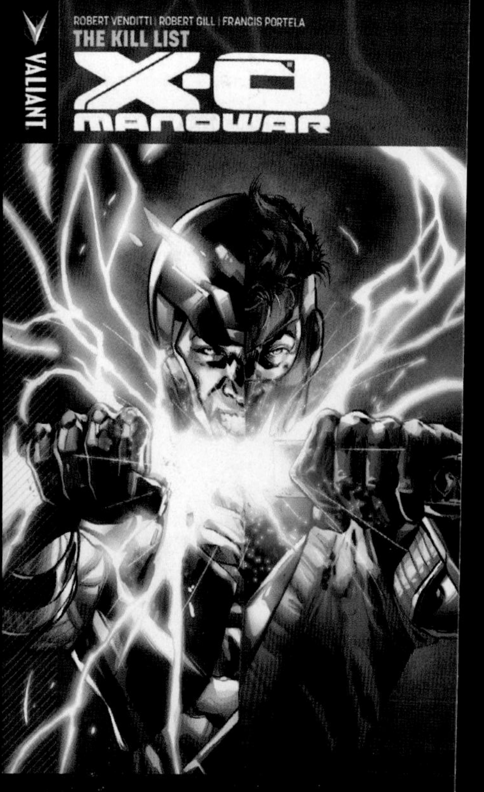
VALIANT
ROBERT VENDITTI | ROBERT GILL | FRANCIS PORTELA
THE KILL LIST
X-O
MANOWAR

TRADE PAPERBACK
ISBN: 978-1-68215-127-3